Earnest

Earnest

Interdisciplinary Work Inspired by the
Life and Teachings of B. T. Roberts

EDITED BY
Andrew C. Koehl
AND
David Basinger

☙PICKWICK *Publications* • Eugene, Oregon

EARNEST
Interdisciplinary Work Inspired by the Life and Teachings of B. T. Roberts

Copyright © 2017 Wipf and Stock Publishers. All rights reserved. Except for brief quotations in critical publications or reviews, no part of this book may be reproduced in any manner without prior written permission from the publisher. Write: Permissions, Wipf and Stock Publishers, 199 W. 8th Ave., Suite 3, Eugene, OR 97401.

Pickwick Publications
An Imprint of Wipf and Stock Publishers
199 W. 8th Ave., Suite 3
Eugene, OR 97401

www.wipfandstock.com

PAPERBACK ISBN: 9781-5326-0633-5
HARDCOVER ISBN: 978-1-5326-0635-9
EBOOK ISBN: 978-1-5326-0634-2

Cataloguing-in-Publication data:

Names: Koehl, Andrew C., editor | Basinger, David, editor

Title: Earnest : interdisciplinary work inspired by the life and teachings of B. T. Roberts / edited by Andrew C. Koehl and David Basinger.

Description: Eugene, OR : Pickwick Publications, 2017 | Includes bibliographical references and index.

Identifiers: ISBN 9781-5326-0633-5 (paperback) | ISBN 978-1-5326-0635-9 (hardcover) | ISBN 978-1-5326-0634-2 (ebook)

Subjects: LCSH: Roberts, Benjamin Titus, 1823–1893.

Classification: BX8413 .E37 2017 (print) | BX8413 .E37 (ebook)

Manufactured in the U.S.A.   08/24/17

Scripture quotations are used from the Revised Standard Version of the Bible, copyright © 1946, 1952, and 1971 the Division of Christian Education of the National Council of the Churches of Christ in the United States of America. Used by permission. All rights reserved.

Scripture quotations are used from the New Revised Standard Version Bible, copyright © 1989 the Division of Christian Education of the National Council of the Churches of Christ in the United States of America. Used by permission. All rights reserved.

Scriptures taken from the Holy Bible, New International Version®, NIV®. Copyright © 1973, 1978, 1984, 2011 by Biblica, Inc.™ Used by permission of Zondervan. All rights reserved worldwide. www.zondervan.com The "NIV" and "New International Version" are trademarks registered in the United States Patent and Trademark Office by Biblica, Inc.™

Contents

List of Contributors | vii

Introduction | ix

Section I: Equality, Holiness, Social Transformation

Chapter 1: Fanatical Women: The Struggle toward Public Ministry in the Early Free Methodist Church | 3
   —Douglas R. Cullum

Chapter 2: Ordaining Women: Discourse of Dissent at the Intersection of Text and Context | 30
   —Elvera B. Berry

Chapter 3: B. T. Roberts as Social Entrepreneur | 55
   —Jack Connell

Chapter 4: B. T. Roberts's Real Estate Debts | 73
   —Matthew Dwight Moore and Carl C. Moore

Chapter 5: Roberts and the Roots of Environmentalism: Contact and Divergence | 100
   —Timothy R. Vande Brake

Chapter 6: Religious Reform in Western New York: B. T. Roberts and Walter Rauschenbusch on Revival and Social Change | 119

—Jeffrey A. McPherson

Section II: Every Relation of Life

Chapter 7: From Primal Harmony to a Broken World: Distinguishing God's Intent for Life from the Encroachment of Death in Genesis 2–3 | 143

—J. Richard Middleton

Chapter 8: Christian Belief and the Challenge of Threats and Inducements | 172

—Andrew C. Koehl

Chapter 9: Amazing Grace in the Life of the Earnest Christian | 190

—Rodney L. Bassett

Chapter 10: Piety, Virtue, Industry, and Economy: The Habits of B. T. Roberts and Christian Nursing Education | 208

—Susanne M. Mohnkern and Cheryl B. Crotser

Chapter 11: Faithful Engagement: The Role of Spirituality and Religion in Social Policy Practice | 226

—Lori M. Sousa

Index | 257

List of Contributors

David Basinger, Professor of Philosophy and Chief Academic Officer at Roberts Wesleyan College, Rochester, NY.

Rodney L. Bassett, Professor of Psychology and Chair of the Human Subjects Review Board at Roberts Wesleyan College, Rochester, NY.

Elvera B. Berry, Professor of Communication at Roberts Wesleyan College, Rochester, NY.

Jack Connell, Provost and Dean of the Faculty, Houghton College, Houghton, NY.

Cheryl B. Crotser, Associate Professor of Nursing and Dean of the School of Nursing at Roberts Wesleyan College, Rochester, NY.

Douglas R. Cullum, Professor of Historical and Pastoral Theology and Dean of Northeastern Seminary, Rochester, NY

Andrew C. Koehl, Professor of Philosophy and Director of Traditional Undergraduate General Education at Roberts Wesleyan College, Rochester, NY.

Jeffrey A. McPherson, Associate Professor of Christian Theology and Chair of the Department of Religion and Philosophy at Roberts Wesleyan College, Rochester, NY.

J. Richard Middleton, Professor of Biblical Worldview and Exegesis at Northeastern Seminary, Rochester, NY.

Susanne M. Mohnkern, Professor of Medical/Surgical Nursing and Dorothy M. Whittingham Chair of Nursing at Roberts Wesleyan College, Rochester, NY.

Matthew Dwight Moore, Associate Professor of Humanities at Roberts Wesleyan College, Rochester, NY.

Lori M. Sousa, Assistant Professor of Social Work at Roberts Wesleyan College, Rochester, NY.

Timothy R. Vande Brake, Professor of English at Roberts Wesleyan College, Rochester, NY.

Introduction

Benjamin Titus Roberts

Benjamin Titus Roberts was born in western New York in a small farming community south of Buffalo, on July 25, 1823. By the time of his death almost seventy years later, Roberts had made a profound impact on church and society. Always a pastor first, his writing, preaching, and ministry focused on true conversion, the disciplines of the Christian life, and holiness. He rejected "prosperity theology," and argued in its stead for simplicity, generosity, evangelism, and global missions. Since holiness for Roberts was inextricably connected to social action, he left behind a legacy of advocacy for temperance, abolition, prohibition, economic justice, and the equality of women. He promoted an inheritance tax modeled after the biblical Jubilee and helped to establish the New York State Farmers' Alliance. His work in favor of "free pews" contributed to his being ousted from the Methodist Episcopal Church and to the subsequent founding of a new denomination, the Free Methodist Church. Roberts's vision for a Christianity that would transform individuals and society led to the founding of the Canal Street Mission in Buffalo, the Bergen Camp Meeting, the *Earnest Christian* magazine, and, in 1866, Chili Seminary, which grew eventually into Roberts Wesleyan College and Northeastern Seminary.

Roberts's intellectual abilities and academic interests were evident early on; he pursued the life of the mind for its own sake as well as for its practical applications. By the age of sixteen, Roberts was a school teacher and a law apprentice. Many in his family and community thought that he was destined for ministry, but Roberts resisted because of his passion to make something of himself in the world. Always a person of integrity, Roberts was perhaps more aware of his yearnings, shortcomings, and need to "count the cost" than many others. He engaged in a spiritual struggle that led him to a complete surrender to God's will shortly before his twenty-first birthday. The initial terms of this surrender included a change of course from his previous professional aspirations to the pursuit of ministry, and he attended Wesleyan University, in Middletown, Connecticut, from 1845 to 1848, where he graduated with high honors, receiving a Master of Arts degree. In 1849, Roberts married Ellen Lois Stowe, who would become a full partner in ministry and his match in terms of intellect, vision, and devotion. He was admitted provisionally to the Genesee Conference of the Methodist Episcopal Church upon graduation, and was formally ordained a deacon in 1850.

In the early 1850s, Roberts became increasingly concerned with practices in the church that seemed to him worldly, unjust, and a departure from the "Old School Methodism" which had been so anointed and fruitful in the earlier part of the century. He was especially distressed by the ways in which the poor and oppressed were marginalized in the church, as well as by the pro-slavery view that was prevalent at that time. Roberts worked to reform the church from the inside, but the publishing of "New School Methodism," in 1857, led in fairly short order to his reproof and then ouster, as well to that of others who had rallied to Roberts's cause.

The movement of "free" churches grew rapidly, and in 1860, the Free Methodist denomination was born. Roberts established a free church in Buffalo at the Old Pearl Street Theater, and founded *The Earnest Christian* magazine, an influential publication that would become widely distributed for the next half century. In November of 1864, Roberts and his wife Ellen moved to Rochester, New York, with plans to establish a school that would provide an affordable, excellent, Christ-centered liberal arts education. In 1866, they purchased the 145-acre Rumsey farm in nearby North Chili and began Chili Seminary in a room of the farmhouse. By the end of the next year, classes were being held in a local tavern. In January of 1869 New York State awarded Chili Seminary a provisional charter, and in November of that same year a new school building (though unfinished) was dedicated and occupied.

Growth and expansion of the campus was steady over the next sixteen years, and after a generous gift in the will of A. M. Chesbrough in 1885, the school name changed to Chesbrough Seminary. In 1945, the school became Roberts Junior College, and in 1949, when it began offering four-year baccalaureate degrees, it was renamed Roberts Wesleyan College. Roberts Wesleyan College gave birth in 1998 to Northeastern Seminary—a Wesleyan seminary that now serves students from over thirty denominations. Together, these two institutions serve over 1,700 students and offer more than sixty undergraduate, thirteen graduate (including one doctoral), and four degree-completion programs.

Purpose of the Book

This book is an interdisciplinary work inspired by the life and teachings of B. T. Roberts, written by current faculty at Roberts Wesleyan College and Northeastern Seminary, on the occasion of the 150th anniversary of the schools that began as Chili Seminary in 1866.[1] The title, *Earnest,* not only references Roberts's signature publication, but also reflects our respect for and fascination with his earnest character. A main theme of this work is the fruitfulness of genuine, hard-wrung faith and holiness, in relationships and society. We witness Roberts's vision worked out in his writings, struggled for, and faithfully won through hardship, opposition, pain, and uncertainty. It is one thing to be idealistic. Many are. It is quite another to pursue those ideals with the kind of genuine practical wisdom that can transform an institution, a society, or a world. Like his contemporary Abraham Lincoln, the brilliance of Roberts came in the patient, daily work, the character that bore up admirably under strain, and the myriad insightful decisions that inched him towards a better reality. It is this genius and character that we explore in the first section of the book, "Equality, Holiness, Social Transformation."

The second section of the book, "Every Relation of Life," explores the trajectory of Roberts's work and ideas as they are *applied,* the implications of his values and his integral Christian worldview for society and for academic disciplines today. In keeping with Roberts's vision of education and scholarship touching on all areas of human life, the essays in Section II explore the implications of Roberts's ideals for the individual, humans in community, and the transformation of society through various contemporary academic disciplines.

Summary of the Chapters

Section I: Equality, Holiness, Social Transformation

Whenever we survey a life, we see it in whole, as a generality; the one who lives it never has that advantage. Here we focus not only on Roberts's ideas, but also on his actions—consistent choices of a powerful personality, under the daily veil of pain and uncertainty, issuing from his carefully and

---

1. One author was an executive vice-president at Roberts, and has now become Dean of the Faculty, Houghton College in Houghton, NY.

consciously chosen character, in pursuit of truth and the kingdom of God. The first six chapters of this book settle in to the particularities of this life well lived, showing the human spirit, divine power, and practicalities of progress.

In the opening chapter, "Fanatical Women: The Struggle Toward Public Ministry in the Early Free Methodist Church," Douglas Cullum explores the ways in which women in nineteenth-century America, and particularly those involved in the founding and early life of the Free Methodist Church, wrestled with conflicting messages. Multiple religious and cultural factors created an environment in which there was a new openness to the full equality of women in both the ecclesial and domestic realms. On the other hand, the young denomination was rooted in a biblical and ecclesiastical conservatism which found some changes to the status quo more challenging than others. This chapter displays the contours of this inner tension in the early Free Methodist Church by examining in detail four real-life accounts. First, the experiences of two Free Methodist women, Mariet Hardy Freeland and Ellen Stowe Roberts, offer representative insight into the joys and struggles encountered by women who felt called by God to enter areas of ministry traditionally held by men. Then, the diversity of opinion on women in ministry is illustrated by the heated verbal interchanges that occurred between two pairs of early Free Methodists—B. T. Roberts and Loren Stiles, and Benson H. Roberts and Emma J. Sellew.

In "Ordaining Women: Discourse of Dissent at the Intersection of Text and Context," Elvera Berry reflects on the writing of an exceptionally learned man naturally inclined toward the art of rhetoric, a biblical scholar committed to living his faith, a charismatic interpreter of the Word, a preacher and evangelist fully engaged in the work of the gospel, a husband and father torn by frequent absence, and a recognized leader in the church. Berry's goal is to look at and beyond the person, B. T. Roberts, through the examination of his rhetoric in *Ordaining Women*, asking such questions as: What is it that seems to empower this man? Which rhetorical tools does he employ once he has come to terms with his Wesleyan call to personal and social piety? How does this solo voice respond to the call to dissent? What enables him to function at the intersection of the rhetorical and theological? In what types of discourse does he engage, and how does he construct his arguments for those who will listen? Berry concludes that just as the social, economic, and theological issues Roberts addressed in his context remain today, the model of analysis and insight offered by Roberts in *Ordaining Women* continues to transcend the particularities of time and place, and remains an exquisitely crafted call for freedom.

In "B. T. Roberts as Social Entrepreneur," Jack Connell explores the entrepreneurial ability that characterized B. T. Roberts's life and ministry. Institutions such as government agencies, churches, businesses, and not-for-profit organizations have important roles to play in addressing the divisions and social injustice of our day. What is also needed, Connell argues, are those rare and remarkable individuals such as B. T. Roberts who see a societal problem, imagine a new way to solve it, and then with persistence, boldness, and creativity gather resources, motivate people, develop strategies, and push through obstacles to get it done. Connell looks at Roberts's life through the lens of what is today called "social entrepreneurship"—the desire and capacity to use entrepreneurial skills to address socio-cultural problems and advance the public good. After discussing social entrepreneurship, the attributes of effective social entrepreneurs, and the ways in which B. T. Roberts exemplifies these attributes, Connell concludes by noting some important contemporary practical implications.

Debt is culturally ubiquitous today, yet in an era before safety nets such as social security, welfare, and disability it is difficult to fathom the kinds of stakes real estate investment and debt represented, especially when conducted charitably on behalf of others. The seminary from which Roberts's Wesleyan College is descended survived the nineteenth century in large part due to such bravura real estate investments made personally by B. T. Roberts. In "B. T. Roberts's Real Estate Debts," Matthew Moore explores the specific actions taken by Roberts that showed his uncanny business acumen and calculated risk-taking in service to a spiritual *telos*. Roberts's own formula for success seems to have consisted of various degrees of earnest prayer, diligence, opportunism, networking, calculated risk, and careful management; the exact proportion of those degrees remains up for debate. Clearly, though, something worked, despite so many ways his debt could have ended in financial ruin for him and his family, not to mention the eradication of myriad opportunities for generations of students locally and around the world.

In "B. T. Roberts and the Roots of Environmentalism," Timothy Vande Brake finds Roberts somewhat at odds with contemporaries John Muir, Teddy Roosevelt, and Henry Thoreau, who are conceiving of nature in a new way. However, a look at Roberts's actions reveals a profound connection between him and these early environmentalists, a connection that is mediated by the exigencies of Roberts's many ministry, interpersonal, and ecclesial concerns. Vande Brake argues that Roberts ultimately affirmed the same things these early environmentalists did, if sometimes from different principles. Roberts's environmental actions were ultimately a living out of his "full-orbed bodily obedience" to God in the world. Whether he was worshipping God beneath the tall hardwoods of the Bergen Camp Ground, teaching and farming on his North Chili campus, or speaking at the Rochester courthouse on behalf of a new association for farmers, he was acknowledging God's good gifts and fighting to preserve them.

The modern stereotype of evangelical/conservative and liberal/modern church tradition pits the former as narrowly concerned with personal spiritual regeneration and the latter as so preoccupied with social issues that church becomes indistinguishable from a social club. In "B. T. Roberts and Walter Rauschenbusch on Revival and Social Change," Jeffrey McPherson demonstrates a profound departure from this stereotype in the theologies of B. T. Roberts and Walter Rauschenbusch, two influential Christians who emerged from Rochester in the second half of the nineteenth century. Roberts is best known for his role in creating Free Methodism and for founding Chili Seminary. Rauschenbusch, the most famous theologian to come from Rochester, is known for helping to create and shape the Social Gospel Movement. McPherson finds that Roberts and Rauschenbusch share a deep conviction that spiritual and social transformation are inseparable. Both men are socially and evangelically engaged theologians. With regards to social issues, Roberts concentrates on slavery while Rauschenbusch focuses on poverty. Both promote prohibition and reformed economics as well. Moreover, they both acknowledge the need of evangelism and conversion as necessary precursors to social change. The lives and writings of Roberts and Rauschenbusch affirm that Christ's gospel requires both revival and reformation.

Section II: Every Relation of Life

Salvation for B. T. Roberts, far from being merely a personal affair, "insists upon the faithful performance of all the duties we owe to others in every relation of life."[2] Salvation is a fully embodied life in the Spirit, touching on every aspect of human experience; inner sanctification will be transformative throughout the physical, intellectual, emotional, spiritual, social, and political realms. The essays in this section apply Roberts's wholistic Christian worldview to contemporary academic issues in the fields of biblical studies, philosophical epistemology, psychology, nursing, and social science.

J. Richard Middleton begins his essay, "From Primal Harmony to a Broken World: Distinguishing God's Intent for Life from the Encroachment of Death in Genesis 2–3," by noting that B. T. Roberts's textual analysis of Genesis 2–3 in *The Ordination of Women* is a model of informed biblical

---

2. Roberts, *First Lessons on Money*, 143.

interpretation. Building on Roberts's insights, especially his understanding of God's original intent (Genesis 2) and the subsequent corruption of that intent (Genesis 3), Middleton clarifies what he sees as the Creator's normative purpose for flourishing in two fundamental human relationships: the relationship of human and earth, which is relevant for understanding the dignity of work, and the relationship of man and woman, which is relevant for understanding male-female equality. He concludes that if we live out this divine intent for flourishing in every dimension of our lives—including our treatment of others (whether male or female) and our work and creative engagement with God's world—we will be on the road to manifesting what B. T. Roberts (following John Wesley) called social holiness.

In "Christian Belief and the Challenge of Threats and Inducements," epistemologist Andrew Koehl explores the impact of choices and desires on knowing God, as well as the challenge that some see to the rationality of Christian belief due to the threats and inducements of the gospel. For B. T. Roberts, coming to know God is not a mere intellectual exercise; it involves the transformation of the will. Given the impact of the will on belief, Roberts encourages life-habits that prepare one for the experience of God, and he also embraces teaching both the promises and the threats of Scripture, the most troubling of which is the threat of hell for the unconverted. Whatever the value of appeals to hell in bringing people to faith, such appeals create a challenge to the epistemic status of Christian belief, given that we generally think that a belief is evidentially tainted if one is intimidated into holding it. Koehl compares this challenge to a difficulty arising from Freud's concept of wishful thinking, and concludes that a response by Alvin Plantinga is useful in dealing with the challenge of threats and inducements. He concludes that Christian beliefs can be warranted and justified even if they are greatly influenced by the dread of damnation or the desire for divinely promised benefits. He also evaluates similar challenges to atheistic beliefs, and concludes with some reflections on B. T. Roberts's view of hell.

Psychologist Rodney Bassett notes in "Amazing Grace in the Life of the Earnest Christian" that B. T. Roberts was convinced of the centrality of grace in redemptive human history. While he affirmed, but didn't explicitly discuss, the various types of grace John Wesley emphasized—prevenient, justifying, and sanctifying grace—Roberts explicitly taught that the experience of God's grace was, is, and will be transformative in the lives of believers. Bassett considers the physiological manifestation of grace—for example, the possibility that the work of grace in someone's life may connect to the roles of oxytocin, vasopressin, glutamate, serotonin, and dopamine within the human brain—before moving on to the key focus of his essay: the psychological implications of grace. Initial studies seem to indicate that grace-salience (the cognitive recognition of the grace one has been shown by God) may make the fruit of the Spirit more abundant in the life of a believer, enhancing the believer's gratitude, humility, forgiveness, and hope. The next step, he concludes, is to empirically clarify the connections between grace-salience, the workings of the human brain, and the fruit of the Spirit.

Concerning the founding of Chili Seminary, B. T. Roberts wrote that "a number of persons . . . desirous of doing all the good in their power, [are undertaking] to establish a school, in which all shall be done that can be done, to train up youth to habits of piety, virtue, industry and economy."[3] Susanne Mohnkern and Cheryl Crotser take seriously Roberts's call for a school in which students develop and apply these habits. In "Piety, Virtue, Industry, and Economy: The Habits of B. T. Roberts and Christian Nursing Education," they find these practices to be as relevant to Christian nursing education today as they were for the students at Chili Seminary. Walking in piety is found to promote the patient-centered care that contemporary nursing literature wholeheartedly recommends. Virtues required in health care practice include courage, honesty, empathy, integrity, and moral imagination. Industry and economy are crucial as well, and they are inextricably connected to development of the other habits. This study of current and former faculty, students, and staff from the School of Nursing at Roberts Wesleyan College finds Roberts's habits to be consistently inculcated in students, essential to the current practice of graduates, and useful for guiding specific curricular changes in nursing education. Mohnkern and Crotser communicate important insights into the nature of nursing today. They also elucidate the core habits of piety, virtue, industry, and economy, and show their relevance to Christian education for character across the disciplines.

B. T. Roberts, desiring to see the Methodist Church return to its original standards, spoke out against the injustices of his day. His yearning to see holiness return to the church fueled his advocacy for the marginalized voices in society. In "Faithful Engagement: The Role of Spirituality and Religion in Social Policy Practice," Lori Sousa reminds us that social policies reflect societal values, and spiritual beliefs often inform these values. The role of religion and spirituality has not only been overlooked historically in social policy analysis, but that lacuna continues to this day. Sousa addresses the following question: "What is the process by which policy practitioners utilize religious and spiritual experiences, beliefs, practices, and values to inform policy practice activities?" Using a grounded-study lens, Sousa examines the process of integrating religion and spirituality in social policy

---

3. Roberts, "A School Project," 161.

practice. Emerging from this study is a new framework for conceptualizing the formative events, beliefs, core values, and experiences that shape the integration of spirituality and religion in social policy practice. Sousa discusses the influence of early core values on later religious affiliations and political leanings, the possibility that the cultural paradigm of separation of church and state in the United States has contributed to the marginalization of religion and spirituality in policy practice, and the fact that spiritual ways of knowing have been ignored in western academic settings. In order to empower individuals and communities to utilize the unique contributions of religion and spirituality, Sousa develops the Spiritually Sensitive Community Assessment Instrument that makes room for religiously inspired values and has the potential to aid policy practitioners with the means to critically assess their own spiritual beliefs and values.

Conclusion

B. T. Roberts exhibited rare and impeccably balanced traits. He displayed the courage and boldness to dissent, as well as the political savvy and communication skills to bring people together. He was a visionary who exhibited patience, tact, and pragmatism. His idealism did not obliterate his attention to details and crucial distinctions. He made people feel loved, respected, and challenged; he was authentic. In his dealings in church and world, we see creativity and flexibility grounded in integrity. A straightforward and natural leader, Roberts inspired trust and devotion; people from all walks of life donated sacrificially to his ministries, and business leaders extended significant credit based merely on his word.

There are, of course, those who are by disposition leaders but do not have much by way of practical skills. Roberts at age twenty surrendered his "wordly ambitions" to God, but this clearly did not compel the latter to remove Roberts's "worldy skills." He was a learned academic, a brilliant rhetorician with an intuitive awareness of audience, and a bold real estate entrepreneur with admirable legal, financial, and management acumen. A lover of the liberal arts who also was committed to manual labor and social change, Roberts was a fitting founder for a school that now trains students in multiple classical disciplines as well as professional programs. His passion for teaching and education ensured that, as much as was possible, his vision and character have been multiplied in lives and eras beyond his own.

Our hope is that this book will contribute to a fuller understanding of the academic and pastoral life of B. T. Roberts, for those who know him well and for those who might become new acquaintances. Most of the issues that were of concern to Roberts are just as pressing today as they were 150 years ago, and our intent is to open new lines of inquiry and fresh vistas of hope. We think readers will find what we have found while editing this volume, an almost physical sense of the man as well as the vitality of his values and ideas for the present day.

Section I

Equality, Holiness, Social Transformation

1

Fanatical Women

The Struggle toward Public Ministry in the Early Free Methodist Church

—Douglas R. Cullum

Nineteenth-century Free Methodist women were the victims of conflicting messages. While there was widespread agreement regarding the pastoral role of Free Methodist clergy*men*, there was no such commonality of opinion concerning the role of women who felt drawn toward public ministry. Indeed, early Free Methodist women were caught in the middle. At the intersection of the young denomination's historic understanding of the vocation of its clergy and its egalitarian affirmation of the role of the laity, women received mixed messages. On the one hand, the rich democratic soil of the so-called burned-over district in western New York—watered by the female-friendly ministries of Charles Finney's revivalism and Phoebe Palmer's holiness camp meetings—provided fertile ground for women's involvement in the formative years of the Free Methodist Church.[1] On the other hand, a biblical and ecclesiastical conservatism, inherited from one stream of its roots in the Methodist Episcopal Church, made the new denomination more than hesitant to move quickly toward the full enfranchisement of women in ministry. This chapter displays the contours of this inner tension in the early Free Methodist Church by recounting four

---

1. For further analysis of the influence of Finney and Palmer, see Cross, *The Burned-Over District*, 177–78, 237; Smith, *Revivalism and Social Reform*, 80–82; Dayton, *Discovering an Evangelical Heritage*, 16–17, 88–89; Richardson, "B. T. Roberts and the Role of Women in Ministry in Nineteenth-Century Free Methodism," 14–25.

real-life accounts. First, highlights of the experiences of two Free Methodist women offer representative insight into the joys and struggles encountered by those who felt called by God to enter areas of ministry traditionally held by men. Then, the diverse opinion on women in ministry is illustrated by the heated verbal interchanges that occurred between two pairs of early Free Methodists.

Women in the Pulpit

Mariet Hardy Freeland

In the spring term of 1851 when twenty-two-year-old Mariet Hardy finally had opportunity to enter Genesee Wesleyan Seminary, it was her desire to study the New Testament in its original language. Her hopes, however, were quickly dashed when she learned that school policy deemed the classical course appropriate only for men. Instead of studying Greek and Latin, she was required to take French and German, "as more becoming to the training a young lady should receive."[2] Hardy continued in the course of study open to her and graduated at the head of her class in 1854. This experience kindled in Hardy a keen awareness of the contemporary injustice regarding gender equality "and led her to make numerous defenses of woman in connection with debates, essays, etc., during her seminary course."[3] During these years Hardy participated in a group of holiness students whose custom it was to visit area churches to assist with special meetings. It was during one of these meetings that Hardy first felt prompted to speak out in public services. Timid at first, Hardy finally could not resist what she believed were the Spirit's nudgings. On one occasion in the spring of 1854, Hardy felt that she must obey this inner prompting. She remained standing after the second hymn of the morning service and asked the pastor if she might say a few words.

> He made no reply although she repeated the request. He had risen to commence his sermon, but as Miss Hardy began speaking he sat down. As she continued speaking the presence of the Lord was felt in power, and the truth was blessed to many hearts . . . Two others followed her testimony, and then the pastor commenced his sermon. He was wonderfully helped, the Holy Spirit resting upon the congregation in an unusual manner.[4]

2. Shay, *Mariet Hardy Freeland, a Faithful Witness*, 41.
3. Ibid., 41–42.
4. Ibid., 65–66.

Though many people were not sure how to respond, with some calling her insane and others regarding her as a fanatic, Hardy had never felt such an "enduement of divine power."[5] In the fall of 1854 Hardy and her close friend, Cynthia Eldridge, opened the Gainesville Female Seminary in Gainesville, New York, and served as its co-principals. After working at this endeavor for several years, Hardy began to sense a deepening burden to work "more exclusively for the direct promotion of God's cause."[6] At the same time, declining health pointed her toward the necessity of a vocational change. On February 11, 1859, Hardy resigned her post at the seminary and stepped out in faith. This formal change was both preceded and followed by events which were formative in her developing ministerial self-understanding.

In September 1858, Hardy attended the Gasport Camp Meeting in Niagara County, New York, where the preacher was B. T. Roberts. After Roberts had concluded his Sunday morning sermon, Hardy "arose and delivered an affecting exhortation before the vast auditory."[7] A Methodist clergyman from the Philadelphia Conference who reported the event commented affirmatively: "I am glad to see this feature of Methodism revived among us," he wrote. "When Methodism was young and vigorous, we had female class-leaders and exhorters."[8]

In late spring or early summer of 1859, Hardy spent two weeks in Buffalo with Ellen and B. T. Roberts. During this visit, she not only enjoyed first-hand the influence of the Roberts couple, but also met and was exposed to the ministry of Dr. J. W. Redfield.[9] In the summer, Hardy went to both the Bergen camp meeting and the Layman's camp meeting at Black Creek, near Belfast, New York. While at both meetings, Hardy was increasingly drawn toward a more public involvement in ministry. Ellen Roberts recorded that during one service at the Bergen camp meeting, "Sister Hardy talked before [the] preaching" and that her doing so had "made a commotion."[10] Yet, the net result of this constellation of meetings and contacts in 1858–1859 was that Hardy's previous apprehensions about her calling were swept away. She had received an internal sense of confirmation that she was to serve as an extraordinary minister of the gospel:

> She felt set apart for God. Her time was no longer her own, but God's. She felt she was not again to engage in secular

5. Ibid., 66.
6. Ibid., 95.
7. Roberts, *Why Another Sect*, 128.
8. Ibid.
9. Shay, *Mariet Hardy Freeland, a Faithful Witness*, 98.
10. Roberts, "The Diary of Ellen Lois Stowe Roberts."

employment, but that she should devote herself to spiritual work. She did not feel called to the regular ministry, but to write, pray, exhort, reprove, instruct, in public as well as in private. She felt called to be a practical teacher of the gospel, rather than a preacher of theological sermons.[11]

These experiences led Hardy to leave the Black Creek camp meeting with a feeling of being sent out "as a laborer in the vineyard of the Lord." She settled down for a short time at Belfast and gave her energies to holding prayer meetings and conducting altar services" under the oversight of the pastor of the Methodist Episcopal Church.[12]

In the following months, opportunities for Hardy to employ her ministry of public exhortation gradually increased. On Saturday evening, August 6, 1859, she attended a general quarterly meeting in Varysburg, and, because the scheduled preacher for the evening had not arrived, she was called forward by the Rev. Joseph McCreery to address the congregation. Though ambivalent about the propriety of assuming a role normally reserved for the clergy, Hardy assented, speaking to the people for half an hour and concluding her exhortation by inviting persons to come forward for prayer. In February 1860, Hardy again had preaching opportunities at Bear Ridge and Pendleton. A few days later, on Wednesday, February 22, 1860, Hardy was invited by B. T. Roberts to speak at the Thirteenth Street Church in Buffalo. The next week found her at Lockport.[13] Then, though not without opposition, Hardy's preaching opportunities took a marked increase, with the result that she was invited to preach some thirty-one times in her first year of pulpit availability, from the summer of 1859 to through the summer of 1860.[14]

In November 1859, Hardy married the Rev. Jonathan B. Freeland, whom she had met in July 1859 at the same Black Creek camp meeting at which her calling was confirmed. This caused her life and ministry to take on the additional features of pastor's spouse, and, later, mother of children. Yet, she continued to preach and minister in various ways as the doors opened in succeeding years. In 1861, having visited the Rev. J. B. Freeland on his circuit at Caryville and Shelby, New York, B. T. Roberts commented in his diary about Mrs. Freeland. "His wife also preaches," Roberts wrote. "She was formerly principal of the Gainesville Seminary, and is a woman of strong sense, good education and deep piety. Her public labors are well

11. Shay, *Mariet Hardy Freeland, a Faithful Witness*, 99.
12. Ibid., 101.
13. Ibid., 102–3.
14. Ibid., 121.

received."[15] Indeed, preaching opportunities continued in the ensuing years. In 1884, for example, Hardy Freeland's pulpit-supply ministry in the Genesee Conference afforded her twenty-five preaching opportunities during the year.[16] Three years later she was officially appointed as supply pastor for the Mt. Vernon circuit in the Dakota Conference, where she and her family had moved in 1885 to serve the denomination as home missionaries in the expanding West.[17] In the later years of her life until her death in 1912, Hardy Freeland continued to exhort, preach, and write as her health permitted. Those who knew her expressed appreciation for both her preaching and her piety. The Rev. Moses Downing was impressed with both the homiletical organization and theological soundness of her sermons. "Of all the women preachers of the Free Methodist Church in those years," Downey recalled, "she was superior. First, in being more methodical, having the ability to see her points clearly and present them in such a manner as to be clear to others. Second, she was sound in doctrine."[18] Bishop Wilson T. Hogue remembered Hardy Freeland as a "dignified, simple, sweet-spirited, zealous, uncompromising Christian woman" whose enduring motif was the message of holiness.[19] Having known her as an older woman, Hogue was struck by her undying passion and stamina for ministry. He spoke of her energetic involvement in camp meetings, noting that even in her old age she would "lead the 5:30 a.m. holiness meetings each morning, preaching with effectiveness, and then laboring with her accustomed zeal to help those who presented themselves as seekers."[20]

Ellen Stowe Roberts

Another well-respected early Free Methodist woman who maintained long involvement in public forms of ministry was none other than Ellen Stowe Roberts. As the spouse of Free Methodism's most prominent figure, Ellen Roberts enjoyed broad exposure and name recognition among people across the developing denomination. In the summer of 1859—during the same time period and at the same camp meetings that Mariet Hardy came to an internal confirmation of her call to public ministry—Ellen Roberts was

15. Roberts, "The Diary of Benjamin T. Roberts," February 2, 1861.
16. Shay, *Mariet Hardy Freeland, a Faithful Witness*, 142.
17. Ibid., 163–68. See also the sketch of the ministry of J. B. and Mariet Hardy Freeland in Hogue, *History*, 2:58–59.
18. Shay, *Mariet Hardy Freeland, a Faithful Witness*, 142–43.
19. Ibid., 223.
20. Ibid.

in the midst of an intense personal struggle about whether she also should speak in public services.[21] At the Black Creek "Laymen's" camp meeting in July 1859 Ellen began to sense a spiritual burden to labor more fully for the salvation of souls. She felt she was being guided by God to go into the pulpit, yet everything in her seemed to resist such a public form of Christian witness. The following excerpts from her 1859 diary reveal internal struggle in which she found herself:

> Sunday, 10 July: I woke feeling so burdened—knew not why—but finally God said, "Go to the stand this morning and tell your experience." I said I would, and the burden left me for a little—it came again. Mr. R[oberts] preached, God helping; then I tried to tell of God's dealings with me. I was blest but greatly tempted after it . . . I stopped in the prayer meeting at the stand for awhile till I was seized with pain in my head. I went to the tent and was taken deathly sick—I soon found it was a burden.
>
> Monday, 11 July: Sis[ter] Kendall told her experience after preaching. I ought to have rose after her and said a few words about duty—conviction is increasing. I feel burdened for the ministers. They are not clear in their experience, not in the light.
>
> Tuesday, 12 July: God let me see just how He loved some of the poor, weak sisters who were trying to do his will. The sight was almost too much for me. He let me see the cross again and, oh, what a cross—it seemed to live. I said how long must I? and the reply came instantly, "Not long," and again I screamed.[22]

In the weeks and months following the Black Creek camp meeting, Ellen Roberts continued to wrestle with her role in public ministry. Occasionally she would speak after the sermon—which was usually given by one of the clergymen—and tell of her experience. But still her internal struggle remained at a high pitch. In late August, at a grove meeting near Wilson, New York, Ellen had opportunity to discuss her inner turmoil with a "Bro[ther] Louis." Because of this conversation Ellen came to recognize that she "had allowed fear and anxiety to come into [her] heart about being led by the Spirit." Her resolve was to trust more fully in God: "I saw that I must not be anxious about that—must have no will about it: trust and

---

21. Though his narrative does not expand upon it, Zahniser also observed Ellen's "bondage as to whether she should speak or refrain from speaking in public services." See Zahniser, *Earnest Christian*, 161.

22. Roberts, "The Diary of Ellen Lois Stowe Roberts," July 10–12, 1859; emphasis added.

confidence will drive away anxiety and fear ... Jesus will lead us."[23] Finally, in December 1859, Ellen came to a clear understanding of the commitment to which she felt she was being called as her long months of spiritual struggle came to a head:

> We spent the day—Sis. Smith and I—at Bro. Rose's—a memorable day. She was greatly burdened. It left her and came upon me—a veil seemed lifted and I saw crosses I had viewed in a distance now close by. I had come up to them—I saw I must, when God required, hold meetings to get souls saved. I must take my place by the altar or, if He led inside the altar, or on the stand or pulpit. I hardly dare write it, yet I saw it. I saw I must go, go, go, as God led me. I did not see any resting place.[24]

In the remaining days of December 1859, Ellen began to pray earnestly for "light and knowledge of spiritual things" and "the gift of wisdom" to guide her in the uncharted ground that lay before her.[25] In the early months of 1860 Ellen Roberts began gradually to flesh out her sense of public calling, though each opportunity seemed to require a specific act of spiritual surrender. On Friday, 5 January, when Ellen spoke after the love feast at Porter's Corners, "the people melted" and a number came forward for prayer. In a prayer time at the end of the same day Ellen was drawn to pray for herself. "[I was] led to ask God," she recorded, "[to] set me apart for his work."[26] In the remaining days of January 1860, Ellen conquered her final reservations about speaking out in public services. The following excerpts from her diary reveal both her lingering struggle and the spiritual resolution with which it was finally replaced as she first anticipated and then participated in a meeting at West Falls:

> Tuesday, 10 January: At prayer I was led out and greatly blessed—had to settle it I would go into the pulpit at West Falls if the Lord led me there ... Evening wrote to Sis. Cady—in writing saw I had not taken the whole cross at Tonawanda. The Stand was a horror to me all the time. I would not look at it. Started for W[est] F[alls]—blessed in going—went right to meeting. I was distressed in meeting—suffered very much—first I knew I was talking out what I felt about going into the pulpit. All night that pulpit was before me.

23. Ibid., August 27, 1859.
24. Ibid., December 10, 1859; emphasis added.
25. Ibid., 24 December 1859.
26. Ibid., January 5, 1860.

> Friday, 13 January: Bro. Hudson opened the way for me to do my duty. I did not start at the time so the way was shut up again. Bro. W. tried to preach. Afterwards I was pushed to do what I ought to have done before—did not realize the help I should, had I started before. I had to go into the pulpit and read a portion of the Word given me and talk some after it. Some came forward—there was conviction and coming up to the cross. As I knelt to pray, oh, how Jesus said to me, "You continue to take this cross and I will hide you." I felt assurance I should have all the grace I needed and wanted.
>
> Tuesday, 17 January: I saw the Lord could give me that which would qualify me for the work He has for me to do. I saw in the "gift of prophecy" was what I needed and must have.
>
> Sunday, 22 January: Bro. Stearns came—the power of God came on me as soon as I saw him. I was filled with the Spirit—and had to tell him I had the "gift of wisdom," and then to tell him what I ought to have told him at Tonawanda, about my feeling I must go into the pulpit. I was relieved and free when I told it out. Evening—I had to tell the Lord I would go into the pulpit here if he led me there. Oh, such power and glory as rested on me.[27]

In the remaining days of the meeting at West Falls, Ellen hesitantly took advantage of opportunities to speak out in the public services, usually in the form of giving testimony to her own religious experience or exhorting after the regular preaching. The pivotal spiritual and emotional point, however, came on Friday, 27 January. "I claimed today the 'gift of prophecy' to fit me for my work," Ellen wrote, and continued, "saw if I went straight through I should soon be by Jesus' side." In the evening service, she spoke to the congregation and later reflected on the meeting. "God spoke through me after Sis. S[mith] talked. I was lifted clear up, [and] could glory in the cross."[28] From this crucial moment onward, Ellen's public ministry was a regular feature of most of the meetings she attended. The very next evening found Ellen in the stand speaking to the people on the theme of justification. In the closing days of the West Falls meeting, B. T. Roberts returned home, leaving Ellen and Sister Smith to continue the revival effort. During these days Ellen wrote to her husband about the recent developments in her sense of calling to public ministry, evidently sharing something of her initial hesitancy to take such a bold step. In his response, B. T. Roberts attempted to remove any doubt that she might have of the propriety of her actions. His

---

27. Ibid., January 10–22, 1860; emphasis added.
28. Ibid., January 27, 1860.

letter sought to encourage Ellen in the authenticity of her calling to "labor for souls" in public meetings:

> I am very glad and thankful to hear that God is blessing your labors. Do not be discouraged at any trial you may encounter. The Lord calls you and Sis. Smith to labor for souls. Of this, I have no doubt—none whatever. God bless, and comfort you, my Love, and make you instruments in the salvation of thousands of souls.[29]

Later the same year, the confidence that B. T. Roberts placed in Ellen Roberts's pulpit abilities was revealed again in another letter. Because most of Mr. Roberts's preaching appointments during this period—between his expulsion and the formal organization of the Free Methodist Church—were scheduled by a letter of notification that he would be in town, and then announced in the local church, he sometimes found himself without confirmation of his itinerary. On one such occasion, after he thought that the announcement might have been made for him to preach in Brockport, Roberts realized that his schedule might not allow him to be there. So, while at another preaching engagement, he wrote to his spouse to ask for her help. "If [the appointment] was given out," Mr. Roberts requested, "I wish you would be at B[rockport] and preach for me if I cannot be there in time."[30]

The following year (1861), Ellen Roberts's preaching ministry began a steady expansion that continued for many years. Like Hardy Freeland, Roberts was normally a guest preacher, pulpit supply, or an assistant at the meetings of the regular clergymen. Nonetheless, there was wide acceptance of her presence in the services. In January 1861 Ellen Roberts and Martha Kendall went with "Bro. Perry" to Allegany, where the society had, as B. T. Roberts recorded it, "sent for Mrs. R. and were very urgent that she should go and assist them."[31] When she returned home over a week later, B. T. Roberts noted that she had "had a good time" and that the "work there [was] in a hopeful state."[32] The very next week, Ellen and B. T. Roberts were once again in West Falls, New York, for a revival meeting. On Thursday, Mr. Roberts found himself called upon to preach the funeral sermon of a seventeen-year-old young lady "who dropped dead going home from school." As a result, Roberts was too weary to attend the meeting that evening, so "Bro. Metcalf was to preach." However, when Metcalf declined, "Sisters Horace, Roberts and Kendall went into the stand" and preached in his stead. B. T.

29. Roberts, "The B. T. Roberts Family Papers," January 30, 1860.
30. Roberts, "The B. T. Roberts Family Papers," July 28, 1860.
31. Roberts, "The Diary of Benjamin T. Roberts," January 23, 1861.
32. Ibid., February 1, 1861.

Roberts was delighted with the outcome, reporting that the women preachers that evening "had a greater break than we have had at any time during the meeting."[33]

In the ensuing years, Ellen Roberts quietly pursued her preaching ministry simply by being available to serve as needed. In 1865, for example, while the family was living in Rochester, New York, Ellen often served as the preacher for one or both regular Sunday services at the Rochester Free Methodist Church. Her diary for 1865 reveals that she was in the pulpit at least once on each of twenty-nine Sundays of the year, sometimes preaching in both the morning and evening.[34] Of course, as the years unfolded Ellen Roberts became a busy person in the tasks of parenting, shepherding the day-to-day functions of Chili Seminary, managing her husband's preaching and travel schedule, and doing correspondence and other chores for The Earnest Christian. Yet, Ellen Roberts's willingness to serve yielded many opportunities for public ministry. In the first half of the year 1871, for example, Ellen preached an average of two times per month, presumably at the Free Methodist Church in North Chili.[35] In the late summer of 1872, Ellen was called to assist the Rev. E. P. Hart at a camp meeting in Coldwater, Michigan. Mr. Roberts recounted his conversation with Hart in a letter: "Bro. Hart seems quite satisfied with having you at the Coldwater C[amp]M[eeting]," Roberts wrote to his spouse. "He said the main thing he wanted was someone to help him over the Sabbath. I told him I thought the Lord would help you to talk to the people and he seemed satisfied."[36]

The experiences of Mariet Hardy Freeland and Ellen Roberts are illustrative of numerous nineteenth-century Free Methodist women preachers. Though often bound by the social and cultural mores of the day to a primarily supportive role, in nearly every place they worked constantly in the background, and, in significant ways, in the foreground as well.[37]

33. Ibid., February 7, 1861. For Ellen's account of the same event, see Roberts, "The Diary of Ellen Lois Stowe Roberts," February 7, 1861.

34. Roberts, "The Diary of Ellen Lois Stowe Roberts," January–December, 1865.

35. In this period, Ellen Roberts often did not indicate the location of her preaching appointments, but only that she had preached on a given day. The Roberts family lived in North Chili at the time. See, for example, Roberts, "The Diary of Ellen Lois Stowe Roberts," January 22, 1871; February 12, 1871; February 26, 1871; March 12, 1871; April 2, 1871; April 30, 1871; May 14, 1871; June 4, 1871.

36. Roberts, "The B. T. Roberts Family Papers," August 21, 1872.

37. For further insight into the roles of various women in early Free Methodism, see Freeland, "Women of Early Free Methodism," May 3, 1898, 11–12 (as well as this whole issue, which was a "Woman's Number"); Gould, "Mothers in Israel," January 4, 1898, 4–5; Shay, *Mariet Hardy Freeland, a Faithful Witness*, 107–13; Richardson, "B. T. Roberts and the Role of Women in Ministry in Nineteenth-Century Free Methodism," 31–34; Gramento, "Those Astounding Free Methodist Women."

Ideological Ferment

Not everyone, however, was comfortable with the public role of women in spheres that traditionally had been almost exclusively reserved for men. In fact, throughout the founding era of the Free Methodist Church, the view that women ought to be ordained to Christian ministry was a minority position. The ideological ferment that bubbled up around this issue may be illustrated by noting the diversity of opinion between two pairs of close friends: first, in the early 1860s, between B. T. Roberts and Loren Stiles; and, second, in the mid-1870s, between Emma J. Sellew and Benson H. Roberts. The former pair enjoyed a long friendship, having been classmates at Genesee Wesleyan Seminary and kindred spirits in the originating struggle of the denomination. The second pair were childhood acquaintances and second cousins, who were joined in marriage only two years after expressing to one another their divergent views about women in ministry.

Loren Stiles and B. T. Roberts

As the activity of women in the public sphere began to become more widespread in early Free Methodist meetings, the Rev. Loren Stiles became increasingly uncomfortable. From Stiles's perspective, the matter of women preaching was merely another expression of the extreme form of Nazarite fanaticism that had no place in the new denomination.[38] One of the first public indicators of Stiles's concern came in the winter of 1861 at the general quarterly convention in Albion. This was a particularly crucial meeting in the early development of the denomination, especially due to the open discussion and disagreement that occurred regarding the young denomination's understanding of the present-day work of the Holy Spirit. In particular, there were some who were pushing the church to take a clear position on the availability of physical healing for all who would come to God in true faith. On the other hand, there were those who believed that such a doctrine of healing was fanatical.[39] Though no formal position on this issue was adopted at the quarterly convention, the meeting placed on the table a set of concerns that would continue to percolate.

38. For further observations on the question of Nazarite enthusiasm, along with excerpts from the diary of B. T. Roberts, see Roberts, *Benjamin Titus Roberts: A Biography*, 321–25; Zahniser, *Earnest Christian*, 161–61, 170–73; Marston, *From Age to Age*, 320–22, 330–33; Richardson, "B. T. Roberts and the Role of Women in Ministry in Nineteenth-Century Free Methodism," 39–51.

39. See B. T. Roberts's account in his diary; Roberts, "The Diary of Benjamin T. Roberts," February 15, 1861.

Perhaps with the issue of fanaticism now out in the open, the Rev. Loren Stiles felt free to make a symbolic gesture regarding the role of women in public services. On Sunday, during the love feast on the final day of the quarterly convention, Mariet Hardy Freeland took liberty to speak in the service. But, as B. T. Roberts recorded, because Hardy Freeland spoke "longer than Bro. Stiles thought she ought to, he stopped her."[40] Though no one outwardly challenged Stiles's exercise of authority, neither did there appear to be any backing down from the more demonstrative members. During the same service Ellen Roberts was "led to speak of love and how glad the Enemy was to get the cloven foot between the Brethren and Sisters, [even] if it was no larger than a case knife." After speaking, as she began to take her seat, Ellen felt she must first "go round and shake hands with Bro. Stiles and Wood and Brooks." In continuing her account of what she experienced in this love-feast expression of Christian unity, Ellen made it clear that she was one of those with whom Stiles was particularly annoyed:

> Oh, I was never so blest in my life. It seemed as if Heaven was let into my soul . . . I was led to those who have been most tried with me. I never felt such unutterable glory in all my life. I was burdened for Bro. Stiles at once.[41]

In the afternoon meeting on the same day, B. T. Roberts recorded that another woman, "Sis. Janette Whitney[,] was specially drawn out. She walked and talked and shouted." Yet, Roberts's own evaluation of the meeting was that "the power of God was among the people."[42] By the time the quarterly convention had concluded, it was clear that trouble was already brewing in the young denomination.

At the Lyndon camp meeting in early September 1861, Stiles's frustrations reached the boiling point. During one of the afternoon services, Hardy Freeland once again "went into the stand" to speak.[43] Her presentation that day, however, was evidently far less effective than desirable. B. T. Roberts's account attempted to place it in the best possible light. "What she said was good and instructive," Mr. Roberts recorded, "but she spoke too long."[44] El-

---

40. Ibid., February 17, 1861.

41. Roberts, "The Diary of Ellen Lois Stowe Roberts," February 17, 1861; emphasis added.

42. Ibid.

43. Roberts, "The Diary of Ellen Lois Stowe Roberts," September 2, 1861.

44. Roberts, "The Diary of Benjamin T. Roberts," 3 September 1861. Note that there is a discrepancy between B. T. Roberts's diary and Ellen Roberts's diary concerning whether this event took place on Monday, September 2, 1861 (Ellen Roberts) or Tuesday, September 3, 1861 (B. T. Roberts).

len Roberts's evaluation was not as affirming. In addition to being "very lengthy," Ellen Roberts recalled that Hardy Freeland's exhortation "was too formal." She was "on many points not clear or correct," and, moreover, she stifled others who would also have spoken, had she not been "so lengthy."[45] As for Loren Stiles, Hardy Freeland's public ministry that day was more than he could tolerate. When Freeland had finished speaking, Stiles "arose, and after professing to be a child of the Lord, went on to disclaim for half an hour against women preaching, gifts, and fanaticism."[46] Stiles further charged that the Eastern Convention of the Free Methodist Church had been misled about the state of things in the West, and supported his charge by reading from "letters which he said he had received from the West to the effect that they were greatly troubled with fanaticism and badly divided."[47] Regarding spiritual gifts, both Ellen and B. T. Roberts appear to have been somewhat baffled by Stiles's comments. From their recollection, there had been no mention of the gifts on the camp grounds, "till he opposed them, classing them with women's preaching."[48] It was the latter, of course, that Stiles was most concerned about. Concerning women preaching, Stiles minced no words:

> He said that if God called women to preach, he would call them as he did men through the church. The church would endorse them, or, in the language of another, "He would call them so loud that the church would overhear the call."[49]

Ellen Roberts's diary recalled another facet of Stiles's speech: He made a bold contrast between the recognized ministry of Phoebe Palmer and that which was presently occurring in their own context. "He did not think anyone in western N[ew] Y[ork] was called to labor in the way Sis. P[almer] did."[50]

B. T. Roberts was grieved by Stiles's outburst. "I felt afflicted," Roberts recorded.[51] From his perspective, the meeting until then "had gone on with the utmost harmony."[52] Furthermore, Roberts noted, "Bro. Stiles and I had always had a good understanding. He had not intimated to me that he had

45. Roberts, "The Diary of Ellen Lois Stowe Roberts," September 2, 1861.
46. Ibid.
47. Roberts, "The Diary of Benjamin T. Roberts," September 3, 1861.
48. Ibid.
49. Ibid.
50. Roberts, "The Diary of Ellen Lois Stowe Roberts," September 2, 1861.
51. Roberts, "The Diary of Benjamin T. Roberts," September 3, 1861.
52. Ibid.

any such letters, nor asked any explanations" [53]about matters in the West. But, refusing to be derailed by Stiles's lumping together of separate issues, Roberts offered a brief, but effective, response to the actual issue at hand—the matter of women in ministry:

> I said but little. In reply to what he said about there not being a woman in the college of Apostles, I briefly remarked that the Apostle sent his salutations to "the women who labored with him in the Gospel" Rom. 16:12, etc. I said that I was willing to leave the matter where Bro. Stiles had put it. I believed if God called a person to labor, the spiritual would recognize the call.[54]

Roberts then proceeded to illustrate his point by asking the congregation to indicate their opinion on the matter. As Ellen Roberts recorded, "Mr. R[oberts] asked the people who thought God called these Sis[ters] to labor as they [were] doing to rise—nearly the whole congregation rose, and only a very few thought otherwise."[55] Stiles, however, was not convinced. He objected to the charade by noting that the congregation's response "was not a fair representation, as the church was not there."[56]

There is no doubt that Stiles believed he had ample evidence to support his conviction that the push for women's preaching was but another expression of the Nazarite fanaticism that was troubling the young denomination. Indeed, Stiles was correct that there had been significant discussion of the problem of fanaticism at the Western Convention which had met earlier, in June 1861. Specifically, a resolution was presented to put the Western Convention on record against the exercise of miraculous gifts.[57] Roberts, however, spoke against the resolution, arguing that "it assumes things to exist among us that have no existence." That is, Roberts continued,

> It claims that there are those who profess to have the power of working miracles. Whereas all that any of our people profess is that God has, in answer to prayer, raised some from sickness

---

53. Ibid.

54. Roberts, "The Diary of Benjamin T. Roberts," September 3, 1861.

55. Roberts, "The Diary of Ellen Lois Stowe Roberts," 2 September 1861. B. T. Roberts reported the same outcome in the following words: "I then asked all who believed that God had called the sisters whom they had heard on that ground to labor as they were laboring to manifest it by rising up. Nearly all arose. All who think they are not called arise. But three or four arose." See Roberts, "The Diary of Benjamin T. Roberts," September 3, 1861.

56. Roberts, "The Diary of Benjamin T. Roberts," September 3, 1861.

57. A similar resolution offered by Loren Stiles had been approved by the Eastern Convention in 1860. See Roberts, "Editorial," 392–93; Zahniser, *Earnest Christian*, 172; Marston, *From Age to Age*, 267.

and restored them to health. Their testimony cannot be called into question.[58]

Roberts's argument, which carried the day at the Western Convention, attempted to steer the infant organization down a middle path that would keep it from forfeiting the blessing of God out of fear of fanaticism. Roberts's hope was that his balanced explanations that day would put the issue to rest once and for all:

> A great deal of confusion has been occasioned by opposition to what some have called fanaticism, but what is in reality the power of God. The term "gift of faith" has also occasioned confusion. The explanations calmed and were satisfactory to all and I trust that the matter will rest forever. Let God work in any way, and let us not be afraid of what is truly His work.[59]

Unfortunately, the issue would not die quite so easily. Only two days later at the same convention, Dr. Redfield's Sunday morning sermon was interrupted by "some sisters who broke in upon him with ejaculating prayers."[60] After Redfield encouraged them to continue their praying, one of them soon "began to jump and scream, and two or three went upon the stand and exhorted him to look to the Lord to be healed of the palsy."[61] Roberts dead-panned his own brutally-honest evaluation: "They had a time, but nothing was effected."[62] For Stiles and others who heard about these events, it was not hard to come to the conclusion that fanaticism, spiritual gifts, and women's role in public worship were somehow part of the same package.

Likewise, back East, Stiles had no problem finding ammunition for his cause. For example, on one occasion at the 1861 Bergen camp meeting one of the leaders of the Nazarite faction, the Rev. Alanson Reddy, "took the stand and told of a vision which he said he had seen. He said that Bro[thers] Abell, Stiles, and Roberts were in the way of the work of the Lord—putting their hands upon it."[63] A similar event happened at the Pekin camp meeting in August 1861. Libbie Wheeler, a woman with Nazarite sentiments, went to the stand and announced that "the Lord wanted her to say that Bro[ther] Roberts had a devil" and that "Bro[ther] Abell had been preaching for the devil ever since the camp meeting began."[64] Then things went from bad to

58. Roberts, "The Diary of Benjamin T. Roberts," June 14, 1861.
59. Ibid.
60. Ibid., June 16, 1861.
61. Ibid.
62. Ibid.
63. Ibid., June 24, 1861.
64. Ibid., August 20, 1861.

worse, as the radical group attempted to exploit the oratory skills of women in order to attract people to its unofficial meetings:

> They tried to get up a demonstration in [the] rear of ground. A wagon was drawn up behind the tents and an app[ointment] was given out for "women preaching." Three or four women mounted the wagon, but no one felt the cross to preach. Presently a half-witted, dirty man from the poor house began to walk around the wagon and shout. Others joined in—a scene of indescribable confusion followed. All sorts of demonstrations occurred. The rowdies cheered and shouted. The more sober among the Nazarites felt ashamed of it. They said there was a degree of self-will in the matter and the devil got control of the meeting.[65]

The following week at a camp meeting near Rose, New York, the fanatical extravagances continued. There, a Methodist Protestant woman "of good character and considerable influence was strangely exercised." In an extraordinary demonstration—evidently during a private tent-prayer meeting—that lasted into the early morning hours, this woman "fell and jumped about and threw her limbs so that she would have been indecently exposed had not some of them held down her clothes." To make matters worse, "her language was vulgar and she sang dancing tunes."[66] When Roberts heard that this had occurred on the camp ground, he went immediately to the tent to set things right. Though he found the woman "in a most sweet and blessed state of mind," Roberts gave a strong exhortation against such excesses. Against the woman and the others with her who claimed that she had been led by God "into these exercises to mortify her and bring her nearer to God," Roberts insisted that "the whole affair was of the devil." He explained to them that the devil

> had pushed this sister into excesses and got the rest of them to endorse them in order to bring the whole work into contempt. God never contradicted himself. But some of her exercises were in plain contradiction to the Bible.[67]

Roberts left the tent believing that God had helped him in his explanation of the event, so that he thought "they were all convinced." For that round, at least, Roberts believed "the devil was defeated."[68]

65. Ibid.
66. Ibid., August 27, 1861.
67. Ibid., August 28, 1861.
68. Ibid.

All of this, and more, lay in the background of Stiles's outburst at the Lyndon camp meeting in early September 1861. Even at the very meeting that Stiles had publicly expressed his concerns, there were further expressions of the very things that troubled him. After Stiles spoke, the Rev. E. W. Dunbar addressed the congregation about the danger of "the devil getting in to make dissension. Sis[ter] Roberts exhorted the people not to allow their attention to be diverted. Sis[ter] Smith also exhorted."[69] Then there were physical manifestations that Stiles would undoubtedly have seen as at least bordering on the fanatical:

> The power of the Lord came down upon the people. Some five or six fell. Bro. Wilcox and others leaped like David before the ark. Three or four were converted. We had no such time of power either before or after upon the Camp Ground.[70]

The day ended with Roberts and others offering an olive branch to Stiles by urging him to come to the stand and preach. Stiles, however, "stoutly refused,"[71] preferring instead to leave the camp ground, after a parting word to Roberts that these matters should be dealt with before the annual meeting of the Eastern convention in October. "He was determined," as Ellen Roberts reported, "to put some things down—women preaching and the gifts."[72]

B. T. Roberts, on the other hand, remained convinced that the young denomination must be careful to distinguish between the fanatical extravagances with which they had been plagued and the authentic power of God to work through whom and in whatever manner God might choose. Throughout the same year in which he had to deal with this abundance of Nazarite excesses, Roberts repeatedly affirmed his ideological and theological commitment to women in public ministry. For example, on 29 April 1861, when Ellen Roberts spoke to a large congregation at the Thirteenth Street Church in Buffalo, B. T. Roberts recorded that "they listened not only attentively, but many seemed to be very much affected. There was more of a melting down than I have seen in Buffalo in a long time." Then, in a moment of theological reflection, Roberts commented more generally on the matter of women's preaching:

> I cannot discountenance there wherein God is pleased to use for the furtherance of His cause. If the Lord gives a sister liberty in

69. Ibid., September 3, 1861.
70. Ibid.
71. Ibid.
72. Roberts, "The Diary of Ellen Lois Stowe Roberts," September 3, 1861.

speaking and gives her the hearts of the people who shall say she shall not speak in the name of Jesus? I dare not.[73]

Similarly, in June 1861 after having listened to "Sister Blatchly" preach at a grove meeting near Chittenango, Roberts exclaimed, "How absurd the prejudice against females laboring for the salvation of souls."[74] The next day, perhaps inspired by Blatchly's sermon, Roberts announced during the Sunday morning service that Ellen Roberts would preach in the afternoon. Even though the patriarchal culture of his day peeked through his own egalitarian commitments in his having announced the meeting before arranging it with his spouse, Roberts's intention was to affirm her giftedness for public ministry. Noting Ellen's response to his surprise announcement, Mr. Roberts was clearly pleased both with himself, for having nudged her into the stand, and with his spouse, for her pulpit ministry that day:

> She was wonderfully tried with me for doing so. But when she consented and went to the stand she was greatly blessed. The congregation was more melted and moved than I have seen them since I have been here. God got hold of many hearts.[75]

At the end of October when the Eastern Convention met in Perry, New York, Stiles was prepared to do battle. Early in the gathering Roberts noted that there was "an evident plan preconcerted to come out against the labor of women in our meetings." For his own part, however, Roberts did not feel free to enter into any political scheming. "[T]he Lord will not let me counterplot," wrote Roberts two days before Stiles's resolutions reached the business of the convention. Instead of plotting a way to defeat the imminent resolutions, Roberts committed it to God with the prayer, "I trust in thee my Saviour, and thou wilt bring me through. The cause is thine, and thou wilt care for it better than I could."[76]

On Monday, 28 October 1861, Stiles's resolutions against women preaching were presented to the convention. Put in the form of two questions, the key to Stiles's argument was his distinction between "female labors" and "female preaching." On the question of whether the Free Methodist Church should approve of female labors in public meetings, such as "prayer, personal testimony, or exhortation, according as their abilities may warrant, or the occasion may offer," Stiles encouraged the convention to

---

73. Roberts, "The Diary of Benjamin T. Roberts," April 29, 1861.
74. Ibid., June 29, 1861.
75. Ibid., June 30, 1861.
76. Ibid., October 25, 1861.

agree heartily.[77] But on the matter of female preaching, Stiles insisted that they should adopt the opposite response, on the basis of the following six arguments:

1. We do not find it authorized in the Old Testament.
2. We do not find it authorized in the New Testament.
3. On the contrary, it is clearly intimated in the Word of God that woman is not designed for the office of the holy ministry.
4. It clashes with the ordinary duties and relations of the female sex.
5. It tends to awaken prejudice, and produce confusion in carrying on the work of God.
6. It is contrary to the usage of the church in all ages, the Methodist Church forming no exception.[78]

Though Roberts spoke against the resolutions, these six points of rationale carried the large majority of the delegates. They were referred to the General Convention of 1862 with the recommendation that the position they expressed against women's preaching be incorporated into the Free Methodist Discipline. As it turned out, due to a disruption of the 1862 General Convention by another issue, the Eastern convention's resolutions regarding women were not presented at all.[79] Moreover, Loren Stiles's untimely death from typhoid fever in May 1863 removed the Genesee delegation's most articulate spokesperson for the resolutions from future involvement for the cause. Nonetheless, Stiles's disagreement with Roberts in 1860–61 was but the tip of an iceberg. Even though—as it was but the opinion of an annual conference—there was no legal authority involved in the resolutions, the Eastern convention's vote in October 1861 provided a clear indicator that there was a substantial and vocal group of early Free Methodists who embraced a fundamentally different view than that of the young denomination's most prominent leader. It was immediately and painfully evident to Roberts that progress on the question of the full enfranchisement of women in ministry would be a long process.[80]

77. *Minutes of the Genesee Annual Convention*, 13–14.
78. Ibid.
79. The disruption swirled around whether Roberts overstepped his authority when, on April 10, 1862, he formed the Susquehanna Conference without the sanction of the General Convention. For a helpful analysis, see Richardson, "B. T. Roberts and the Role of Women in Ministry in Nineteenth-Century Free Methodism," 60–64. For background issues and documentary evidence, see Hogue, *History*, 1:360–70; Zahniser, *Earnest Christian*, 191–96.
80. After the convention both B. T. and Ellen Roberts struggled with discouragement

Emma J. Sellew and Benson H. Roberts

Nearly a decade and a half later than the Stiles-Roberts disagreement, another pair of early Free Methodists engaged in a conversation via correspondence that provides additional insight into the strength of the ideological and theological ferment that lingered around the issue of women in ministry. In 1875, Emma Jane Sellew and Benson Howard Roberts were both 21 years old, both had attended Oberlin College, and now Benson was studying at Dartmouth. Emma was teaching languages at the Chili Seminary in North Chili, New York, where Benson's family also lived and worked. Benson, of course, was the son of Ellen and B. T. Roberts. At the time of their correspondence in May 1875, each of them was involved in an intense period of personal and vocational searching. Emma was sensing a very clear call to become a preacher of the gospel. Benson, on the other hand, was in the midst of a personal struggle about whether he should join the Episcopal Church.[81] Though Benson's letter to Emma is not extant, Emma's reply to Benson gives ample clues to the content of Benson's original letter. From Emma's letter, it is clear that Benson had changed his view on the matter of women in ministry, very likely because of his new-found affinity with the Episcopal Church. Ironically, earlier letters from Benson to Emma had actually been formative for her own affirmation of the appropriateness of women's preaching. Thus, it can be assumed that Benson had earlier held the view of his parents, and then, while at Dartmouth, reversed his position. Emma's reply to Benson is valuable both for the strength of her argument and the light it sheds on the nature of the debate in Free Methodism's second decade.

Emma Sellew pitied what she perceived as the narrowing of Benson's position on the subject. On exegetical grounds, Emma had come to believe that the Bible was strongly in favor of women's preaching. She found the calling to motherhood and care of the home to be an honorable one, but was

---

for several days. For example, on October 29, 1861, B. T. Roberts wrote, "If our preachers would only stop fighting and regulating the work, it would go on with much greater power." Again, on November 2, 1861, Roberts confessed, "I have felt sad, dejected and disheartened in view of the prospects before the Free Methodist Church. I greatly fear the tendency of some of the measures adopted at the late convention." (Roberts, "The Diary of Benjamin T. Roberts.") See also Roberts, "The Diary of Benjamin T. Roberts," November 1 and 3, 1861; Roberts, "The Diary of Ellen Lois Stowe Roberts," October 29–30, 1861.

81. See, for example, Roberts, "Benson H. Roberts to B. T. and Ellen Roberts," April 21, 1875; "Benson H. Roberts to B. T. Roberts," April 29, 1875; "Benson H. Roberts to Ellen Roberts," May 6, 1875; "Benson H. Roberts to B. T. Roberts," May 10, 1875; "Benson H. Roberts to Ellen Roberts," May 14, 1875.

adamantly opposed to the view that the domestic vocation defined the full range of a woman's appropriate work. Moreover, Emma resisted Benson's view that if a woman were involved in public work, such work ought to be in the arena of social reform rather than the proclamation of the gospel. Further, Emma was offended by Benson's intimation that women's work ought to be in relation only to the needs of other women or domestic issues, but not in relation to, or with implied authority over men. Regarding this volley of correspondence with Emma, Benson made his position on this question crystal clear in a private letter to his mother:

> I have thought of Emma's letters—how much more favor she with her abilities and education could do by devoting her life to raising the standard of desire of the working women and training them to be true and faithful to the duties than she can ever do by engaging in a field from which Scripture excludes her, not as I think because of unfitness, but because her sphere lies in another direction. She cannot realize the need that there is for earnest true women in the noble work of reforming the evils under which the laboring women of the cities are crushed to the earth, or she would never have such an opportunity to which everything points her for, a field of such bountiful expediency.[82]

Convinced that his view was biblically correct, and perhaps operating in the petulance of youth, Benson even took a jab at his father's well-known view in favor of women preachers. "I wonder if Father has seen so few poor or unfortunate preachers" Benson wrote to his mother, "that he is willing to spoil a good Mother and a great reformer to add to the number of those who excite wonder and amazement rather than to accomplish great and lasting good."[83] Moreover, the regular preaching ministry of Ellen Roberts notwithstanding, Benson was even able to place the work of his mother over the years within his framework of his own understanding. Perhaps because Ellen Roberts was not licensed as an evangelist, and her ministry was based out of her home, Benson did not see his mother as a contradiction to his view. "My mother," wrote Benson, "has not needed to usurp what Scripture assigns to her husband to accomplish an untold amount of good."[84] It is thus clear that Benson Roberts's position in 1875—against that of his parents—was essentially the same as that of the 1861 Eastern convention: a strong affirmation of women's labors in Christian work, but an equally strong rejection of women's preaching. Emma, however, was convinced of

82. Roberts, "Benson H. Roberts to Ellen Roberts," May 1875.
83. Ibid.
84. Ibid.

the validity of the position of those who would—though she did not know it at the time—become her future in-laws. Echoing the sentiments of B. T. Roberts, Emma boldly exhorted Benson: "Let every woman use the ability God has given her, do the greatest work she can, and in her own way. May no man say to her thus far shalt thou go and no farther."[85]

Though it is unclear from Emma Sellew's letter, it is quite likely that she was considering a call to become a licensed evangelist. At the 1874 General Conference, just six months before Emma Sellew wrote to Benson Roberts in defense of her sense of vocational direction, the Free Methodist Church had approved the licensing of women evangelists. Licensure as an evangelist was thus opened to "any brother or sister in good standing" who felt "called of God to preach the Gospel, to labor to promote revivals of religion, and to spread abroad the cause of Christ in the land."[86] While such licensure was not to be confused with ordination, which also granted the right of pastoral appointment and participation in church governance, nonetheless a beginning was made by this action of the General Conference in 1874. Finally, Free Methodist women had the opportunity to be recognized and officially set apart for a role that many had played since the denomination's earliest days.

In the succeeding years, women continued to be active in ministry while the official machinery of denominational politics and deliberation moved at a slow but steady pace.[87] After a heated debate, the 1886 General Conference adopted a motion to make licensed evangelists members of the quarterly conference. Because those who were licensed evangelists included persons of both genders, this move had the important effect of cracking open the door for the official participation of women in the governing structures of the denomination. In 1890, at what would be his last General Conference, B. T. Roberts pushed hard for the adoption of a resolution approving the ordination of women. Most delegates, however, saw otherwise. Thus, as the denomination neared the end of its founding era, the full ordination of women still lay in an uncertain future.[88]

---

85. Sellew, "Emma J. Sellew to Benson H. Roberts," May 13, 1875.

86. *The Doctrines and Discipline of the Free Methodist Church (1874)*, 84.

87. The best historical overview of Free Methodist deliberations on the role of women is Richardson, "B. T. Roberts and the Role of Women in Ministry in Nineteenth-Century Free Methodism," 65–121.

88. The mounting interest in woman's sphere in the church caused a flurry of articles to appear in *The Free Methodist* in 1886. For a list of some of these articles, see Richardson, "B. T. Roberts and the Role of Women in Ministry in Nineteenth-Century Free Methodism," 138–41. See especially Wetherald, "Shall Women Be Ordained?"; Wetherald, "Shall Women Be Ordained? (Concluded)"; Griffith, "The Woman Question."

With the defeat of the 1890 General Conference behind him, B. T. Roberts set to work expanding and revising his earlier pamphlet, *The Right of Women to Preach the Gospel*.[89] His new book, *Ordaining Women*, was published in 1891. In it Roberts sought to provide biblical and practical rationale for the ordination of women. With the women's rights and suffrage movements challenging the ethics of the nation, Roberts specifically disclaimed any attempt to accommodate the denomination to the prevailing political climate. "I have purposely avoided all appeals to sentiment and to 'the spirit of the age', wrote Roberts, "and based my arguments mainly on the Word of God."[90] Roberts began by reminding his readers of the complicity of the church in the matter of human slavery. Using the Methodist Episcopal Church and Episcopal bishop, J. H. Hopkins, as examples, Roberts challenged his readers to consider the possibility that well-meaning Christians might also be mistaken on the issue of women in ministry. Then, based on a sixteen-chapter analysis of the matter from biblical, historical, and psychological perspectives, Roberts drew a final soteriological conclusion:

> The Gospel of Jesus Christ, in the provisions which it makes, and in the agencies which it employs, for the salvation of mankind, knows no distinction of race, condition, or sex, therefore no person evidently called of God to the Gospel ministry, and duly qualified for it, should be refused ordination on account of race, condition, or sex.[91]

In these words, Roberts summarized what he had believed and worked toward for many years. As it turned out, this was his last word on the matter. Roberts died on 27 February 1893, before he would have opportunity to shepherd the issue through another General Conference.

When the 1894 General Conference met, without Roberts at the helm, there was little doubt that the issue of women's ordination would at least be discussed. Strikingly, however, in the void of Roberts's presence, no actual resolution was presented; instead, the conference was merely poled by the presiding officer as to its sentiment on the question, "Do you believe in the ordination of women?" By a 65 percent majority the delegates voted in the negative.[92]

Nor was any headway made on the issue at either of the next two General Conferences in 1898 and 1903. For Ellen Roberts, as she grieved the loss of her husband, this lack of definitive action was doubly disconcerting. In

---

89. Roberts, *The Right of Women to Preach the Gospel*.
90. Roberts, *Ordaining Women: Biblical and Historical Insights*, 8.
91. Ibid., 104.
92. Marston, *From Age to Age*, 418.

undated holographs, which were written after the death of her husband, and after either the 1898 or 1903 General Conferences, Ellen Roberts expressed her frustration about the apparent lack of denominational determination to carry the matter forward.[93] "We have had a notable Gen[eral] Conf[erence] come and go," Ellen bemoaned, "with as far as I could hear a dead silence on this subject." She then clarified her position:

> I am no advocate for extravagance in this matter. I believe in a right decision being helpful to the church, and if women do the work of a man in God's vineyard, give her all that you give a man. I think my sisters will give all due deference to the other sex.[94]

Ellen also revealed that from her perspective things had gotten to the point that she felt compelled to speak out. "I confess I am stirred and cannot keep still much longer," Ellen confided. She then offered the additional revelation that the combination of Mr. Roberts's absence, her own passion about the issue, and the poor arguments of those on the other side, served only to steel her resolve:

> When my husband was here I could afford to keep still, though there was more than once in Gen[eral] Conf[erence] when I would gladly have stood up and testified that the opposition to ordination was making a strong convert of me that woman should have every privilege of men while capable of taking her place in all the hard work connected with preaching the gospel.[95]

Ellen Roberts also expressed gratitude that some in the church had indicated interest in her husband's published thoughts on the issue. She wished people to know that the substance of Mr. Roberts's earlier pamphlet, *The Right of Women to Preach the Gospel*, was contained in expanded form in his latest book, Ordaining Women. She even intimated that some members of the denomination might be resistant to reading it out of fear that it might change their minds. "Many have never read it," Ellen recognized, and then quipped: "Perhaps they do not like to trust themselves to read it. I am convinced the book is greatly needed, [and even] more so since the notable dead silence on the subject at the last Gen[eral] Conf[erence]."[96]

---

93. These two holographs were probably drafts of short editorial pieces intended for publication in either *The Earnest Christian* or *The Free Methodist*, but their actual appearance has not yet been located.

94. Roberts, Ellen, "Handwritten Note by Ellen Roberts, No. 1."

95. Roberts, Ellen, "Handwritten Note by Ellen Roberts, No. 2."

96. Ibid.

Indeed, Ellen Roberts wished for a readership much broader than the Free Methodist Church for her husband's book. She even believed that it could contribute to the national debate on the matter of women's rights. In a move that was indicative both of her desire to share her husband's work and her own engagement in the larger women's movement of the time, on May 4, 1905, Ellen Roberts gave a copy of *Ordaining Women* to Susan B. Anthony. Though there is no record of Anthony's response, the actual volume eventually made its way into the local history collection of the Rochester Public Library, Rochester, New York. In Ellen Roberts's handwriting, the flyleaf inscription reads, "To Susan B. Anthony from Ellen L. Roberts, wife of the Author, A. M. Chesbrough Seminary, N. Chili, N. Y., May 4, 1905."

Finally, in 1907, four years after the death B. T. Roberts and just months before the death of Ellen, the General Conference approved the ordination of women to the office of deacon. However, even this victory was only partial. The General Conference still restrained the ministry of women by including the proviso that the ordination of women to the office of deacon "shall not be considered a step toward ordination as elder."[97]

These narratives offer insight into a young denomination dually rooted, on the one hand, in what they understood to be the authority of Scripture and the Methodist tradition, and, on the other, in the right of private judgment. The net result of this dual emphasis was a denomination in which the leveling influence of democratic opinion was a determinative factor in discerning who could be authorized for various roles of church leadership. Tethered around a central core of common soteriological affirmation, a significant level of diversity flourished in which the voices of the people—laity and clergy—demanded to be heard. Even the women, who in the founding era were never granted full participation in the governing structures of the church, kept on speaking.

Bibliography

Cross, Whitney R. *The Burned-Over District: The Social and Intellectual History of Enthusiastic Religion in Western New York*. Ithaca: Cornell University Press, 1950.
Dayton, Donald W. *Discovering an Evangelical Heritage*. Peabody, MA: Hendrickson, 1988.

---

97. Marston, *From Age to Age*, 419. The ordination of women as elders was not approved in the Free Methodist Church until the General Conference of 1974. For additional discussion and promotion of this issue in the late nineteenth and early twentieth centuries, see Sellew, *Why Not?*; Meyer, *Deaconesses*; Roberts, Ellen L. "Shall the Free Methodist Church Employ Deaconesses?"; Rowe, "The Ordination of Women: Round One."

The Doctrines and Discipline of the Free Methodist Church (1874). North Chili, NY: Earnest Christian, 1875.

Freeland, Mariet H. "Women of Early Free Methodism." *The Free Methodist* (3 May 1898) 11–12.

Gould, William. "Mothers in Israel." *The Free Methodist* (4 January 1898) 4–5.

Gramento, Jean Hall. "Those Astounding Free Methodist Women: A Biographical History of Free Methodist Women in Ministry with an Extended Bibliography of Free Methodist Women's Studies." DMin thesis, United Theological Seminary, 1992.

Griffith, G.W. "The Woman Question." *The Free Methodist* (18 May 1892) 2.

Hogue, Wilson T. *History of the Free Methodist Church.* 2 vols. Chicago: Free Methodist, 1915.

Marston, Leslie R. *From Age to Age a Living Witness: A Historical Interpretation of Free Methodism's First Century.* Winona Lake, IN: Light and Life, 1960.

Meyer, Lucy R. *Deaconesses, Biblical, Early Church, European, American, with the Story of the Chicago Training School, for the City, Home and Foreign Missions, and the Chicago Deaconess Home.* Chicago: Message, 1889.

"Minutes of the Genesee Annual Convention of the Free Methodist Church." Perry, NY, October 24–28, 1861, 13–14, cited by Hogue, *History*, 1:345.

Richardson, Jack D. "B. T. Roberts and the Role of Women in Ministry in Nineteenth-Century Free Methodism." MA thesis, Colgate-Rochester Divinity School, 1984.

Roberts, Benjamin T. "The Diary of Benjamin T. Roberts." *Collected Papers of Benjamin T. Roberts Family (Covering the Years 1832–1924).* Library of Congress.

———. "Editorial." *Earnest Christian* (December 1860) 392–93.

———. *Ordaining Women: Biblical and Historical Insights.* 1891. Repr., Indianapolis: Light and Life, 1992.

———. *The Right of Women to Preach the Gospel.* Rochester, NY: Roberts, 1872.

———. *Why Another Sect, Containing a Review of Articles by Bishop Simpson and Others on the Free Methodist Church.* Rochester, NY: Earnest Christian, 1879.

Roberts, Benson H. *Benjamin Titus Roberts: A Biography.* North Chili, NY: Earnest Christian, 1900.

Roberts, Ellen L. "Handwritten Note by Ellen Roberts, No. 1." Holograph document. *Collected Papers of Benjamin T. Roberts Family (Covering the Years 1832–1924).* Library of Congress.

———. "Handwritten Note by Ellen Roberts, No. 2." Holograph document. *Collected Papers of Benjamin T. Roberts Family (Covering the Years 1832–1924).* Library of Congress.

———. "Shall the Free Methodist Church Employ Deaconesses?" *The Free Methodist* (1 February 1898) 3.

Rowe, Kenneth E. "The Ordination of Women: Round One: Anna Oliver and the General Conference of 1880." In *Perspectives on American Methodism: Interpretive Essays*, edited by Russell E. Richey et al., 298–308. Nashville: Kingswood, 1993.

Sellew, W. A. *Why Not? A Plea for the Ordination of Those Women Whom God Has Called to Preach the Gospel.* North Chili, NY: Earnest Christian, 1894.

Shay, Emma F. *Mariet Hardy Freeland, a Faithful Witness: A Biography by Her Daughter.* Chicago: Free Methodist, 1913.

Smith, Timothy L. *Revivalism and Social Reform: American Protestantism on the Eve of the Civil War.* Baltimore: Johns Hopkins University Press, 1980.

Wetherald, Clara L. "Shall Women Be Ordained?" *The Free Methodist* (14 May 1890) 2.
———. "Shall Women Be Ordained? (Concluded)." *The Free Methodist* (21 May 1890) 2.
Zahniser, Clarence H. *Earnest Christian: Life and Works of Benjamin Titus Roberts*. Published by the author, 1957.

2

Ordaining Women

Discourse of Dissent at the Intersection of Text and Context

—Elvera B. Berry

A century and a half ago, the culture was rife with dissent in areas of race, religion, and gender as western New York became the geographic seat of organized communities of dissent and change. *Race* was epitomized in the Civil War, as well as in the Underground Railroad with its own form of rhetoric and ideological as well as literal movements via that "train." *Religion* was no longer seen as the sole province of established churches but found expression, instead, in newly developing religious organizations and approaches to faith—the Mormons in Palmyra and Spiritualists in Lily Dale, for example, along with a strong Society of Friends movement and periodic revivalism under itinerate preachers like Charles Grandison Finney, Presbyterian minister and later president of Oberlin College. *Gender*, too, gained a new voice with its first-wave highly organized suffragettes, the Seneca Falls Convention, and the publication of the *Declaration of Sentiments*.[1]

---

1. Stanton et al., "The Declaration of Sentiments and Resolutions Seneca Falls Conference."

The Man in Context

Benjamin Titus Roberts had been born into a farmer's family in the rural community of Gowanda in southwestern New York, on July 25, 1823, about one hundred miles from Rochester and within fifty miles of centers of newly attractive ideas, Lily Dale and Chautauqua. He was academically gifted, began teaching school at age sixteen, and apprenticed with an attorney—his intended profession. At age twenty, he underwent a spiritual conversion and entered Wesleyan University in Connecticut, where he graduated with high honors and a highly esteemed Master of Arts degree. Having proven himself as an educator while at Wesleyan, and influenced by President Stephen Olin and revivalist, John Wesley Redfield, he was offered the presidency of a seminary but returned, instead, to western New York to join the Genesee Conference of the established Methodist Episcopal (M. E.) Church.

In 1849, he married the woman with whom he had a life-long love affair and who became a true partner in all his endeavors: Ellen Lois Stowe (relative of Harriet Beecher Stowe). For a decade, he pastored churches throughout western New York between Rochester and Buffalo, and between Lake Ontario and the Southern Tier. Almost immediately, he was "on the hot seat" for writing and speaking against established church practices that, to Roberts, defied Scripture and the theology of John Wesley. By the time he died in 1893, he had been the major influence in the formation of a related but distinct denomination, Free Methodism (1860 in Pekin, NY), and had evidenced his commitment to education through the founding and support of a "seminary" (i.e., a place of study) in 1866—a school that eventually became Roberts Wesleyan College, in Rochester, New York.

The Discourse of Dissent

The written discourse of B. T. Roberts reflects one who was increasingly called to multiple "freedoms" grounded in his understanding of biblical text and human context: equality of both access and rights regardless of gender, race, or economic status. His was, in many ways, a discourse of dissent. On one hand, Roberts was an exceptionally learned man naturally inclined toward the art of rhetoric: a diligent student steeped in classical learning that permeated his writing, a would-be lawyer familiar with tenets of argument and debate, a university-trained scholar, and a natural teacher. On the other hand, he was a biblical scholar committed to living his faith: a charismatic interpreter of the Word, a preacher and evangelist fully engaged in the work of the Gospel, a husband and father torn by frequent absence, and a recognized leader in the church. Joining the voices of such contemporaries as Abraham Lincoln, Frederick Douglass, Susan B. Anthony, and Charles G. Finney, he found himself challenged on all fronts: political, social, and theological.

From whatever angle one views Roberts, one sees a man caught between personal commitment and contextual exigency—between individual piety and cultural norms. The demands of his faith at another historical juncture might not have led to the final break with his beloved M. E. Church in 1860.[2] Indeed, it is conceivable that he might have been able to argue successfully on behalf of one or another of his several calls to "freedom." Perhaps he could have persuaded at least one individual Methodist congregation to reconsider the ravages of human slavery and take a humane and theological stand. Some might also have become leery, as Roberts was, of secret societies. The church could possibly have revised its stance on raising money by "selling" discriminating rights to congregational seating, and some might even have been willing to compromise on allowing women to become educated and, ultimately, fully ordained as clergy.

Reviewing his wide-ranging corpus of articles, books, letters, magazines, pamphlets, petitions, position papers, and tracts, one discovers the interrelatedness among these concerns and other pietistic commitments that would have made it impossible for him to focus on any one issue to the exclusion of the others. Taken together, his many documents represent not only significant aspects of day-to-day ministry and teaching, but also vision-driven principles foundational to political, cultural, and labor-related issues of social justice. Whether short pieces or long, whatever the topic, his writing exemplifies astonishing contact with history, literature, philosophy, and theology as well as enviable understanding of language and mastery of rhetoric. *Ordaining Women*, however, represents his culminating masterpiece—a work that can be treated as what literary and social critic Kenneth Burke would call a "representative anecdote" of his carefully honed rhetoric. Examination of that particular text is an instructive study that is in many ways no less relevant today than it was when it was published in 1891, some thirty years after Ellen Stowe Roberts had gained "wide acceptance" as "guest preacher, pulpit supply, or assistant at the meetings of the regular clergymen."[3] That was seventeen years after women had gained licensure as "evangelist" in 1874, sixteen years before licensure as "deacon" in 1907, and eighty-three years before full-ministerial ordination of women as elders in

---

2. Roberts, *The Bishop and His Lady*, 54–57.
3. Cullum, "Fanatical Women," 11.

the Free Methodist Church was finally approved in 1974—a full century after the earliest "evangelist" licensure.[4]

The goal of this study is to look at and beyond the endlessly fascinating "person," Benjamin Titus Roberts, through the examination of his rhetoric in *Ordaining Women*, asking such questions as: What is it that seems to empower this man? Which rhetorical tools does he employ once he has come to terms with his Wesleyan call to personal and social piety? How does this solo voice respond to the call to dissent? What enables him to function at the intersection of the rhetorical and theological? In what types of discourse does he engage, and how does he construct his arguments for those who will listen?

Introduction to the Text

Ordaining Women is among the last of the many articles, treatises and books in which Roberts addressed specific issues of great concern: abolition of slavery, "free" churches, holiness, need for education, responsible use of money, rudiments of preaching, social justice, temperance, and women's roles. Published just two years before his death, it represents the culmination of an extended argument first, with mainline Methodism and then, with leaders of his own Free Methodist Church who had long since acquiesced regarding slavery, equality in the worship space, and the like. As still evidenced in many areas 125 years later, including church circles, women complicate things! They belong to the human species, having been created in God's image, but often remain "separately" equal. Roberts had tried unsuccessfully to convince decision makers at all levels to embrace theological equality of women, but he had been forced to be content with baby steps moving a woman from preacher's "assistant," or guest preacher—when men were not available, to no further than "evangelist" by the time he died. Even the next step of woman's licensure as "deacon" did not occur until three years into the twentieth century, a decade after his death and seventy-one years before full ordination as "elder" in the Free Methodist Church. What accounts for Bishop Roberts's inability to witness the ordination of women, and how can we call his rhetoric successful?

Progress had, indeed, been made in all other areas, both within and outside of the church. By the time he gathered his rhetorical forces in publishing *Ordaining Women*, the slaves had been declared free, and the fifteenth amendment to the Constitution had already been ratified for twenty-one years: "The right of citizens of the United States to vote shall not

4. Ibid., 27 n. 97.

be denied or abridged by the United States or by any State *on account of race, color, or previous condition of servitude* [*italics* added]."[5] Struggles regarding race would continue, and new federal laws and acts would be needed—and continue to be needed—to address ongoing challenges, but the die had been cast. Not until fifty years later, however, would the vision cast alongside suffrage for Negro men be ratified for women in the nineteenth amendment: "The right of citizens of the United States to vote shall not be denied or abridged by the United States or by any State *on account of sex*" [*italics* added].[6]

Regarding women, therefore, Roberts was facing opposition on two significant fronts, both of which were male-dominated: cultural and religious. Clearly products of the dominant culture in which rights were determined and practiced by men, most male decision makers stayed that unexamined course in both social and religious contexts. To suggest that women be allowed to become equal in terms of using their gifts, intellect, and calling was at best problematic. To further suggest biblical endorsement of equal access to interpretation of Scriptures, preaching, and church governance was beyond the pale. Truths long held inviolate were being brought into question in a context of moral, social, and theological upheaval—a context in which Roberts's movement toward women's ordination paralleled the struggles of women seeking the right to vote, the opportunity for an education, and the desire to engage in work beyond "homemaking" on their own terms. Notable suffragettes and women fiction writers had begun to publish on culturally controversial topics: e.g., slavery in Harriet Beecher Stowe's *Uncle Tom's Cabin* (1852), and women's independence in Charlotte Perkins Gilman's *Yellow Wallpaper* (1892) and Kate Chopin's *The Awakening* (1899). Few, however, were concerned about changing the roles of women in the church. Remaining sympathetic to broader freedoms for which he had fought, Roberts turns once more to what had no doubt been his greatest disappointment: lack of ordination for women.

Ordaining Women opens with what becomes his signature verse:

> "There is neither Jew nor Greek, there is neither bond nor free, there is neither male nor female: for ye are all one in Christ Jesus."
>
> —Galatians iii, 28.[7]

The Title page is followed by a Dedication to the author's "beloved wife":

---

5. *U.S. Constitution*, amendment 15.
6. *U.S. Constitution*, amendment 19.
7. Roberts, *Ordaining Women*, 1.

TO

My Beloved Wife,

WHO FOR FORTY-TWO YEARS

HAS FAITHFULLY STOOD BY ME IN THE GOSPEL MINISTRY,

Who has never shunned to be a partaker of the

AFFLICTIONS OF THE GOSPEL,

But has faced undismayed the fires of persecution,

WHO HAS BEEN TO ME A CONSTANT INSPIRATION
TO A FULLER UNDERSTANDING OF THE

Mysteries of the Kingdom,

These Pages Are Affectionately Dedicated

BY THE AUTHOR[8]

The book includes a brief stage-setting preface and sixteen chapters of uneven length (from four to twenty-one pages each). In the two-page seventeenth chapter, "Conclusion," Roberts lists six "propositions [that] have been clearly proved,"[9] followed by a totally capitalized statement written in the style of the fifteenth and nineteenth amendments to the Constitution—with comparable substance: ". . . THEREFORE NO PERSON EVIDENTLY CALLED OF GOD TO THE GOSPEL MINISTRY, AND DULY QUALIFIED FOR IT SHOULD BE REFUSED ORDINATION ON ACCOUNT OF RACE, CONDITION, OR SEX."[10]

Challenges to Ordination

From the arresting opening lines of the preface—"I have written this book from a strong conviction of duty. Christ commands us to let our light shine."[11]—to the closing statement of his "final CONCLUSION [sic]," Roberts exhibits the culmination of a lifetime's attention to the use and power of words. His language is clear, his appeal direct, his references abundant, and his arguments persuasive. The preface, while straightforward in alerting the reader to his intent to prove the equality of women based "mainly on the

---

8. Ibid., 5.
9. Ibid., 159.
10. Ibid.
11. Ibid., 6.

Word of God,"[12] recognizes the likelihood of an unsympathetic audience and immediately invites thoughtful consideration: "There is no reason why this subject should not be considered as calmly and candidly as any other."[13] Within two more sentences, he has invoked both "Scripture and reason" and has pointed to the 200-year history of the Society of Friends in which:

> woman has been accorded the same rights as man, and yet she has lost none of her womanliness in consequence. Among no class of people are women more true, and modest, and domestic, and noble, and refined, and given to every good work than among them. Nowhere else can be found more beautiful, happy homes than in the Society of the Friends.[14]

Lest the rights of a woman be viewed too narrowly, he immediately widens the lens to the State of Wyoming in which women had already been voting for twenty years. "Nor need we have any fearful forebodings, if giving to women equal rights in the church should lead to giving her equal rights in the state."[15] He invites readers to consider the reported conscientiousness and positive influence of women "on the side of good government and for the selection of the best men for office,"[16] always functioning against corruption and "the ignorant and criminal elements which have such control in the municipal affairs of the leading cities of the United States."[17] (In 1891, Roberts has pointed to arguments regarding the need for female ameliorative perspectives that continue to be made in politics and industry 125 years later.) Having now become one with the reader by invoking "we," he emphasizes his reliance on reason as he interprets the Word of God and invites the reader into the conversation: "I ask as a special favor of those who have decided not to agree with the position I have taken that they will read before they condemn. The subject is worthy of patient and prayerful investigation."[18]

Each chapter's title serves to both encapsulate the chapter and move the argument logically forward. Each title is followed by a carefully targeted quotation (sometimes two) primarily from the works of highly esteemed poets who represent a range of religious expressions. Chapters themselves are replete with biblical exegesis and approximately one hundred references

---

12. Ibid., 8.
13. Ibid., 6.
14. Ibid.
15. Ibid., 8.
16. Ibid.
17. Ibid.
18. Ibid.

to and quotations from seminal bishops, educators, explorers, historians, martyrs, monarchs, philosophers, political leaders, preachers, priests, professors, reformers, rhetoricians, scientists, and theologians, spanning cultures from ancient Greece and Rome to current nineteenth-century Europe and the United States. Liberally interspersed throughout the entire book, the references not only confirm the breadth and depth of a highly learned man, but also exemplify his ability to draw upon disparate and debatable perspectives to construct his own compelling case for the ordination of women. Overall, the chapters move as a debatable argument might be framed and rhetorically unpacked for greatest persuasiveness: the definition of "woman" in terms of current practice and some of the problems with that definition; identification of problems inherent in the limitations of words and language; range of current views regarding ordination; careful analysis of theological and secular objections to ordination; examples of women apostles and prophets, deacons, and deaconesses; need for evangelists and biblical injunction regarding evangelism; proof of scriptural and secular fitness for leadership and governance; and precedence of equal treatment under early law.

The intent here is not to delineate full details of every chapter, but to examine the overall flow of argument and to elaborate on some of the pivotal rhetorical choices Roberts made in his last published discourse of dissent. Women's equality had been a concern from early on in his ministry, one which readily accompanied his concerns about slavery and free access to worship. He had witnessed the effectiveness of women who were taking on the work of ministry but being denied full expression of their calling.[19] And surely, his enduring love and respect for Ellen throughout their long and mutually happy marriage-partnership had exacerbated his frustration with the role women were allowed to play in both society and the church. What had been a series of repeatedly failed attempts to move his own denomination to accept the full ordination of women now became a 159-page document and lasting legacy paralleling his abolitionist arguments. Equality under the law had come to mean equality under both scriptural and secular law for all!

As one reads the text, one cannot help but observe not only its organizational "rhetorical" flow referenced above, but also the many ways in which it mirrors both historical and contemporary communication theory. While Aristotle, whom Roberts recognizes as "one of the greatest of the old Greek philosophers,"[20] would not typically be quoted in support of women's

19. See Cullum, "Fanatical Women."
20. Ibid., 10.

rights, let alone scriptural interpretation, Roberts recognizes his primary goal as part of a much larger hegemonic and interpretive issue. Similarly, while contemporary theories related to hegemonic forces (e.g., Stuart Hall: "Cultural Studies"; Julia Wood plus Patricia Collins and Sandra Harding: "Standpoint," *Cheris Kramarae*: "Muted Group") further applied to the marginalization of women in the church certainly would not have been Aristotle's concern, Roberts understands the broader implications of Aristotelian insights, especially "in his [Aristotle's] book on Politics and Economics."[21]

The fundamental argument of reason in "Prejudice," the opening chapter of *Ordaining Women*, rests on recognizing the ordination of women as an emancipatory act not unlike abolition of slavery. Roberts cites Aristotle regarding the natural condition of slavery, italicizing portions he wants to emphasize:

> By nature some beings command, and others obey, for the sake of mutual safety; for a being endowed with discernment and forethought is, by nature, the superior and governor; whereas he who is merely able to execute by bodily labor is inferior and a *natural slave*; and hence the *interest of master and slave is identical* . . . (from Book 1, Chapter 2, p.4) [and later] . . . it is clear then, that some men *are free by nature, and others are slaves, and that in the case of the latter, the lot of slavery is both advantageous and just*. (from Book 2, Chapter 5, p. 13)[22]

Roberts notes Aristotle's resultant justification of "the art of war" as "a part of the art of acquisition" used against those who "*are unwilling to submit*" to the slavery to which they were born, and then points to the contextualism built into analogous conclusions among 1860s churches. An 1836 M. E. Church resolution opposes "modern Abolitionism, and wholly disclaim[s] any right, wish, or intention to interfere in the civil and political relation between master and slave as it exists in the slave holding States of this Union."[23] Roberts cannot resist pointing out that once "slavery was abolished by war, the above resolutions were repealed, and another General Conference of the same Church passed a resolution to the effect that it was a matter of congratulation that the M. E. Church had always taken the lead of the sister churches in the anti-slavery movement."[24] Similarly, the Right Rev. John Henry Hopkins, Protestant Episcopal Bishop of the diocese of Vermont, had written that "human slavery, as it then existed in these United States,

21. Ibid., 10–11.
22. Ibid., 10.
23. Ibid., 11.
24. Ibid., 12.

was supported by 'the authority of the Bible, the writing of the Fathers, the decrees of Councils, the concurrent judgment of Protestant divines, and the Constitution.' The efforts to overthrow it he characterized as the 'assaults of mistaken philanthropy, in union with infidelity, fanaticism, and political expediency.'"[25]

The strength of the argument lies in recognizing that there is precedent for change even among those guided by "Reason and Revelation," be they ancient thinkers or contemporary bishops. If they were "so greatly mistaken on a subject which we now think so plain that it does not admit of dispute, that every man has a right to freedom, is it not possible that the current sentiment as to the position which WOMAN [sic] should be permitted to occupy in the *Church of Christ* may also be wrong?"[26] Note that Roberts has framed his argument not with regard to "slavery," per se, but with the "right to freedom." Returning to the language of Law, he incorporates grammatical direct address: "Reader, will you admit this possibility? Will you sit as an impartial juror in the case, and carefully weigh the evidence we may present?" Finally, acknowledging that understandings can be proven imperfect, he appeals to reason, equating slavery with denial of a woman's right to ordination: "Let us decide that as the church did, for ages, misinterpret the teachings of the Bible on the subject of slavery, so it may now fail to apprehend its teaching on the question of woman's rights."[27]

Having thus introduced the "problem" and his intent (chapter 1), Roberts must ascertain "Woman's Legal Condition" (chapter 2) in order to show why the current state of women makes the "right to freedom" impossible. He traces forms of slave-like subjugation to a husband from laws of Rome across the continents of Africa, Europe, and North America with the help of first-hand accounts, including David Livingstone's *In Darkest Africa*;[28] to L. P. Brackett's accounts of "German women of the lower, and to some extent of the middle classes"; and to John Stuart Mill's extended description of the woman's "bondservant" place in England.[29] Mill details the many ways in which a wife is owned by her husband through vows of matrimony, common law in which "whatever is hers is his, but the parallel inference is never drawn that whatever is his is hers," slavery "at all hours and all minutes,"[30] and the raising of children who "are by law his children" and hers upon his

25. Ibid.
26. Ibid., 13.
27. Ibid.
28. Ibid., 16.
29. Ibid., 14–21.
30. Ibid., 19.

death only if his will declares her "legal guardian."[31] Roberts observes that while legal conditions are more favorable in this country, many of the same "laws" are practiced, and "yet in thirty-six of our [forty-three] states the woman with a husband living is not the legal owner of her children. The husband has the legal control, and in some of the states he can will the child away from his wife before the child is born."[32] Acknowledging that "it is no wonder that our prejudices against the rights of woman . . . infused into us from early childhood, should be so strong,"[33] he returns to the first chapter's awakening to the problem with hope, declaring simply: "But reason and grace serve to overcome *prejudice* [*italics* added]."[34]

The first two chapters are illustrative of awareness of audience, fluidity of thought, and tightness of reasoning one finds throughout the book. With astounding agility, Roberts accesses clerical, cultural, historical, literary, philosophical, political, and scientific resources to augment and strengthen his fundamental assertion of biblical equality. He clearly assumes an educated audience whom he hopes to woo primarily through artful use of reason in support of revelation. When viewed through Aristotle's lens of artistic proofs, *logos* dominates and results in countless examples of syllogistic or, in some cases, enthymematic proofs. Roberts uses the rhetorical enthymematic form of syllogism, for example, when he leads the reader implicitly to equate slavery with denial of women's rights in order to conclude that having been wrong about slavery, the church may very well also be wrong about ordination of women.

Overt *pathos*—appeals (to emotions) are virtually lacking in the text—and would not have been deemed appropriate for an argument deliberately framed to invite serious re-consideration of a long-debated issue. Roberts reserves personal responses grounded in *pathos* primarily for matters of his own heart and for work on behalf of those suffering physical pain, cruel injustice, or heartbreaking circumstance. Sensitivities to his own and loved ones' distress, to the overwhelming needs of the many who were struggling with life's adversities, and to the urgency of redemption and grace are given voice in letters, speeches, and sermons—but not in *Ordination of Women* lest the strength of the audience- and reason-centered argument be threatened.

Ethos appeals, on the other hand, are built into the fabric of *logos* exhibited in the text. Concerned with maintaining credibility as a scholar and man of the cloth, he continually refers to carefully selected women and men

31. Ibid., 20.
32. Ibid., 21.
33. Ibid.
34. Ibid.

whose names will be recognized and ideas respected by his readers. How could one go wrong with admired thinkers, biblical characters, cherished poets, respected teachers, revered clergy, venerated bishops, and acclaimed martyrs? How can one argue with a case resting on evidence related to over 125 named persons, including at least thirty-five from the Bible, along with over ninety biblical passages? Even while he argues against positions taken by some whom he quotes, rightfully acknowledging their perceived legitimacy, Roberts is reminding the reader of the significance of human interpretation in matters of great consequence.

In light of the centrality of interpretation in every aspect of argument, the master-teacher takes a detour from the topic he has so carefully framed. On one hand, the next chapter (chapter 3) includes no mention of freedom, ordination, rights, or slavery. On the other hand, this shortest chapter, "Words,"[35] may be the most salient from a rhetorical perspective and, ultimately, in terms of providing linguistic tools for making his case in the remaining fourteen chapters. Everything in the first two chapters of *Ordaining Women* attests implicitly to the significance of words, and few would have had difficulty following the ideas laid out in the preface and first two chapters. Whereas some readers might now be disagreeing with the intent of the book or the arguments Roberts has introduced, others might be applauding his carefully framed evidence pointing to the possibility of change. Whatever their current position, Roberts recognizes that *all* need to be reminded of the nature and power of language, of words: the undisputed human means of understanding and communicating—concerning the past, present, and future.

A quotation from Samuel Johnson sets the stage for both the necessity and ambiguity of words: "I am not so lost in lexicography as to forget that words are the daughters of earth, and that things are the sons of Heaven."[36] While the implied hierarchy of sons "above" and daughters "below" might be perceived as problematic, if we add a bit more of the quotation than appears in the text, we see the very complexity that Roberts goes on to recognize and address. Johnson continues, "Language is only the instrument of science and words are but the signs of ideas . . ."[37] From a rhetorical perspective, we are absolutely bound to language and words for access to both things and ideas.

As twentieth-century literary and rhetorical critic Kenneth Burke points out in *The Rhetoric of Religion* and develops in theoretical and

---

35. Ibid., 22–25.
36. Ibid., 22.
37. Ibid.

practical terms, we engage language related to four realms: words for the "natural" things, the tangible things of our world; words for the "sociopolitical realm," including words for ideas, laws, relationships, etc.; "words about words," including words related to grammar, etymology, rhetoric, etc.; and finally, words for the "supernatural." Burke observes that since:

> the supernatural is by definition the realm of the "ineffable." And our language by definition is not suited to the expression of the "ineffable." So, our words for the fourth realm, the supernatural . . . are necessarily borrowed from the sorts of things we can talk about literally, our words for . . . the world of everyday experience.[38]

Roberts applies similar understanding of how language works to the biblical text in 1 Corinthians 15:46, "Howbeit that was not first which is spiritual, but that which is natural; and afterward that which is spiritual." (His use of the King James translation provides further evidence of the complexity and time-bound nature of linguistic interpretation. Today, the New International Version might better serve understanding for many: "The spiritual did not come first, but the natural, and after that the spiritual.") He understands that the distinction between words and things "is true, not only of things, but of words which represent things"[39] and concludes, like Burke, that "all the ecclesiastical terms of the New Testament . . . had primarily [i.e., originally], a secular meaning."[40] Tracing several Greek words, he illustrates the challenges of translation, definition, and usage: "*pneuma*, spirit, in its primary meaning signifies *wind, air, the air we breathe*, . . . *kerux*, preacher, was a *herald*, who summoned the assembly . . . *apostolos*, apostle, was *one sent*, a messenger . . . *presbus*, elder—one of mature years . . . *episkopos*, bishop, was an overseer, watcher, guardian . . . *diakonos*, deacon, a servant, waiting-man or woman. The word is of common gender."[41] Noting the "common gender" of *diakonos* foreshadows discussions of "Deacons" (chapter 10) and "Deaconnesses" (chapter 11).

In many ways, Roberts has already moved ahead to modern times in which language has come to be understood as honorifically rather than pejoratively arbitrary and, by definition, interpretive. He understands that no word fully captures the intended referent because words are loaded with history and implications. Seventy years later, Burke summarizes the elusive nature of words: "Words are to non-verbal things they name as Spirit is

38. Burke, *The Rhetoric of Religion*, 15.
39. Roberts, *Ordaining Women*, 22.
40. Ibid., 23.
41. Ibid., 22–23.

to Matter... There is a sense in which the word 'transcends' the thing it names."[42] Thus, while we seek one-to-one correspondence between word and substance, as well as definitive closure regarding meaning and intent, we know that language—as life itself—"is more complicated than that."[43] We recognize, as did Roberts, the complexity of dealing with words, words-in-translation and, especially, words related to a spiritual realm outside our own. We also recognize that while some continue to debate the total inerrancy of biblical texts, all of which involve human translation, "words are arbitrary signs of ideas or of things. And often the same word represents things which have no relation to each other"[44]—whether used in matters of everyday life, academic debate, or religious faith. Here, Roberts uses examples with which we might not resonate today but with which his readers would have been familiar:

> The mother who brings up her children to obey her is sometimes obliged to use the *switch* upon the refractory child. The railroad man, by turning the *switch* wrong, wrecked the train. The fashionable woman when she buys a *switch* is careful to have it match her own hair. The farmer cuts his wheat with a *cradle*. His wife rocks the baby in a *cradle*.[45]

He explains: "These illustrations show that in ascertaining the meaning of a word we must look at the connection in which it stands"[46]; his stated intent is to remain cognizant of the context, giving "to words the signification intended by those who used them."[47]

Quoting nineteenth-century Max Müller, German scholar of comparative language (especially Sanskrit) and religion, Roberts concludes the chapter on "Words" with a summarizing statement on language that continues to speak today. The study of words, Müller says:

> may be tedious to the school-boy, as breaking of stones is to the wayside laborer: but to the thoughtful eye of the geologist these stones are full of interest; he sees miracles on the high road and reads chronicles in every ditch. Language, too, has marvels of her own, which she unveils to the inquiring glance of the patient

---

42. Burke, *The Rhetoric of Religion*, 16.
43. Ibid., 277.
44. Roberts, *Ordaining Women*, 24.
45. Ibid.
46. Ibid.
47. Ibid., 25.

student. There are chronicles below her surface; there are sermons in every word.[48]

The sermonic nature of our value-laden language has been recognized and explored by such twentieth-century rhetoricians as Kenneth Burke[49] and Richard Weaver,[50] and continues to be a focus of contemporary rhetorical studies.[51] Roberts has resonated with Müller's wedding of the secular and the sacred as he moves from the miraculous nature of language to the sermons hidden in every word. That wedding of concrete-word with ever-elusive-antecedent, of "spirit with matter," is foundational to the argument Roberts will now construct.

"Ordination, while it does not, in the rite itself, convey any supernatural, or magical power, yet it should be the occasion of great and permanent blessing to the person ordained."[52] Before addressing arguments for and against women's ordination, Roberts lays the definitional foundation of "Ordination" in his fourth and longest chapter: twenty pages, over half of which is devoted to what Protestant ordination is not. Placing proper ordination between extremes of non-sacramental Friends, on one hand, and power-conferring ordination of male priests in Roman Catholicism, on the other, he upholds ordination as a community-based symbol of an individual's response to the Holy Spirit's calling and "dedication to the work of the Gospel."[53] He includes just a brief, matter-of-fact conclusion regarding women toward the end of the chapter: "There is nothing, then, in the nature of ordination which indicates that no woman should ever be ordained. If she is *called of God* to his work, and this is evident to the church, then may the church *separate* her to this work by ordination."[54]

Almost a third of the way through *Ordaining Women*, having now defined the terms and parameters, Roberts turns to the classic rhetorical strategy of naming and addressing opposing arguments, to which he devotes three chapters. "The objections to the ordination of women may be classed under two heads—*Scriptural* ["Old Testament," chapter 5, and "New Testament," chapter 6] and *natural* [chapter 7]."[55] He begins both *Scriptural* chapters with a frontal attack before identifying and refuting others'

48. Ibid.
49. Burke, *A Rhetoric of Motives*.
50. Weaver, "Language is Sermonic."
51. See Brummett, *Reading Rhetorical Theory*, 671–928.
52. Roberts, *Ordaining Women*, 44.
53. Ibid., 35–45.
54. Ibid., 44.
55. Ibid., 47.

arguments. His opening *Old Testament* argument speaks directly to those who deem the woman inferior and subservient to the man because she was created last, to which Roberts responds: "If this proves anything, it proves her superiority. For the work of creation proceeded in regular gradation from the lower to the higher."[56] His opening *New Testament* argument is simply: "In all that we have heard and read against the right of woman to be, in the fullest sense, a minister of the gospel, we have never heard or read a single quotation from the words of Jesus against this right. This is significant. Christ applied the same rules of moral conduct to the woman as to the man,"[57] to which he adds Paul's Galatians 3:28 definitive inclusion of Jews, Greeks, bond, free, male, and female as "all one in Christ Jesus."[58]

The rest of the two *Scriptural* chapters contain carefully developed supporting evidence in favor of ordination. Since his case rests most heavily on conflicting interpretations of Paul's letters of instruction to the early churches, the New Testament chapter is twice as long as the Old.[59] Both chapters, however, follow the same pattern of addressing "objections" one by one using a combination of Scripture and support from respected scholars and theologians who had produced extensive biblical commentaries that are still valued today: Methodist Adam Clarke and Presbyterian Matthew Henry. To every objection, Roberts has a reasoned response.

As still debated today, objections related to the Old Testament focus first on the wording of the creation story and implications of the fall. Who was created to "have dominion" when both male and female were created in God's image? Do laws of subjugation referred to in portions of the Old Testament still obtain once Christ has come and re-introduced the desired state, or has Christ "*restored the primitive law?*" Roberts emphasizes, "[Christ] said nothing about the *subjection of woman—not one word.*"[60] He goes on to decry the objection that functioning as a "'domestic society requires the wife to be subject to the husband.' This is a great mistake. If it did, Christ would doubtless have given directions accordingly. But it does not."[61] Here, we see his strong stance by declaration and analogy:

> The greatest domestic happiness always exists where husband and wife live together on terms of equality. Two men, having individual interests, united only by business ties, daily associate

56. Ibid.
57. Ibid., 54.
58. Ibid., 55.
59. Ibid., 54–68.
60. Ibid., 51.
61. Ibid.

> as partners for years, without either of them being in subjection to the other. They consider each other as equals; and treat each other as equals. Then, cannot a man and woman, united by conjugal love, the strongest tie that can unite two human beings. Having the same interests, live together in *the same* manner?[62]
>
> Christ came to repair the ruin wrought by the fall. In Him, and in Him only, is Paradise *restored*. The Gospel belongs to woman as much as to man.[63]

Finally, he agrees with the claim that "under the Aaronic priesthood men only were priests . . . But the priests were not the only or the chief religious teachers of the Jews. The prophets ranked in this respect above the priests . . . but women prophesied,"[64] as evidenced in four prophetesses, Miriam, Deborah, Huldah, and Noadiah. "Then we conclude that there is nothing in the creation of woman or in her condition under the law which proves that no woman should be ordained as a minister of the Gospel."[65]

In "Objections—New Testament" (chapter 6), Roberts sees "for ye are all one in Christ Jesus" as the "KEY-TEXT (*sic*)" related to rights of women.[66] He fully develops five scriptural and reason-based arguments to counter the basic objection that Paul intended equality only in terms of salvation and extension beyond salvation constitutes misinterpretation of Scripture.[67] The arguments are enhanced by analyzing and cross-referencing biblical texts, quoting ancient and contemporary scholars, naming the many women engaged in all forms of ministry in the New Testament, identifying rhetorical strategies, parsing linguistic nuance, acknowledging differences among denominations, distinguishing between contextual and *literal* application of admonitions, and appealing to the unmistakable logical conclusion: There is no meaningful distinction between the rights of women and the rights of men! A summary statement of each major argument conveys the essence and tone:

1. "We must understand [Galatians 3:28] to teach, as it actually does, the perfect equality of all, under the Gospel, in rights and privileges, without respect to nationality, or condition, or sex."[68]

---

62. Ibid., 52.
63. Ibid.
64. Ibid.
65. Ibid., 53.
66. Ibid., 55.
67. Ibid., 55–56.
68. Ibid., 58.

2. In Christ, women and men are "the children of Abraham," but not subject to what Clarke discusses as "a great disparity among the Jews . . . Under the blessed spirit of Christianity, they have equal *rights*, equal *privileges*, and equal blessings, and, let me add, they are equally *useful*."[69]

3. While Clarke's analysis may not be totally clear, St. Paul is clear by all other references that the two passages (1 Cor 14:34–35 and 1 Tim 2:11–12) "in which he appears to forbid, in general terms, women to speak in meeting, or to teach, either in meeting or out, are not to be construed literally."[70]

4. Even Peter (2 Pet 3:15) "says that in all of Paul's epistles *are some things hard to be understood*."[71]

5. Contextual understanding has set the course: "We must either give her equal rights with men or we must reduce her to the servitude of bygone ages. Either we must be governed by the Christian law of love and equity, or we must take a step back into barbarism and be governed by the law of brute force. Which shall it be?"[72]

New Testament "objections" are laid to rest with a choice echoing a call to political action: Will it be liberty or will it be a silencing death? "If woman, in using her voice, in praising God, or declaring His truth, in your churches, is a transgressor, then silence her at whatever cost; if she is doing right then remove all shackles and give her the liberty of the Gospel."[73]

The switch to *natural* objections (chapter 7) is rhetorically dramatic. No longer relying on his understanding of Scripture and interpretive acuity, he turns to past and present influential voices as he appeals directly to reason in response to the objection that women are by nature unfit for what men do naturally. Where Aristotle and others may have seen women as "naturally" subservient to men and incapable of doing what men can do, Roberts sides with John Stuart Mill in concluding all the more reason not to legislate; if natural, such inclinations will take care of themselves.[74] Just as women can be physicians and lawyers, some can compete even in war. According to Herodotus, examples of female warriors that violate the stereotypes abound during major wars: e.g., "Amazons," in the ancient world of

69. Ibid., 59.
70. Ibid., 64.
71. Ibid.
72. Ibid., 68.
73. Ibid., 69.
74. Ibid., 70.

Greece and Rome. Henry Morton Stanley encounters such in Uganda, and Joan of Arc turns the tide in the Hundred Years' war.[75] Roberts uses what might be deemed extreme examples analogically to convince his clergy colleagues "that some women may possess the physical strength and endurance, and the courage to discharge all the duties of an ordained minister of the Gospel."[76]

In the next four chapters (7–11), Roberts presents an evidence-based litany of biblical apostles, prophets, deacons, and deaconesses. He includes exemplary biblical names in each category, returns to original texts and their translations, calls upon the work of renowned clergy (including Luther and Wesley), quotes commentators who support his position, questions commentators who do not, compares women in ministry with women in secular leadership, and presents his arguments with increasing boldness and urgency. One summarizing statement from each chapter may serve to illustrate the depth and progression of argument:

- "Women Apostles" (chapter 8): "It is high time that the tyranny of sex was overthrown. And the church of Jesus Christ should lead the way in treating all human beings with absolute impartiality."[77]

- "Women Prophets" (chapter 9): "Prophets are an established order of ministers . . . they rank next to the Apostles . . . are those called of God, and inspired by His Spirit to preach the Gospel[78] . . . In the prophetic office not the slightest distinction is made between women and men . . . women who give equally satisfactory evidence that they are called of God to preach should be ordained."[79]

- "Deacons" (chapter 10): After extensive attention to debated issues of translation (see discussion above) and contextual prejudice—e.g., only for Phebe was "deacon" translated as "servant"[80]—Roberts declares that: New Testament "*deacons* were preachers of the Gospel . . .some of the deacons were women . . . provision was made for [qualified] women to be deacons in the church of Christ for all time to come . . . Then the New Testament gives to the church ample authority to ordain women for the work of the ministry."[81]

75. Ibid., 73–75.
76. Ibid., 78.
77. Ibid., 85.
78. Ibid., 91.
79. Ibid., 92.
80. Ibid., 95–96.
81. Ibid., 104.

- "Deaconesses (chapter 11): "The office was one—the functions the same."[82] If "a postmistress discharges all the duties, and enjoys all of the privileges of a postmaster . . . A queen, who succeeds to the throne in her own right, possesses all the prerogatives of a King . . . So a deaconess, in the New Testament sense of the term, is simply a woman who possesses the functions and discharges the duties of a deacon."[83]

With animated certainty, and increased impatience with disparities between terms and roles in churches where they do not even exist in the State or schools, Roberts confronts those who have been slow to concede.

> The practice of some of our modern churches of placing deacons where they belong, as an order in the ministry, eligible to promotion, and classing deaconesses among lay-workers, without any possibility of ever rising to the higher ministries of the church, has neither reason nor Scripture for its support. It is giving a stone to those who call for bread. It is conferring a shadow and withholding the substance; it is bestowing a name and keeping back that which is implied in the name. In short it is a stupendous sham, of which any body of men claiming common honesty should be ashamed. It is an insult to womankind, and should be resented by them as such. Every woman should refuse to accept the name unless there is given with it all that is implied in the name."[84]

The focus in "Evangelizing the World" (chapter 12) and "Required" (chapter 13) is not only on the biblical injunction to "go, teach, and baptize," (Matt 28:19) but also on what stands in the way of executing that injunction: namely, *"that the vast majority of those who embrace the Gospel are not permitted to labor according to their ability, for the spread of the Gospel."*[85] With two-thirds of the 1891 membership in Protestant churches women, women remain, in effect, silenced. Except among the Friends, "the competent coward must command, if no competent man is found, while the competent woman is relegated to the rear."[86] As may remain true today regarding opportunity for advancement, "she is, of set purpose, kept back, while cunning contrivances are adopted to make her think that she is accorded all the

---

82. Ibid., 105.
83. Ibid., 106.
84. Ibid., 107.
85. Ibid., 115–16.
86. Ibid., 116.

liberty she wants"[87]—this, notes Roberts, despite the work of extraordinary reformers such as Frances Willard.

The argument in "Required" (chapter 13) is a logical extension of desiring the wedding of title and function. Roberts is on a mission greater than "fairness" and common sense; he is seeking the culmination of ordination for women—for the good of the Gospel! "Going" is not enough, nor is "teaching," for without the right to "baptize," currently reserved for a man, she can complete neither her calling nor the "the last, great Command of Christ . . . *baptizing* [italics mine] them in the name of the Father, and of the Son, and of the Holy Ghost."[88] For Roberts, "woman must either be permitted to baptize, or she must not be permitted to make converts,"[89] to which he adds a poignant example of missionary Fanny J. Sparkes having to intervene when a woman in India was about to be lost because contextual laws forbade being touched by a man—even for the laying on of hands in baptism.[90] If, in schools and the courts and professions of all sorts, a woman is able to prove herself worthy, and if she is fully worthy in Christ, "justice, then, demands that all barriers placed by men in the way of the elevation of woman to any office in the gift of the church be removed."[91]

The chapters on "Fitness" (chapter 14) and "Governing" (chapter 15) include fascinating insights and instructive examples of the natural fit of women for godliness, teaching, nursing, sensibility, mental ability, and ministry, both in temperament and skill. Roberts includes biblical and secular examples of woman's propensity to be "on the lookout," whether for Christ after the resurrection or for influence over monarchs and clergy. Fifth-century pagan Clovis, King of the Franks, was converted through his Christian wife Clothilde; John Wesley's mother urged him to allow laypreachers;[92] and Mary Sewel changed Adam Clarke's dismissal of women in ministry, leading Clarke to quote a "shrewd man, who having heard her preach, and being asked his opinion of the lawfulness of it, answered, 'An ass reproved Balaam, and a cock reproved Peter, and why may not a *woman* reprove sin?'"[93]

> If, then, woman has the spiritual discernment, the aptitude for teaching, the prudence and courage necessary to qualify her for

87. Ibid.
88. Ibid., 118.
89. Ibid., 119.
90. Ibid., 120–22.
91. Ibid., 124.
92. Ibid., 129–30.
93. Ibid., 130–31.

the work of the ministry in all its departments, why not ordain her? Why deprive the church and the world, in any degree of the services they need, and which she is able and willing to render?[94]

"Governing" (chapter 15) opens new doors of support for Roberts, for if there is one area feared by men in authority, it is that others will enter their arena. Ordination will open doors of church governance, not only to men but to women—a violation of 1 Tim 2:12: "I suffer not a woman to usurp authority over the man." "But," declares Roberts, "to exercise authority with which one is *lawfully invested*, is not to *usurp* authority. Queen Victoria exercises authority over men; but she is not a usurper."[95] He then attacks the "violation" on two fronts: the correct reading of Scripture in light of translations showing that "women took a prominent part in the government of the apostolic church,"[96] and a recitation of women who have more than "successfully" ascended to and occupied the throne: Queen Elizabeth, Catharine II of Russia, and highly revered Queen Victoria. In his closing statements of "Governing," Roberts brings out the big guns, tying race to sex:

- The church has no right to forbid the free exercise of abilities to do good which God has given. To do so is usurpation and tyranny.
- Men had better busy themselves in building up the temple of God, instead of employing their time in pushing from the scaffold their sisters, who are both able and willing to work with them side by side.
- All restrictions to positions in the church based on race have been abolished; it is time then that those based on sex were also abolished.[97]

Just before his concluding his treatise, Roberts plays his trump rhetorical card: an entire chapter devoted to analyzing an exchange of letters between Pliny the Younger, Italian Consul, and Emperor Trajan around AD 100. The title of the chapter, "Heathen Testimony" (chapter 16), is potentially misleading in that one might assume he will be arguing with heathens about the validity of Christianity. Instead, he can use, as testimony, the writing of one who had studied rhetoric with the most revered Roman educator and teacher of rhetoric and moral responsibility of the era: Marcus Fabius Quintilianus.[98] Known for his view of rhetoric as necessitating "a good man speaking well," Quintilian remains among the most highly regarded

94. Ibid., 138.
95. Ibid., 139.
96. Ibid., 140.
97. Ibid., 149.
98. Quintilianus, "The *Institutio Oratoria.*"

scholars of rhetoric. Pliny's letter illustrates the understanding of rhetoric as more than transmission of information; in it he seeks to do the "right" in following ill-defined laws. He implores the emperor to assist him in determining proper guilt or innocence of increasing numbers of "Christians" who are meeting to eat together and to sing "to Christ, as a God, and bind themselves by an oath . . . not to be guilty of theft, or robbery, or adultery, never to falsify their word, nor to deny a pledge committed to them, when called upon to return it."[99] Pliny admits that he has not discovered any evil doing except "a bad and excessive superstition," even after judging it necessary to "examine, and that by torture, two maid-servants, which were called *ministers* [*italics* added]."[100]

Here is proof, not only of the spread and influence of Christianity, the "purity of character of these Christians," and the perceived divinity of Christ to whom they sang hymns "as a God,"[101] but also that Pliny, a man trained by the best in giving as accurate an account as possible, "says, 'they are called ministers,' that is, by the Christians."[102] Roberts ends this special chapter with a tone born of frustration with the reality of human behavior: "Women, it seems, could be ministers of the church at this early age, while it was poor and persecuted, but afterwards, when it became rich and popular, they were set aside."[103]

But for Woman to Lead Us!

> What are we, what our race, How good for nothing and base, Without fair woman to aid us?
>
> What could we do, where should we go, How should we wander in night and wo,
>
> But for woman to lead us!
>
> Cristoval DeCastilley, A. D. 1590[104]

Thus begins the "Conclusion" (chapter 17), which apart, perhaps, from its opening verse is no surprise. In short shrift, Roberts simply lists six

---

99. Ibid., 153.
100. Ibid.
101. Ibid.
102. Ibid., 157.
103. Ibid.
104. Ibid., 158.

numbered propositions he declares "have been clearly proved,"[105] along with his final statement. His rhetorically powerful synthesis has involved over 150 pages of meticulous research, considered opinion, painstaking analysis, and circumspect deliberation:

1. Man and woman were created equal, each possessing the same rights and privileges as the other.
2. At the fall, woman, because she was first in the transgression, was, as a punishment, made subject to her husband.
3. Christ re-enacted the primitive law and restored the original relation of equality of the sexes.
4. The objections to the equality of man and woman in the Christian church, based upon the Bible, rest upon a wrong translation of some passages and a misinterpretation of others. The objections drawn from woman's nature are fully overthrown by undisputed facts.
5. In the New Testament church, woman, as well as man, filled the office of Apostle, Prophet, Deacon or preacher, and Pastor. There is not the slightest evidence that the functions of any of these offices, when filled by a woman, were different from what they were when filled by a man.
6. Woman took a part in governing the Apostolic church.[106]

> We come, then, to this final CONCLUSION: THE GOSPEL OF JESUS CHRIST, IN THE PROVISIONS WHICH IT MAKES, AND IN THE AGENCIES WHICH IT EMPLOYS, FOR THE SALVATION OF MANKIND, KNOWS NO DISTINCTION OF RACE, CONDITION, OR SEX, THEREFORE NO PERSON EVIDENTLY CALLED OF GOD TO THE GOSPEL MINISTRY, AND DULY QUALIFIED FOR IT, SHOULD BE REFUSED ORDINATION ON ACCOUNT OF RACE, CONDITION, OR SEX.[107]

The issues Roberts raised and addressed in his context have not disappeared in 2016: Slavery remains in forms of human bondage, servitude, trade, and trafficking; the church falls prey to class, gender, and race distinctions, as well as to pernicious exegetical argument; and women are still taught that while "man and woman were created equal," each may *not* possess "the same rights and privileges as the other." In *Ordaining Women*,

---

105. Ibid.
106. Ibid., 159.
107. Ibid.

Benjamin Titus Roberts offered a model of analysis and insight that continues to transcend the particularities of time and place. At the intersection of his text and context, his discourse of dissent resulted in an exquisitely crafted call for freedom—the abiding call to human identity for *all* in Christ Jesus. That call resounds today!

Bibliography

Burke, Kenneth. *A Rhetoric of Motives*. Los Angeles: University of California Press, 1969.
Burke, Kenneth. *The Rhetoric of Religion: Studies in Logology*. Los Angeles: University of California Press, 1961.
Brummett, Barry. *Reading Rhetorical Theory*. New York: Harcourt, 2000.
Cullum, Douglas. "Fanatical Women: The Struggle toward Public Ministry in the Early Free Methodist Church." In *Earnest: Interdisciplinary Work Inspired by the Life and Teachings of B. T. Roberts*, edited by Andrew C. Koehl and David Basinger, 3–29. Eugene, OR: Pickwick, 2017.
Griffin, Em, Andrew Ledbetter, and Glenn Sparks. "Muted Group Theory of Cheris Kramarae." In *A First Look at Communication Theory*, 457–67. 9th ed. New York: McGraw Hill, 2015.
Hall, Stuart. "Introduction" and "The Work of Representation." In *Representation: Cultural Representations and Signifying Practices*, edited by Stuart Hall et al., 1–64. London: Sage, 1997.
Johnson, Samuel. *A Dictionary of the English Language*. London: Strahan, 1755.
Quintilianus, Marcus Fabius. "The Institutio Oratoria of Quintilian." In *Reading Rhetorical Theory*, edited by Barry Brummett, 295–354. New York: Harcourt, 2000.
Roberts, Benjamin T. *Ordaining Women*. Rochester, NY: Earnest Christian, 1891.
Roberts, Esther M. *The Bishop and His Lady*. Winona Lake, IN: Light and Life, 1962.
Stanton, Elizabeth C., Susan B. Anthony, and Matilda Joslyn Gage. "The Declaration of Sentiments and Resolutions Seneca Falls Conference." In *A History of Woman Suffrage*, 1:70–73. Rochester, NY: Fowler and Wells, 1889.
Weaver, Richard. "Language Is Sermonic." In *Reading Rhetorical Theory*, edited by Barry Brummett, 774–84. New York: Harcourt, 2000.
Wood, Julia T. "Critical Theories of Gender: Standpoint Theory." In *Gendered Lives: Communication, Gender, & Culture*, 51–53. Stamford, CT: Cengage, 2015.

3

B. T. Roberts as Social Entrepreneur

—Jack Connell

B. T.'s Father and the Walnut Tree

B. T. Roberts was two years old when his father Titus had an idea. Plagued by financial troubles and intrigued by the commercial potential of the newly-constructed Erie Canal, Titus and his friend Halsey Stearns seized what they believed to be a unique business opportunity. A mammoth black walnut tree felled by a storm three years earlier had become a local curiosity and minor tourist attraction. Thirty-one feet in circumference, the hollow trunk was large enough on its side for a horse and rider to pass through. When the tree became available for purchase, Titus and his friend saw an opportunity they could not refuse. They managed to scrape together the $200 asking price, tied the tree to a wagon, and headed toward the Erie Canal for an exhibition tour that they hoped would draw large audiences of paying customers. The hoped-for audiences did not materialize, however, and Roberts and Stearns ended up giving the tree to their lender and returning home to their families as broke as ever. To add insult to injury, the tree later made its way to New York City where thousands of patrons did in fact pay to see it, increasing its value to $3000.[1] The entrepreneurial vision of BT's father may have been prescient; perhaps it was his insight into the tactical matters of time and place that was slightly off.

---

1. Snyder, *Populist Saints*, 14–15.

Despite Titus Roberts's failure to turn a colossal tree into a revenue stream for his family, it seems that the entrepreneurial spirit that characterized this venture may have been part of the legacy that he passed along to his son. The entrepreneurial flair that characterized Roberts's life and ministry is unmistakable, and the purpose of this paper is to explore the ways in which the profound impact of B. T. Roberts's life is attributable to this entrepreneurial disposition. Specifically, I will look at his life through the lens of what is today called social entrepreneurship, i.e., the desire and capacity to use entrepreneurial skills to address socio-cultural problems and advance the public good.

I am mindful of the potential danger of arbitrarily imposing a twenty-first century paradigm on a nineteenth-century historical figure. However, even a cursory familiarity with B. T. Roberts's life leads one to the observation that he conducted himself with a bold willingness to launch and nourish new enterprises that he believed would advance the causes to which God had called him. A partial list of his entrepreneurial endeavors includes a new denomination, a new camp meeting, a new publication, and a new educational institution in North Chili, N.Y. I believe it will enrich our understanding of both B. T. Roberts and social entrepreneurship to explore the ways in which his life was marked by the qualities described in this emerging and rapidly growing field of study. This study will proceed through three primary sections: a discussion of social entrepreneurship and the attributes of effective social entrepreneurs, an analysis of the ways in which the life and leadership of B. T. Roberts are consistent with the attitudes and practices of a social entrepreneur, and a brief exploration of some contemporary practical implications.

Defining Social Entrepreneurship

The starting point for understanding the emerging field of social entrepreneurship must be an understanding of entrepreneurship in general. The idea of entrepreneurship originated in the French study of economics in the early nineteenth century and literally means "one who undertakes." The term came to be used as a means of identifying those "venturesome individuals who stimulated economic progress by finding new and better ways of doing things."[2] Entrepreneurs are the innovative visionaries who create economic value by seeing and seizing new opportunities. They are the change agents who bring transformational new ideas to the marketplace that drive economic growth. In contrast to administrators and managers who tend to

---

2. Dees, "The Meaning of Social Entrepreneurship," 2.

be constrained by current resources and structures, entrepreneurs are able to mobilize new resources and imagine new possibilities that allow them to achieve their objectives.[3]

For entrepreneurs in the business world, the motivation behind their entrepreneurial activity is typically to build an organization and to maximize profits. Their desire is to create economic value. Social entrepreneurs, on the other hand, utilize their entrepreneurial disposition and skills to create social value. Instead of being on a mission to create wealth, they are on a mission to serve humanity, solve social problems, and create a better world. They utilize the same types of savvy, creativity, and determination that characterize business entrepreneurship, but they use it in the passionate pursuit of societal good. The difference between a social entrepreneur and a commercial entrepreneur, then, is not in the nature of the entrepreneurial process, but in the nature of the mission being pursued.[4]

As one might expect in a nascent field of study, an agreed-upon formal definition of social entrepreneurship remains elusive. A sampling of definitions by some of the leading scholars in the field, however, provides a clear sense of what is foundational to an understanding of social entrepreneurship. Greg Dees, identified by some as the father of social entrepreneurship, defines it as follows:

> Social entrepreneurs play the role of change agents in the social sector by adopting a mission to create and sustain social value, recognizing and relentlessly pursuing new opportunities to serve that mission, engaging in a process of continuous innovation, adaptation, and learning, acting boldly without being limited by resources currently at hand, and exhibiting a heightened sense of accountability to the constituencies served and for the outcomes created."[5]

David Bornstein and Susan Davis define social entrepreneurship as "a process by which citizens build or transform institutions to advance solutions to social problems in order to make life better for many."[6] The Center for Social Entrepreneurship at Duke University's Fuqua School of Business defines social entrepreneurship as the process of "recognizing and resourcefully pursuing opportunities to create social value by crafting innovative approaches to addressing critical social needs."[7]

3. Ibid.
4. Brooks, *Social Entrepreneurship*, 5.
5. Dees, "The Meaning of Social Entrepreneurship," 2.
6. Bornstein and Davis, *Social Entrepreneurship*, 1.
7. The Center for Entrepreneurship.

What these definitions share is a conception of social entrepreneurs as people who have transformative approaches for solving social problems. Compelled by a desire to improve the lives of people who are needy or disadvantaged, they drive social change. They develop innovative solutions to such profound societal needs as poverty, illness, illiteracy, environmental threats, human rights abuses, crime, and injustice. By starting a new program, developing a new initiative, gathering new resources, or building an entirely new organization, social entrepreneurs address urgent human needs that are not being met by current structures or institutions.

Attributes of Social Entrepreneurs

The literature on social entrepreneurship discusses at length the qualities or attributes that tend to characterize the individuals who pursue and achieve entrepreneurial social change. Before we look at B. T. Roberts through the lens of social entrepreneurism, it will be helpful to have some of these qualities in mind. What follows is certainly not an exhaustive list of characteristics commonly exhibited by social entrepreneurs, nor does this list intend to suggest that an effective social entrepreneur will always embody all of them. Rather, this brief list is intended to give a snapshot of some of the attributes that are most commonly suggested in the literature as foundational to the effective social entrepreneur.

Innovation

Bornstein identifies two types of innovation that characterize social entrepreneurs. First, they possess a visionary creativity that enables them to see "over the horizon" and identify opportunities for meeting a specific social challenge. Second, they possess a problem-solving creativity that allows them to address the inevitable challenges that will come as they seek to meet that challenge. Their innovativeness allows them to recognize an opportunity to reshape part of the world, and then develop the strategies and solutions that will actually get the job done. [8] Dees describes social entrepreneurs as creative individuals who "break new ground, develop new models, and pioneer new approaches."[9]

---

8. Bornstein, *How to Change the World*, 124.
9. Dees, "The Meaning of Social Entrepreneurship," 5.

Action-orientation

When they see an opportunity to change the world, social entrepreneurs do not wait around for someone else to solve the problem. They are highly proactive people who "take direct action" by creating a new service or strategy or product.[10] They do not see problems as intractable, nor do they view themselves as victims of the status quo. Rather, they tend to be goal-oriented activists who believe they can bring about change—or at least give it their very best shot. One key dimension of this action-orientation is a willingness to tolerate risk.[11] Social entrepreneurs understand that any kind of innovation carries with it the possibility of failure, and yet they are willing to assume that risk and uncertainty to pursue with bold action the vision that has captured their hearts.

Collaboration

Social entrepreneurs are team-builders. The visionary idea and the initial steps forward might be theirs alone, but social entrepreneurs learn quickly that they can accomplish little by themselves. As a result, successful social entrepreneurs are networkers and collaborators who intentionally cultivate relationships with others who can add value to the venture. They recruit, motivate, and inspire. They are effective at " . . . pulling together people from different spheres, with different kinds of experience and expertise, who can, together, build workable solutions that are qualitatively new."[12] The new configurations of people assembled and coordinated by the social entrepreneur allow for the innovation to be advanced with greater success and dispatch.[13] The new organization often grows larger—perhaps ultimately involving staff, board, and other volunteers—and the size and scope of the organization's social impact is hopefully enlarged as well.[14]

Bornstein notes insightfully that central to the social entrepreneur's ability to involve others in the vision is the level of her own integrity. Speaking of the people who could conceivably invest their own time, energy, and resources in the social entrepreneur's movement, he states:

> You're asking a lot of them. And if they don't trust you, your probability of success is greatly reduced. The trustworthiness of

10. Martin and Osberg, "Social Entrepreneurship: The Case for Definition," 33.
11. Brooks, *Social Entrepreneurship*, 12.
12. Bornstein, *How to Change the World*, 242.
13. Bornstein and Davis, *Social Entrepreneurship*, 24.
14. Brooks, *Social Entrepreneurship*, 6.

the social entrepreneur—their integrity—is one of their most important assets. People sense that—and if they don't trust you, they won't follow you.[15]

Resource Acquisition

In addition to finding the human resources required to realize their vision, social entrepreneurs must also determine how to acquire necessary financial resources.[16] Social entrepreneurs may have an abundance of vision and passion and creativity, but rarely do they also possess an abundance of capital. Their action-orientation means that they will not allow limited resources to stand in the way of forward progress, and they look for innovative ways to address this challenge. They use scarce assets wisely and explore all possible avenues for generating additional resources, incorporating ideas " . . . from pure philanthropy to the commercial methods of the business sector."[17]

Determination

Bornstein describes social entrepreneurs as possessing "the fixed determination of an indomitable will."[18] It is the nature of catalyzing meaningful change to encounter resistance, apathy, misunderstanding, doubt, criticism, and almost limitless obstacles, disappointments, delays, and setbacks. In the face of these challenges, successful social entrepreneurs have the dogged determination to stay the course. They believe so deeply and so stubbornly in their mission that they are willing to do whatever is necessary to continue advancing it. Rather than give up when facing potential defeat, they continually ask questions like: How can we surmount this challenge? How can we overcome this obstacle? How can we adjust course to find success? How can we make this work?[19] A social entrepreneur regularly comes face-to-face with the difficulties intrinsic to initiating and anchoring social transformation, yet has the fortitude to remain steadfast and resolute in pursuit of the new day she envisions.

---

15. Bornstein, *How to Change the World*, 127.
16. Brooks, *Social Entrepreneurship*, 6.
17. Dees, "The Meaning of Social Entrepreneurship," 5.
18. Bornstein, *How to Change the World*, 41.
19. Dees, "The Meaning of Social Entrepreneurship," 5.

The Social Entrepreneurship of B. T. Roberts

As we turn our attention now to some of the ways in which B. T. Roberts can be understood as a social entrepreneur, it seems appropriate to inquire about the validity of viewing a nineteenth-century historical figure through the lens of a twenty-first century theoretical construct. Is this discussion an inappropriate and pointless exercise in imposing upon Roberts and his contemporaries an anachronistic set of ideas?

I share the opinion of many in the field of social entrepreneurship, namely, that while the language of social entrepreneurship is a recent development, the phenomenon of social entrepreneurship is not.[20] St. Francis of Assisi, Florence Nightingale, Mahatma Gandhi, and Martin Luther King Jr. are among those named in the literature as exemplars of social entrepreneurship. As Dees notes, "We have always had social entrepreneurs, even if we did not call them that."[21] Perhaps they were called reformers or visionaries or agents of change, but what they did is consistent with the contemporary notion of social entrepreneurship. Social entrepreneurism simply gives us a new language and lens for understanding and evaluating their work. The remainder of this study is devoted to exploring the ways in which the life, leadership, and legacy of B. T. Roberts were marked by the qualities and perspectives of social entrepreneurship, with the hope that this will enrich our understanding both of B. T. Roberts and of this emerging field. For the narrative contours of Roberts's life and ministry, I acknowledge with gratitude my reliance on Howard A. Snyder's definitive biography of B. T. and Ellen Roberts, *Populist Saints*.[22]

Entrepreneurial Roots

Bornstein and Davis note that social entrepreneurs often report being inspired to entrepreneurial activity by the encouragement or example of a significant adult in their lives.[23] The story of the walnut tree that opened this paper is just one illustration of the fact that B. T. Roberts grew up under the influence of a father who clearly possessed an entrepreneurial spirit. A certain level of entrepreneurial activity would likely be required of anyone who lived on the rural frontier of western New York State in the early nineteenth

---

20. See Dees, "The Meaning of Social Entrepreneurship"; Bornstein and Davis, *Social Entrepreneurship: What Everyone Needs to Know*.
21. Dees, "The Meaning of Social Entrepreneurship," 1.
22. Snyder, *Populist Saints*.
23. Bornstein and Davis, *Social Entrepreneurship*, 27.

century, but Titus Roberts seemed to be particularly disposed toward this type of activity. His efforts with the walnut tree as a twenty-two-year-old man were not particularly successful, but his later entrepreneurial efforts enabled him to provide for his growing family. As a young married couple, Titus and Sally opened and operated an inn and also began buying and selling real estate. Titus opened a store that became a successful enterprise, later purchased and operated a dairy farm, and continued to invest in real estate throughout his life. Snyder notes that "Titus Roberts became fairly well-to-do through his varied business ventures, buying and selling over 150 properties between 1823 and his death in 1881."[24] Titus's entrepreneurial activity was clearly driven by economic (not social) factors, but it seems reasonable to suggest that young B. T. would have seen in his father an entrepreneurial disposition and learned from his father the nature and value of entrepreneurial skills. His father's example and tutelage would have exposed B. T. to such attributes as opportunity recognition, risk-taking, persistence, and innovation—attributes that B. T. would later deploy in service to the grand calling God placed upon his own life.

The Mission

Social entrepreneurs are gripped by a desire to change the world. They see a societal problem that is not being sufficiently addressed by current structures or organizations, and that problem stirs their personal passion to the point it becomes their life mission to solve that problem and improve people's lives. For B. T. Roberts, the societal need that gripped his heart was for all people to experience biblical Christianity. His conversion to Christianity at the age of twenty was a watershed moment in his life, and from that point on his life's passion was to enhance and extend the transformative mission of Christ's work in the world. In an article that offered his critique of the Methodist Episcopal Church, Roberts articulated his understanding of the church's true purpose: "She has a special mission to accomplish. This is not to gather into her fold the proud and fashionable, the devotees of pleasure and ambition, but to spread Scripture holiness over these lands."[25] At the time of the founding of the Free Methodist Church, Roberts stated his passion similarly: "We do feel an intense desire to see, all over the world, churches in which the Gospel standard of experimental and practical godliness shall be held up, and the Spirit of God be allowed to

---

24. Snyder, *Populist Saints*, 21.
25. Roberts, *Why Another Sect?*, 95.

have free course."[26] The animating mission of B. T. Roberts's life was to see the church flourish and prevail so that all people everywhere (e.g., rich and poor, black and white, free and slave, American and international) could experience the hope and transformation of the biblical Christian faith. The entrepreneurial vision and behavior that characterized so much of Roberts's life was clearly driven by this profoundly religious impetus. He saw churches that were ineffective, Christians whose faith seemed lifeless, people who were being marginalized and oppressed, and the cause of Christianity being compromised and hindered. His holy discontent with these realities and his deep desire to change them drove the entrepreneurial activity that he relentlessly pursued throughout his life.

Intrapreneurial Efforts

Social entrepreneurs are typically thought of as people who begin new organizations. Sometimes, however, social entrepreneurs seek to be catalysts for change by working within and seeking to transform existing organizations.[27] These so-called "intrapreneurs" bring their innovative spirit to established structures and attempt to redirect and renew those structures in ways that will enhance missional effectiveness.

B. T. Roberts is known primarily for the organizations he started, most notably the Free Methodist Church and Roberts Wesleyan College. But before these organizations were founded, Roberts was engaged for ten years in the intrapreneurial work of attempting to renew and revive the Methodist Episcopal Church. His catalog of concerns with the denomination in which he served is well known: the practice of renting or selling pews, growing acceptance of fashion and worldliness, a lack of devotion among ministers, spiritual and numerical decline. Roberts wrote in 1853, "We are a Conference low in spirituality. There is great want of the power and even of the form of godliness. In many and perhaps most of our charges, probably not one half of our members are enjoying justifying grace, according to the scriptural and the Methodist standard."[28]

Roberts believed that the Methodist Episcopal Church was spiritually adrift in ways that were inconsistent with biblical Christianity and amounted to betrayals of authentic Methodism. Yet it was not his intention or desire to start a new denomination; rather, in the fashion of the social intrapraneur, he sought to redirect his denomination from within. He stated this clearly in a

26. Roberts, "Free Churches," 192.
27. Bornstein, *How to Change the World*, 241.
28. Roberts, "Genesee Conference," 2.

denominational newspaper in 1853: "I love Methodism for what it has done, and what it is capable of doing. I do not think her mission is accomplished. She has not finished her work. But she is neglecting it. I would, if possible, aid in recalling her to the stern toils of the harvest field."[29] Roberts engaged in numerous activities that he hoped would "recall" or reform the Methodist Church: e.g., revivalistic preaching and speaking, writing, networking with other like-minded church leaders, and influencing conference policy and elections. His reform efforts culminated in the 1857 publication of an article entitled "New School Methodism,"[30] which outlined his critique of the church and gave his impassioned appeal for a return to "Old School Methodism." It was the publication of this article, however, that set in motion the series of events that led to Roberts's trial by the church and ultimately to his expulsion from the Methodist Episcopal Church in 1858—thereby ending his ability to reform the church from within. The birth of the Free Methodist Church was now a not-too-distant reality, but it did not occur until B. T. Roberts had spent a decade of his life attempting the intrapreneurial task of driving for change within an existing organization. During those years, he did not have "any thought of forming a new church."[31] But with the door of change-from-within now closed to him, Roberts reluctantly turned his innovative energies and leadership skills to the more classic function of the social entrepreneur: starting a new organization.

New Organizations

Perhaps the most compelling piece of evidence for viewing B. T. Roberts as a social entrepreneur is his proclivity for starting new organizations. Time and again throughout his life and leadership, Roberts saw a societal need that was not being addressed by any existing organization and became a catalyst for launching an organization that would fill the gap. While a thorough discussion of Roberts's organizational start-ups is far beyond the scope of this brief paper, the following summary will hopefully provide a glimpse of his entrepreneurial vision and activity. These new organizations are listed in approximate chronological order.

---

29. Roberts, "Causes of Religious Declension."
30. Roberts, "New School Methodism."
31. Roberts, *Why Another Sect?*, 186.

The Bergen Camp Meeting

In the revivalist tradition, the summer camp meeting was an opportunity for God's people to come apart from the normal patterns of life for fellowship, worship, prayer, and preaching. It was a time for promoting holiness, reviving the church, preaching sanctification, and reaching the unconverted. B. T. Roberts was clearly not the originator of the camp meeting concept; he was, however, concerned at what he believed to be a decline in the camp meeting movement in Methodist circles.[32] He took it upon himself, therefore, to organize a new camp meeting in 1854 in Bergen, New York, near the church he was pastoring in Brockport. Celebrating the success of the first year's camp, Roberts exulted to his father: "There were a goodly number of conversions, but the greatest work was in the church. Formalists were aroused, backsliders reclaimed and believers sanctified."[33] In addition to being the primary visionary behind the Bergen camp meeting, Roberts's involvement included such details as selecting the initial site and helping clear the land, raising money, purchasing land, and forming a camp association to provide oversight. Roberts saw camp meeting as an indispensable means of renewal and reform in the church, and so went to great lengths to fill a gap he saw in the opportunities available to Christians in the region. Interestingly, the control and purpose of the Bergen camp meeting later became a source of controversy in the broader deliberations and disputes in the Methodist Episcopal Church that led ultimately to Roberts's expulsion.

The Free Methodist Church

As previously noted, it was not Roberts's original intention to start a new denomination. However, with the opportunity for ongoing ministry in the Methodist Episcopal Church taken from him, with his continued passion for a church that would be faithful to biblical Christianity and minister to the poor, and with growing interest among other church leaders in such a church being formed, Roberts was willing to take on a primary leadership role in the founding of the Free Methodist Church. As he notes in his diary in 1860, since there was "no existing church that makes the salvation of souls its prominent and main work, we then had to form a new church or live outside of any and have no place to put those that God converts through our instrumentality."[34] Many people played pivotal roles in the birth of the new

---

32. Snyder, *Populist Saints*, 349.
33. Ibid., 284.
34. Ibid., 522.

church, but Roberts's role was uniquely prominent. He issued the call for the organizing convention in his *Earnest Christian* magazine, wrote many of the founding documents, was elected the first general superintendent, and immediately gave vigorous leadership to the fledgling and rapidly-growing denomination. Although Roberts was the reluctant founder of a new denomination in 1860, he did not shrink from the moment and instead offered his substantial vision, skill, energy, and *gravitas* to its launch and development.

The Earnest Christian Magazine

In the months immediately leading up to the birth of the Free Methodist Church, B. T. Roberts saw the need for a new publication that would advance the causes about which he was passionate. He wanted a magazine that would be "a revival journal; our aim shall be to set up the Bible standard of religion."[35] While the idea had been talked about previously by others, in true entrepreneurial fashion, Roberts took the lead and devoted himself to making it happen. He raised the money needed to begin the enterprise, made the necessary arrangements with a printing company, served as editor-in-chief, wrote much of the copy, provided proof-reading services, and enlisted his family in the monthly task of mailing each issue—all in addition to his expanding responsibilities in launching and leading the Free Methodist Church. The *Earnest Christian* achieved a circulation of over 7000 readers by the late 1860s, and Roberts continued to publish it until his death in 1893.[36]

The Canal Street Mission

A less-well-known example of Roberts's social entrepreneurism is the catalytic role he played in the birth of a mission in the city of Buffalo. While giving leadership to the new denomination and publishing the *Earnest Christian* magazine, Roberts also noticed the need for a Christian outreach in the waterfront region of the city that was notorious for its bars and brothels. He began by preaching on a dock in the area, and later rented a hall over a saloon that was suitable for holding regular meetings.[37] Roberts's passion for social justice is evident in his appeal to fellow Christians to provide

---

35. Roberts, "Object and Scope of this Magazine," 6.
36. Snyder, *Populist Saints*, 563.
37. Ibid., 589.

housing for the young women being ministered to at the mission: "Many of them are quite young, and to hear the sad stories of the wrongs they suffered, which brought ruin upon them, would make your hearts bleed."[38] The Canal Street mission was constrained by a lack of funds and by the fact that Roberts's time and energy were pulled in so many other directions.[39] Its launch, however, is further evidence of his passion for producing social change through innovative entrepreneurial efforts.

Chili Seminary

B. T. Roberts believed strongly in the value of Christian education. As he noted in the *Earnest Christian*, "We know of no branch of Christian effort that promises more good for the world than the Christian education of the young."[40] On another occasion, he observed: "God has never chosen ignorant, untrained men to be leaders in any important work . . . "[41] Shortly after the founding of the Free Methodist Church, then, Roberts began taking steps to open up a new school that would provide an affordable, high-quality Christ-centered education for boys and girls. His efforts in launching Chili Seminary read like a how-to manual for social entrepreneurism: he had the vision for the school, raised the money, purchased the 145-acre farm property, recruited the board members, hired the first teacher, and served as principal. Roberts also oversaw the farming operation, which helped fund the new educational enterprise and provided what today would be called work-study opportunities for the students.

Snyder tells the story of Roberts's concern about the existence of a tavern near the school. Roberts organized a fund-raising event to purchase the tavern and put it out of business; when that event failed to generate the required funds, Roberts found a way to purchase the tavern himself. Snyder writes, "This was another example of B. T. Roberts's entrepreneurial spirit, his activism and determination, and his ability to make things happen."[42] The legacy of the entrepreneurial spirit that started Chili Seminary is flourishing 150 years later in the thriving institution of Christian higher education that is Roberts Wesleyan College.

---

38. Roberts, "Righteousness," 188.
39. Snyder, *Populist Saints*, 591.
40. Roberts, "Camp Meetings," 36.
41. Pfouts, *A History*, 11.
42. Snyder, *Populist Saints*, 616.

The Farmers' Alliance

The organizational start-ups described to this point all flow directly from Roberts's passion for the expansion of a vital Christian faith. He played a key role in the launch of a camp meeting, a denomination, a magazine, an inner-city mission, and a school because of his urgent desire to see people converted to living in transformative union with Christ. This final example of Roberts's disposition toward and skill in starting new organizations is unique in that the organization he envisioned would not be explicitly Christian. Roberts's motivation for starting an organization for farmers was deeply consistent with his Christian faith, however, because it was rooted in his fervent belief in the biblical idea of justice for the oppressed and disenfranchised.

Roberts's father was a farmer, he was himself responsible for the administration of the farm at Chili Seminary, and he lived in a region in which farming was a dominant profession. As such, Roberts had substantial knowledge of and appreciation for the needs of farmers. When Roberts became concerned in the early 1870s about economic and social structures that were disadvantageous to farmers (most surrounding the growing power of the railroads), it is perhaps no surprise that he became an activist for the rights of farmers. He spoke and wrote on the topic, and began to promote forming a new organization that would advocate for the interests of farmers. Roberts's efforts led to the formation of a Farmers' Alliance in Rochester in 1875, and his push for a statewide organization led ultimately to the birth of the New York State Farmers' Alliance in 1877. While many others were involved in the launch and development of these political organizations for farmers, this new farmers' movement "was largely Roberts's idea and came at his initiative."[43] His non-stop social entrepreneurism thus spread beyond the confines of the Christian church and extended to another population group for which he had great affinity and concern.

Entrepreneurial Traits

As noted previously, the literature on social entrepreneurship identifies several traits that are typically found in those who are effective in this arena: innovation, action-orientation, collaboration, resource acquisition, and determination. I believe Roberts's innovation and action-orientation are self-evident from the entrepreneurial achievements just outlined. I would like to highlight very briefly, however, a few of the ways in which his life

43. Ibid., 761.

exhibits the remaining three qualities of collaboration, resource acquisition, and determination.

Roberts was clearly a networker who was highly effective at inviting other people into his entrepreneurial endeavors and utilizing their talents in ways that strengthened the work. While he was seeking to reform the Methodist Episcopal Church, he was consistently meeting with other church leaders in an intentional effort to collaborate.[44] His friendships with various members of the Chesbrough family were pivotal in the founding of the Free Methodist Church and bore fruit at several times in his ministry. In starting Chili Seminary, Roberts recruited the members of the first board of trustees. The birth of every organization mentioned previously was accompanied by Roberts's impassioned appeals to church members, preachers, donors, friends, and farmers to join him in his efforts. The full story of B. T. Roberts could not be told without the stories of John Wesley Redfield, Loren Stiles, Vivian Dake, William Kendall, Jane Dunning, David Newton, and countless others who were his co-laborers and partners in ministry.

As effective as Roberts was in assembling and leading human resources, he was perhaps even more effective in acquiring the financial resources required to fund his ministry ventures. Ironically, much of the impetus for his reformation efforts was his objection to the common ecclesial fund-raising strategy of renting and selling pews. Roberts opposed that approach because of the ways in which it favored the wealthy and oppressed the poor, but he was consistently creative in developing other means of fund-raising and resource acquisition. He raised the money for the purchase of the land for the Bergen campground by taking out a note and soliciting funds from numerous individuals and congregations.[45] When Roberts needed $5000 to purchase a theatre in downtown Buffalo for use as a church, he acquired the funds through selling his own home, seeking pledges from friends, and publishing a written appeal (by his wife Ellen) in an issue of *Earnest Christian* magazine.[46] Some of the funds required for the founding of Chili Seminary came from profits realized from real estate transactions in downtown Rochester, and the operation of the school was partially subsidized by the farming operation.[47] B. T. and Ellen Roberts were sacrificially generous with their own resources, but also bold in soliciting gifts from others and creative in identifying other means of acquiring resources that would support their ministries. Roberts had an astute financial mind and deployed it in order to

---

44. Snyder, *Populist Saints*, 353–54.
45. Ibid., 349.
46. Ibid., 502–3.
47. Ibid., 612–14.

advance his work. At no point did he attempt to sell admission tickets for the viewing of a colossal walnut tree, but one gets the impression that he might have tried had the opportunity presented itself.

A final trait of successful social entrepreneurs is relentless determination in the pursuit of their goals. They face the inevitable challenges and setbacks with a persistent dedication rooted in their passionate conviction. Without question, Roberts embodied the "fixed determination of an indomitable will" throughout his life and ministry.[48] He faced resistance from many powerful Methodist Episcopal leaders and ultimate expulsion from the denomination he loved. He faced numerous financial challenges, organizational problems, failures and disappointments, bouts of exhaustion, and profound personal loss. And yet buoyed by his deep faith in God, his commitment to his calling, and the loving support of his wife Ellen, he kept going. And he poured himself completely into his work. When he was founding the *Earnest Christian* magazine, one of the owners of the printing company said to him, "Mr. Roberts . . . you do the work of four men. You have too much sense to keep on this way. Pardon me, Mr. Roberts, if I say I think you are foolish. Who cares for all this sacrifice you are making?" Roberts replied: "God cares, and I care."[49] Delia Jeffries, the first teacher at Chili Seminary, recalled Roberts's work as follows: "With the work on the seminary, looking after the workmen, seeing that all needed material was at hand, doing a vast amount of preaching, making long journeys, having the care of a large family, overseeing the farm, editing a monthly magazine, many times I, as I lived in his house, and assisted in mailing the paper, thought he did more work than a man ought to do."[50] Even his death at age sixty-nine, likely hastened by the overwork that characterized his entire life, occurred while he was away from home assisting a Free Methodist congregation.

The spirit of B. T. Roberts as a social entrepreneur is captured in these words:

> One effect of true holiness is to make us deeply interested in various benevolent enterprises. It takes us out of ourselves. It enlists our energies in behalf of interests that have no direct bearing on our personal affairs. We give our time and money for that which brings us neither profit nor reputation.[51]

Roberts's enterprises included the founding of a denomination, a mission, a publication, a school, a farmers' movement, and countless other

---

48. Bornstein, *How to Change the World*, 41.
49. Matthews, *Benjamin T. Roberts as I Knew Him*, 106.
50. Roberts, *Benjamin Titus Roberts*, 357.
51. Roberts, "Camp Meetings," 34.

congregations and initiatives that are far beyond the scope of this paper. With uncommon innovation, skill, courage, and determination, Roberts gave his life to entrepreneurial efforts that advanced the cause of biblical Christianity, made the world a better place, and continue to do so today.

Contemporary Relevance

As Roberts Wesleyan College celebrates its 150th year, we find ourselves in a world that still faces the kinds of societal problems that so troubled B. T. Roberts. Racial strife, divisions between rich and poor, declining religiosity, sexism, and social injustice. Institutions such as government agencies, churches, businesses, and not-for-profit organizations all have important roles to play in addressing these most difficult of social problems. But many societal problems are simply beyond the scope of institutional solutions. The problems are too numerous and too complex and require too many resources for existing organizations to be able to solve them all. Institutional solutions are necessary, but not sufficient. What we need are those rare and remarkable individuals who see a societal problem, imagine a new way to solve it, and then with persistence and boldness and creativity gather resources and motivate people and develop strategies and push through obstacles and get it done. What we need are more people who will embrace the social entrepreneurship embodied for us so compellingly by the life and leadership of B. T. Roberts.

One way to achieve this is for colleges and universities to integrate social entrepreneurship into the curriculum and life of the campus. It is not difficult to imagine social entrepreneurship being taught as part of the curriculum in business, education, social work, nursing, technology, ministry, psychology, history, and many other disciplines. Social entrepreneurs could be welcomed to campus as guest lecturers and consultants. Students and faculty could be given opportunities to lead social innovation, perhaps with some modest innovation funding from external or internal sources. Centers for the study and encouragement of social entrepreneurship could be established, such as the Center for the Advancement of Social Entrepreneurship at The Fuqua School of Business at Duke University. I am pleased that at Roberts Wesleyan College, the Enactus program encourages student-led social innovation and that the School of Business has a program in "Management and Social Entrepreneurship." All such efforts should be encouraged and multiplied at our colleges and universities.

I also hope the example of B. T. Roberts will inspire the institutions that see him as a spiritual father to continued diligence in their own efforts to be innovative and entrepreneurial. As we move into the next 150 years of our history, our colleges and churches and not-for-profit agencies must continue to envision and implement new and creative ways of fulfilling our respective missions. Roberts was expelled from an organization that did not welcome his efforts at reform and innovation; may we be much more affirming of the intrapreneurial initiatives of the social entrepreneurs in our midst. Such receptivity to change is indispensable as we seek to advance the cause of Christ in these rapidly changing times. And I believe it affirms the rich legacy that is ours from the first social entrepreneur in the movement—B. T. Roberts.

Bibliography

Bornstein, David. *How to Change the World: Social Entrepreneurs and the Power of New Ideas*. Oxford: Oxford University Press, 2007.

Bornstein, David, and Susan Davis. *Social Entrepreneurship: What Everyone Needs to Know*. Oxford: Oxford University Press, 2010.

Brooks, Arthur C. *Social Entrepreneurship: A Modern Approach to Social Value Creation*. Upper Saddle River, NJ: Pearson, 2009.

The Center for Social Entrepreneurship at Duke University's Fuqua School of Business. "What Is Social Entrepreneurship?" https://centers.fuqua.duke.edu/case/about/what-is-social-entrepreneurship.

Dees, J. Gregory. "The Meaning of Social Entrepreneurship." https://entrepreneurship.duke.edu/news-item/the-meaning-of-social-entrepreneurship/

Martin, Roger L. and Sally Osberg. "Social Entrepreneurship: The Case for Definition." *Stanford Social Innovation Review* (2007) 29–39.

Matthews, J. "Benjamin T. Roberts As I Knew Him." *Earnest Christian* 65 (1893) 106.

Pfouts, Neil E. *A History of Roberts Wesleyan College*. North Chili, NY: Roberts Wesleyan College, 2000.

Roberts, Benson H. *Benjamin Titus Roberts: A Biography*. North Chili, NY: Earnest Christian, 1900.

Roberts, Benjamin T. "Camp Meetings." *Earnest Christian* (July 1885) 36.

———. "Causes of Religious Declension." *Northern Christian Advocate* 13, no. 14 (Apr. 6, 1853).

———. "Genesee Conference—Its Prosperity, Its Decline." *Northern Christian Advocate* 13, no. 7 (Feb. 16, 1853).

———. "Follow On." *Earnest Christian* (July 1885) 34.

———. "Free Churches." *Earnest Christian* (June 1861) 22.

———. "New School Methodism." In *Benjamin Titus Roberts: A Biography*, edited by Benson H. Roberts, 112–26. Rochester, NY: Earnest Christian, 1879.

———. "Object and Scope of this Magazine." *Earnest Christian* (Jan. 1860) 1–6.

———. "Righteousness." *Earnest Christian* (June 1862) 18.

———. "The Weekly Paper." *Earnest Christian* (Dec. 1860) 51.

———. *Why Another Sect?* Rochester, NY: Earnest Christian, 1879.

Snyder, H. A. *Populist Saints: B. T. and Ellen Roberts and the First Free Methodists*. Grand Rapids: Eerdmans, 2006.

4

B. T. Roberts's Real Estate Debts

—MATTHEW DWIGHT MOORE
(based on original research and writing by Carl C. Moore Jr.)

A Personal and Professional Note

This represents a labor of love. Carl C. Moore Jr., a teacher and author who wrote the official history of the town of Chili, New York—my father—loved the kind of history that required the researcher to roll up one's sleeves to get immersed in it. For at least two decades, he rummaged through forgotten archives, church basements, unkempt libraries, decrepit closets, and neglected ruins—a preternaturally patient explorer of lost local facts. A far cry from what Google searchers might call "research," his labor was decidedly difficult and unglamorous work—the kind that could get one dirty, literally.

This love took him away from me. Night after night for years, he would steal away to the rare book room in the Roberts Wesleyan College library, where he would enter into ancient worlds I did not fully understand. On occasion, he would take me as a child with him to measure the beams of a local homeowner's basement or to make an etching from an overgrown and barely legible cemetery headstone. After some time, I started to see what he and only a few others could. I began to perceive the spectral past overlaid onto the neon signs and asphalt that comprised my contemporary world.

For many years, his work focused on the untold story of why Chili Seminary (the forerunner of Roberts Wesleyan College) survived while an overwhelming majority of private educational institutions did not. This led him on the ride of his life. The ride culminated in a full-length unpublished book. He seemed to always be looking to uncover those last remaining facts hiding in some distant archives that would help him to finish the work. Indeed, the book stands as a fascinating and highly-detailed work of mature scholarship, if not perfectly finished by his own standards.

So, when he began to show signs of dementia thirty years ago in 1985, it put more than his book in jeopardy. I began to lose my father in an irretrievable and existential way. Words like fastidious, copious, and slavish come to mind when surveying the trove that is left behind from his decades of research and materials. In order to organize the resources he accrued over the years, he developed his own system of note-taking and archiving, which he actively maintained. Here, for example is his list of B. T. Roberts's real estate transactions in Chili, with record numbers on the right.

Roberts Purchases and Sales in Chili

April 12, 1866 Garret W. Wilcox to B.T. Roberts #17,000 (Rumsey Farm)
Jan 30, 1868 William Wilcox to B.T. Roberts (BT P. Farm Chili)
Feb 22, 1868 William Wilcox to BT Roberts & Thomas Hannah (Tavern & Delano Parcel) #4,300
Sept. 29, 1869 Benj T Roberts to Chili Seminary Trustees #300. Two acres & building
Jan 27, 1870 Execs of Thomas Hannah to B.T. Roberts #1,617 Hannahs Share of Tavern Parcel
June 28, 1870 B.T. Roberts to Elizabeth Porter #300 small lot adjacent to tavern
July 6, 1870 Benj T. Roberts to Benjamin T. Stoutenberg #3,600 Tavern Parcel 5½ acres
Jan. 23, 1872 Oscar D. Vandiveer to BT Roberts #2,500 Five & half acres on West edge (orchards)
June 15, 1872 Charles H. Clark to B. T. Roberts $150. ½ acre adjacent to Delano Parcel
Nov 10, 1874 Charles M. Hovey & Eliza to B.T. Roberts #1,500 4 acres homestead
Nov 10, 1874 Benj T. Roberts to Eliza P. Hovey B 700. ½ acre Delano & ½ Clark Parcels.
May 1, 1880 BT Roberts to Joseph Bittle B 22,000 Rumsey Farm Minus 2 acres
April 15, 1881 John H. Martindale to BT Roberts #19,000 For 186 acres near mill
Jan. 29, 1884 BT Roberts to Edney E Irvine #600. second lot East of tavern
(April 2, 1885 Joseph Bittle to A.M. Chesbrough Seminary $22,500 Rumsey Farm)
May 2, 1883 Elizabeth B. Adams to BT Roberts #500 — NE corner lot to homestead
June 14, 1892 Robert Plant to B.T. Roberts #75. SE corner of homestead lot — ¾ acre
June 22, 1899 Thomas Hurry to Benson H. Roberts #600 Two acres at edge lot 51
April 5, 1915 Benson H. Roberts to Anna Hart #1300 — Elizabeth Adams lot
April 23, 1923 George L. Roberts to Hibbert R Roberts #10. — Rights to homestead
April 24, 1924   "   "   TO   "   "   #1.   "   " Robert Plant lot
May 8, 1928 Benson Roberts & other Roberts heirs to George W. Garlock May 8, 1928 Homestead
March 16, 1917 George Roberts + "   " To Ira R. Richards Adm. Martindale Farm
Oct. 22, 1904 Benson H. & Emma Roberts To Mary C. Patten — Hurry lot

4/1978 C. Moore

(Moore family archives)

As my father's dementia progressed through the late 1980s, he began to surreptitiously destroy most of his records, which once linked his writing to the original primary sources. Ultimately, what was salvaged were several boxes of notes and records and, more importantly, one full, final photocopied draft. Although the manuscript contains no citations whatsoever, using any criteria (whether grammar, logic, or corroborated facts) an objective reader would determine that his tome is untouched by dementia.

Such is the dilemma of this current work. For thirty years, I have wondered how to best preserve his research to share with those who would learn about this fascinating chapter of our history. In all frankness, I am not the primary scholar my father was. As those few and rare intrigued people who had heard of the book would request to look at it over the years, my mother would carefully assess if they would treat it (and him) fairly. Family friend Neil Pfouts, who wrote a history of Roberts Wesleyan College,[1] was one of those who gave my father's work credence and credit. But surely no peer-reviewed academic press would allow work so devoid of even the slightest citation, I thought. Since I am an academic, for years I hesitated to seek its publication, guided by this bedrock principle. After much reflection, I decided that, with this singular qualification, the greater good may be served by offering a form of my father's work here in the hopes of stimulating more primary research to connect the dots between the details my father cited and their original sources. In that spirit, I invite those few and rare intrigued readers motivated and skilled enough to dirty themselves by going into the archives and public records offices to contact me. I have volumes of information I am waiting to share with you. Places where my father's data may diverge from data presented in the classic works on B. T. Roberts, from Benson Roberts[2] to Clarence Zahniser[3] to Howard Snyder[4] should be taken as openings to re-examine (or re-assert) the primary sources. Ironically, my father would be the first to say that one should always go back to the original sources, not blindly take someone's word for it.

Literally every page of this work was written within sight of B. T. Roberts's final home. My father's original handwritten notes and typewritten copies were composed on the Roberts Wesleyan College campus and at my childhood home, just a stone's throw from the old tavern at the crossroads of North Chili. In 1995, then-president Dr. William Crothers championed the preservation of my father's book, even keeping a copy in his safe and

1. Pfouts, *A History*.
2. Roberts, *Benjamin Titus Roberts*.
3. Zahniser, *Earnest Christian*.
4. Snyder, *Populist Saints*.

recruiting Edna Ogden and Mary Lou Bates to type the entire book word-for-word into a computer document for the family to keep. Even this current adaptation was written from my office on Orchard Street, from which I can see the cemetery where the markers for both my father and B. T. Roberts sit. And over the forty or more years this has taken to write, colleagues like archivist Charlie Canon and librarian Al Krober provided great support for both my father and me. Local history does not get any more local than that.

It should be noted that my mother, not unlike Roberts's wife, Ellen Stowe, diligently enabled my father to do such invaluable work (although in his humility he likely would not have used the word "invaluable"). She provided ceaseless encouragement and editorial input to him, not to mention nourishment and care for the children, and has been a loyal and noble champion of my father and his life-work. My mother is at least partially responsible for this work as well and went on to become Chili Town Historian a short time after his death in 1998.

Due to the unusual nature of this current iteration, a methodology of my editing and writing may be helpful. I assume the reader already has some familiarity with B. T. Roberts's life and work, so I typically excluded most of the biographical data. Portions from several different chapters were selected to tell a single story that in such richness of detail has yet to be told. As a rule, I have tried to retain the original sentence structure and narrative coherence, but where it does not compromise the facts, I have edited, revised, and added in order to tell that story as evenly, clearly, and authentically as possible. One way or another, most of what follows derives directly from my father's writings, while some derives from my shaping, framing, and enhancing of this story.

As I write this, I realize that my father was my age when he began this final work. What an uncanny yet appropriate way to connect with him—and with B. T. Roberts—a man in whose footsteps my dad followed, quite literally. Whether in describing the sacrifices of B. T. Roberts or those of my father or mother, love can be found running all throughout this work.

Early Entrepreneurship

Debt is culturally ubiquitous today, as evidenced by the billions of dollars wrapped up in credit cards, mortgages, school loans, and a national economy encumbered by foreign indebtedness. Yet in an era before safety nets such as social security, welfare, and disability, it is difficult to fathom the kinds of stakes real estate investment and debt represented, especially when conducted charitably on behalf of other people. The seminary from which Roberts Wesleyan College is descended survived the nineteenth century in large part because of such bravura real estate investments made personally by B. T. Roberts.

A truly broad-scale examination of Chili Seminary's inception and operation automatically requires a serious attempt to analyze the practices and philosophies which its major leader reflected regarding financial involvement. In this analysis, it will be seen that in addition to a preacher, publisher, abolitionist, and champion of the ordination of women, B. T. Roberts became something of a minor activist in the real estate market. This latter role—in which he had made some surprisingly large financial commitments for a small-income preacher—is indeed worthy of more involved exploration. In the same way that some mythologies such as divine providence and manifest destiny have naively explained America's development, the explanation for Chili Seminary's survival and growth as part of God's plan is, at best, speculative. What this analysis will explore are the specific actions taken by a servant of God that showed his uncanny business acumen and calculated risk-taking in service to a spiritual *telos*. To put it plainly, claiming that Roberts prayed hard enough is hardly as satisfactory an explanation of the seminary's success as exploring in detail the noteworthy investment dealings into which he chose to enter.

B. T. Roberts was born on July 25, 1823 into a family that knew how to manage money. His grandfather, Benjamin Roberts, had owned a one-hundred-acre farm in Pomfret in New York state's westernmost county of Chautauqua. Young B. T. was twelve years old when his grandfather died on this farm. B. T.'s father, Titus, had a notable interest in buying, maintaining, and selling property throughout his life. Perhaps since he was likely the oldest of seven children, Titus seemed to show a successful entrepreneurial drive for most of his life. He and his wife Sally bought a two-acre home nearby in Forestville, NY for $800 in April 1824. As Titus's oldest son, perhaps B. T. intuitively learned Titus's enterprising skills in managing money and property. B. T. studied law, and in those days (as today) much of local law focused on property matters.

Staying closely connected with his family throughout his life would have also exposed Roberts to this reliable paternal model of financial management, even through his most tenuous times. Certainly, his father's penchant for such matters must have acclimated Roberts to such financial dealings. But monetarily his potential by the early 1850s must have been questionable—given such factors as his meager pay as a minister, his marriage to Ellen Stowe, and his need to set up housekeeping (not to mention the death of their first child)—all within three years of graduation.

Between 1851 and 1859, B. T. Roberts personally assumed the full legal risks and benefits of owning property on no less than four different purchases in or near his pastorates. In April, 1853, while Roberts was finishing his first appointments as Methodist Episcopal pastor in Buffalo, New York, he purchased a home for $1,000. This was located on an eighty-nine by twenty-five feet lot on Palmer Street (which was renamed Tenth Street shortly afterwards), just about five blocks from the Erie Canal. The payments were completed on April 11, 1857—the exact day the final payment was contractually due. He possessed the property for a total of seven years, selling it in early 1860.

Following two years of ecclesiastical service at Brockport, the Roberts family moved to Albion, New York, where he purchased a new house at auction on May 30, 1856, for a winning bid of $1,000. Along with the deal, he agreed to assume the $500 principal (and interest) on a mortgage left unpaid by the property's deceased owner, Mary G. Briggs, for which he gained a ¾ acre lot about two blocks east of his church on the same street, which backed onto the Erie Canal. Although the Roberts family only resided there for just over a year, they retained ownership until early in 1863—almost five years in total.

Looking to purchase a summer retreat for Methodist camp meetings in the area, suitable properties were examined. Eventually, Roberts joined with active supporter of the Chili Methodist Church, Asa Allis, in buying a twenty-four-acre site in rural North Bergen, New York for $1,500 on July 11, 1856. It is noted that others such as Hart Smith and Asa Abell were active supporters of this transaction, although Roberts and Allis's names are the only ones that appear in the paperwork. Almost one year later, on June 16, 1857, a summer worship camp trustee board (which had been formed for this purpose) paid the exact sum to Roberts and Abell for the church to officially take over.

Of course, the campground and all other Methodist Episcopal holdings became embroiled in the imminent schism, which for Roberts became personal after he had been tried by the Methodist Church and expelled after a decade of service. Many have written about the tenuousness and poignancy of his state—and the state of those in the Wesleyan-Methodist persuasion—during and soon after this rift. Such a rift immediately resulted in the formation of the Free Methodist Church (of which Roberts became the first superintendent) and was soon overshadowed by the bloody conflict of the Civil War.

By April 18, 1860, Roberts's efforts to provide an ongoing "free" church in Buffalo reached fruition. On that date, he sold his Buffalo home on Palmer Street for $1,500 to a George Jones as a down payment on the Old Pearl Street theater (owned by Jones), for a price of $3,500 plus assuming the unpaid $1,500 part of the principal on a mortgage lien against that lot and theater. Presumably, the Roberts family briefly lived on the premises or rented living quarters nearby until his economic prospects improved. At

$1,500, the Pearl Street facility was the largest of these sums and parcels to date for which he was the sole owner. He held it until that November, while the newly formed Free Methodist congregation was coalescing and formalizing. Then the congregation officially assumed the exact amount of $3,500, which Roberts accepted in addition to the existing mortgage which had come with it (for $1,050), which he had also assumed.

The fourth of his sole property purchases during this period was made official on February 27, 1861—virtually as the first shots of the American Civil War were fired—when he signed the contract for possession of a $1,000 forty-eight by 132 feet house and lot on Ninth Street in Buffalo. For the next three years or so, this property served as the nascent headquarters for overseeing both the Free Methodist Church of North America and much that went into the by-then thriving monthly *Earnest Christian* magazine.

Based on the available facts and figures regarding the known four parcels which he personally owned, during this decade of great tumult and change he had signed to pay a total of $6,500 in purchase prices for real estate. In addition, he signed contracts to absorb an additional $1,950 by assuming existing mortgages on some of those parcels. This might seem like a heavy financial load for a youthful minister with a young, growing family, especially one whose income as a Methodist minister was severed by 1858. But shortly after that termination he started a small publishing business with start-up capital accrued from free will offerings taken on his behalf as he held religious services from place to place across west central New York.

Until Roberts moved to Rochester in 1864, publishing the *Earnest Christian* would continue from Buffalo, which necessitated numerous train rides back and forth across western New York. This study has found no records for any specific salary, travel expenses, or income derived from publishing by Roberts during this time. Nevertheless, it must be assumed that altogether these professions must have provided enough money for him and his family. It should be noted that at the time the Roberts family moved there, Rochester was the headquarters of one of the most significant abolitionist publications during the middle part of the century, a periodical which started in 1847 as the *North Star*, headed by the famed Frederick Douglass. It is inconceivable that Roberts was not in some way inspired by his Rochester neighbor. Years later, on May 2, 1883, Roberts bought a two-story wagon shop building just down the road from the Chili Seminary and had the structure physically moved to his property to be used as the publishing house for the *Earnest Christian*. At its peak, that print shop was putting out 32,000 materials to its subscribers monthly.

However much a financial struggle it may have been for Roberts and his family in those earlier years, the overall tally of his property buying and selling before moving to Rochester looks surprisingly bright. Whereas he had agreed to pay purchase prices amounting to $6,500, his selling prices of those combined properties brought him a total of $7,100 before he left. Furthermore, whereas he had accepted responsibility for $1,950 in mortgages previously made against these parcels, his actual outlay against those debts amounted to only $686 from his own pocket. That meant that $1,264 in existing mortgages was passed on by Roberts to the next buyers. All in all, the indebtedness of the Roberts family regarding real estate encumbrances seems to have been surprisingly well balanced by sales income.

The arrival of the Roberts family to live in Rochester probably took place in the middle of November 1864. This approximation is made on the basis that on November 16, Roberts had officially paid $3,350 for lots seventeen and eighteen (which apparently contained a house) on Asylum Street and here he would stay for close to a year and a half. However, because that property had a lien on it from a deceased former owner, Roberts had to appear at the Monroe County Court House on January 25, 1865, to buy off that debt in order to clear his new property's title. He did this by paying forty-one dollars, which in effect raised the price he paid for his Rochester home site to $3,391. Even so, less than fifteen months later, when he used this Asylum street property as a down payment toward purchase of the Rumsey farm in North Chili, he was credited with a value for it that had risen to $4,200. Of some interest in this regard was the fact that Roberts had apparently paid for that property with cash in the first place and no other liens had existed on it during his time of ownership, which was a period when his financial resources might have been expected to have ebbed. In other words, he not only had an honorable financial status, but was clearly solvent, despite how easy it might have been to succumb to financial problems.

While he was accepting personal liability on each sale or purchase, he must have certainly solicited from other sources. This must have been the case if he was to garner those shockingly large sums such as the down payment totaling over $2,000 for the campus site so soon after producing $3,350 for his home. By this time, he had likely built myriad connections among many people in western New York—Free Methodist or not. He knew Daniel Steele, the first president of Syracuse University, and Martin Anderson, the first president of the University of Rochester, as well as numerous other notables. As early as April 18, 1860, wealthy layman Edward P. Cox aided Roberts until the latter could sell his home as a down payment on the Pearl Street theater in Buffalo. It is likely that benefactors like Cox, friendly to the fledgling denomination of Free Methodism, assisted Roberts because Roberts represented one of the most dynamic leaders of its vanguard. But the fact of the matter is, without extant records, we can only speculate about some aspects of the financial support the Roberts family received during this period.

Chili Seminary

During his fifteen months living on Asylum Street, which was then east of present downtown Rochester, Roberts must have surveyed the outskirts for an appropriate place to start a seminary. Indeed, he may have chosen a downtown location primarily to conduct such reconnaissance. Located fifteen miles west, the hamlet of North Chili proved to be virtually ideal in nearly all respects—almost as though just the right planning had been done from years before. By 1866, the cumulative effect of the east-west railroad (which bisected Chili one mile south of North Chili), the east-west Erie Canal (which ran only a few miles north of North Chili through Spencerport), the east-west stagecoach line (which ran down the middle of North Chili along Buffalo Road), and the north-south former Haudenosaunee road originally known as Cattaraugus trail (later Union Street) brought significant populations and attention to what was once a simple crossroads in the wilderness west of America's first boom-town, Rochester. And for some time before, Roberts had visited the Methodist church just down the road and knew the land and people there.

An objective analyst, however, would quickly note that Roberts's purchase of a vast plot would put him into a financial cycle far more involved than he had hitherto encountered. He likely felt, however, that the stakes in reaching out for the lives of many young people instead of concentrating primarily on his own children's future (as he mostly had up to this point) must be expected to be higher. Furthermore, his religious leadership role in the lives of many church families around his Free Methodist constituency had coalesced to the degree that he was confident that these years of cooperative effort would result in adequate mutual support for success.

Having several personal connections in Chili (not the least of these was his friend, the Methodist pastor William Kendall who had served there), Roberts had visited the area from time to time, years before his plan for a seminary in that locality had taken seed in his mind. It seems that on at least on occasion, Roberts was taken in at the home of Cornelius Rumsey, a farmer who worshipped at the Chili Methodist church. Just northeast of the North Chili crossroads, the Rumsey farmstead contained at least one house, an L-shaped barn for cows, pigs, horses, and sheep, and a carriage shed for two or three carriages and a sled.

The Rumsey farmstead (Moore family archives)

Interestingly, excavations of this site during the middle of the twentieth century revealed mysterious remains whose presence may indicate that at a time pre-dating the Rumsey's predecessors, the area had Haudenosaunee residents.

Having probably seen the peak of his family's fortunes, Cornelius died of cholera at seventy-one years old in 1849, leaving the plot to his son Alexander. By the end of the next year, the Rumsey family had built another rather large house that perched on the gently rolling hill, from which one could oversee at least some of his large plot. Over the course of the next eight years, all four of the family inheritors died mysteriously. (For some reason two otherwise healthy adult sons had predeceased their father.) The result of this family disaster was that the sizeable farmstead just outside the slowly prospering hamlet of North Chili suddenly fell to three women (Alexander's wife, mother, and sister) who presumably could not practically maintain it.

At any rate, Roberts personally signed to pay $17,000 for nearly 145 acres which came as the remaining Rumsey farm acreage. In addition, he assumed two large existing mortgages (one for $2,000 and the next for $8,000). This means that the sellers, Garrett W. Wilcox and his wife, Lydia, accepted the mentioned value placed upon his Rochester home ($4,200) as the only asset which Roberts paid them at the time of trading titles. Furthermore, several diligent efforts have not uncovered any recorded mortgage for the $12,800 Roberts still owed them for the purchase price (not to say anything of the $10,000 in mortgages Roberts had assumed). This suggests that the

Wilcox's reason to accept Roberts's word was that he would guarantee them against loss. Nowhere has been found a reference to when those staggering debts would have to be paid, nor what the Wilcoxes could expect on it from one month to another, or even from one year to the next. Such faith in one man reaches beyond a common friendship.

Not incidentally, in 2016 dollars, the purchasing power parity (factoring in the consumer price index) for B. T. Roberts's $17,000 investment in 1866 would conservatively translate into something between $250,000 and $330,000—and this from one whose regular employment income must have still been dubious at the time. This would prove to be the single-largest real estate investment of Roberts's life to date. Saying that this represented one of his central life decisions even understates the seriousness of the purchase. It may be remembered that Roberts and his father continued to correspond throughout this period. Since his father continued to manage his own business transactions into the 1870s, it is reasonable to assume that Roberts was bolstered by his father's Christian business model. Such strength and inspiration, not to mention practical advice, can mean the difference between a trajectory of success and one of failure.

Upon moving his family into the Rumsey homestead in 1866, Roberts began to lay plans to institute the first tentative classes that fall in this same house.

Original schoolhouse, Rumsey farm (Moore family archives)

However, the reality of the situation soon indicated that a serious education program would require considerably more space than was available in his family home. So, as plans were being made for the Seminary's first full-scale program, Roberts was searching for a building nearby which was large enough to house that school. Monroe County records reveal that Roberts had signed a land contract with William Wilcox on January 22, 1868. Surprisingly, this sale's agreement did not mention the purchase of the tavern at all. Instead it sold him forty-six landlocked acres called the Stillson farm on the south side of Buffalo Road—opposite the southeastern edge of the Rumsey farm. But in that contract was a nearly hidden clue of proof that Roberts actually had been holding classes in the tavern building from the previous November. Obviously, sometime in the previous six to ten months an accommodation had been established between Roberts, who needed to use that building, and Wilcox, who knew that (short of a miracle) Roberts could not pay for it in the foreseeable future. What had happened to help clear up that dilemma?

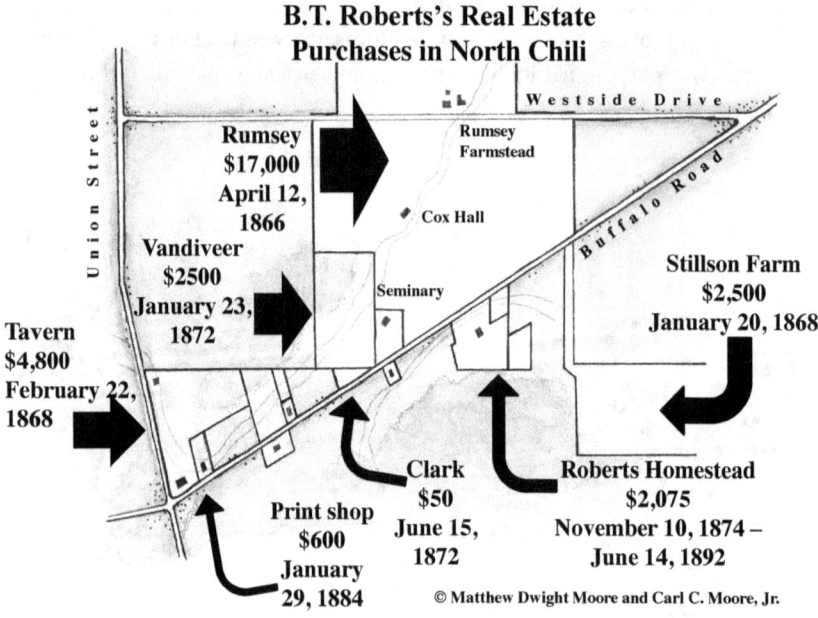

B. T. Roberts's Real Estate Purchases in North Chili

In the spring of 1867, Garrett Wilcox had transferred the tavern ownership and several other properties to William Wilcox. In that shuffle, William had accepted title to the forty-six acre Stillson farm, just south of the Rumsey plot across Buffalo road. In the fall of 1868, the latter Wilcox had clearly reversed the decision not to open the tavern building to Roberts for an advanced education program. But in acquiescing to Roberts's request (probably approached several times during that period), he worked out a contingency in return. By itself the Stillson farm, although relatively useful for pasturing or raising new crops, was clearly limited as a saleable parcel, since it was located far back from the road near the current president's residence and College Greene housing tract.

In 1866, a few students began taking intermittent classes in the Roberts home on the Rumsey farm knoll. Likely several community youngsters and some boarding students attended, although no records survive except laconic confirmation by some participants. In November of 1867, Roberts bargained to rent the North Chili tavern and bought the building on February 22, 1868, no doubt intending to accommodate an adult supervisor's quarters in addition to classrooms and boarding students. Thomas Hannah, one of the greatest land owners in Chili by the end of the 1850s and a leader in the Chili Methodist Episcopal Church (even after that church had split), signed a note to buy the tavern with Roberts. But Hannah died less than two years later and Roberts eventually paid off both shares.

Still today the oldest extant structure in the area, the building had been built sometime between 1815 and 1819, and was known for many years simply as "the Tavern." In that period, Captain John Wetmore, a veteran of the War of 1812, had bought 340 acres encompassing all four corners of present Union Street-Buffalo Road crossroads of North Chili. It was constructed of clay bricks from a site just a stone's throw south on Union Street. The original building boasted two stories and thirteen rooms made of oak and beech beams—a solid construction that survives exactly two centuries later.

The Tavern 1860s (Moore family archives)

Still brand new in 1819, Levi Campbell, a Presbyterian deacon, bought the property for $60 and the tavern flourished. In 1838, Charles Harford bought the property for $3,000 and added another use to the tavern's original one; it was sometimes used as a temporary jail. During the Civil War, William Allen bought the building for $2,500 and the tavern eventually closed. This was perhaps due to the pressure of temperance movements as Chili, once on the outskirts of Rochester, found itself populated by more church-going middle class homesteaders in the wake of the so-called "burned-over district." By 1867, when Garrett Wilcox and then Roberts bought it for $2900, the tavern's serving of alcohol had already been effectively shut down. Indeed, it was later called "Temperance House."

The Temperance House 1870s (Moore family archives)

In November of 1868, Roberts announced in *The Earnest Christian* that the first phase of a major seminary building construction project on Rumsey farm acreage had already begun, transitioning from the traditional "silent phase" of the capital campaign to the more public one.

> We have commenced the task of founding a Seminary of learning at Chili, N. Y. . . . Our building is up, and nearly enclosed. But we need more means—greatly need them; and we trust that if any who read these pages have the means to help on a good work, they will forward them to us without delay.[5]

This fact suggests, in part, that from the beginning of its use for classes the old tavern building's space was not likely to be adequate. Another factor in Roberts's quick move to find another building for this school probably related to his knowledge of the State Board of Regents' guidelines for academic charters. These called for adequate facilities owned by the school's trustee board and valued at least as high as $5,000 over and above all encumbrances (which could not exceed more than one-third of the academy's property value).

Roberts's combined debts on the Rumsey farm and on the tavern building were certainly prohibitive in that respect. This reality, plus the

5. Roberts, "Labor," 160.

limited physical size of the "tavern school house," certainly destined that building's use (for his purposes) to be of short duration. So, virtually from its beginning, the Chili Seminary had a single option. If it could survive long enough, it would one day have a new building of its own with a value of at least $5,000. Furthermore, Roberts, who had personally purchased the Rumsey farm, would have to somehow show that the seminary building was not likely to be swamped with debts from the heavily mortgaged land on which it stood. This challenge of constructing a large school building while disassociating it from the heavy existing debt would have seemed at least formidable, if not potentially disastrous to the life of the seminary.

Perhaps as early as 1866, the location for the new building had been chosen—the site of the current Northeastern Seminary building, whose property at that time was surely surrounded by more wilderness than it would be in the next 150 years. Then as now, the site sat back a little from Buffalo Road and was just a short walk equidistant from both the Rumsey homestead and the former tavern at the crossroads. By October 1868, Roberts announced in the *Earnest Christian*, "the Seminary building is progressing finely,"[6] signaling that the first phase of major seminary building construction on Rumsey farm acreage was underway. In that same notice, he also mentioned that "to complete it we need about three thousand dollars more than have been subscribed."[7]

In 1869, major construction of the Seminary building continued. By the middle of the fall of 1869, the forty by sixty feet basement[8] was firmed up with fieldstone foundation walls that provided support for the three brick-wall stories topped with wooden shingles and octagonal cupola. But going into the winter, all ninety windows were still needed. The State of New York's Board of Regents reflected their confidence in the Chili Seminary's application by granting it a provisional charter in January 1869. While announcing receipt of the charter, Roberts also reluctantly made a passing reference to the fact that a major part of the subscriptions for this construction project had yet to be paid. "The Genesee Conference, last fall, pledged to raise over $2,000, of which about sixty dollars have been paid. The Susquehanna Conference pledged one thousand; they have paid about thirty."[9] Therefore, this represented a serious jeopardy toward the use of the new building (at least in the foreseeable future) along with the possibility that the State might withdraw the school's official charter if the building program

6. Roberts, "Chili School," 125.
7. Ibid.
8. Roberts, "Chili Seminary," 33.
9. Roberts, "Chili Seminary (February 1869)," 66.

became paralyzed. Roberts's frustration is evident in this announcement: "We are perplexed and embarrassed."[10]

Indeed, funds had been so scarce that Roberts had personally borrowed much of the $4,000 needed to finish paying for materials and the workers.

> The building is now ready to plaster. To get it along as far as we have, we have ourselves become personally responsible to the amount of some $4,000. For a portion of this sum we have given bank notes; and the rest is borrowed money.[11]

Some students lived in the unheated structure before it was finished, even through the winter of 1869 to 1870. In that term, there were fifty-six students enrolled. Of those, twenty-nine were residents of Chili and ten were from nearby towns, suggesting that as many as seventy percent of the enrolled students were commuters of some sort. For the next term, 1870–1, enrollment dipped to forty-two or forty-three, a decrease of 25 percent. In today's academic economy, such a percentage drop would no doubt be catastrophic. In fact, from June 1869 to December 1870, the United States economy endured the largest economic recession since the end of the Civil War. Business activity decreased by nearly 10 percent and on September 24, 1869, later termed "Black Friday," the gold market imploded, leaving many financial investors ruined. This was some of the hard ground that Roberts was breaking in the fall of 1869.

Tuition played an interesting role in the global scheme of the Seminary's financial life. Although children representing some affluence were among Chili Seminary's student population on a regular basis, the institution's student body was largely constituted by members of moderate or less than moderate income. Tuition (which was the primary source of funds for the entire annual operating budget) was kept substantially lower than the median of her peer schools in upstate. Board in the fall of 1870 was $2.50 per week, "wood and lights extra. 50c per week extra when tea and coffee are used."[12] Traditionally this was done with success through the religious dedication of the small staff whose sacrificial spirit was to become legendary. Through this practice the adult personnel could accept relatively large numbers of students regularly from homes under which ordinary circumstances could not afford to send them to school. This practice quickly became characteristic of the Chili Seminary from its beginning. It was en-

---

10. Ibid.
11. Roberts, "Chili Seminary," 33.
12. Roberts, "Chili Seminary Announcement," 65.

couraged by the original philosophy of the school founder that each student should spend half of each day on book work and the other half on manual labor. Although this guideline was modified in practice (it never was an official mandate), for at least its first century this school could boast that a preponderance of its students paid most or at least major portions of their own expenses from jobs fulfilled during the school year, whether they were in the laundry or tending the farm.

For the formal dedication of the seminary building on November 16, 1869, the community at large was invited to a speech by University of Rochester president, Dr. Martin B. Anderson.[13] There were no paths or walkways to reach the hollow husk of a building. In empirical terms, it was far from clear on that day that the building would ever be finished. Sometime later, while providing a financial report on the building project, the administration noted that this self-contained seminary and subsidiary buildings such as toilets had cost $11,765 over two years of work. Of that, $10,272 had been received on subscriptions from all sources. But this left a balance due on the building of approximately $1,000. In addition, an estimated $1,000 worth of "seats and furniture" were needed but had not been obtained by that time.[14]

There can be no question that the personal acquisition by Roberts of the Rumsey farm in North Chili in the spring of 1866 was intended for the use of an advanced school of learning. But to acquire that 145 acres, the Roberts family had legally encumbered themselves for $22,800 (including two existing mortgages on the property). In addition, by the time the seminary's construction was well underway in mid-1868, Roberts had accepted another major debt from his purchase of the old tavern building in North Chili. These debts totaled close to $25,000 and certainly could have seemed dubious or even reckless to observers. It must be remembered that these large debts seriously threatened not only his personal solvency and taxed the resources available from the widening circles of supporters, but it had contradicted the terms implicit in the seminary's state charter.

On September 27, 1869, two months before the seminary's dedication had taken place, Roberts legally separated his personal property encumbrances from the young school. He did this unobtrusively by legally transferring the two-and-a-half-acre plot on which the new school building was rising to the Chili Seminary trustee board for the nominal price of $300. In effect, this divorced the school from the overwhelming debts Roberts was carrying on real estate previously tied to the existence of the Chili Seminary. Now any possible foreclosure proceedings on either the debts on the Rumsey

13. Roberts, "Dedication," 190–91.
14. Roberts, "Chili Seminary Announcement," 65.

farm or the old tavern building would not seriously jeopardize the school's life expectancy. For years thereafter, it would serve its several environs as a legal entity, separate and apart from much of Roberts's personal weight of debt which he would carry through his remaining life. As Roberts sought donations in *The Earnest Christian*, his language evidenced the weight he felt from this debt: "Ask the Lord if He would have you help us; and if He would, do so promptly. It is not the will of the Lord that we should bear this heavy burden alone."[15] This didn't mean that he regretted his actions. Taking on reasonable debt in service to the Lord was something he even encouraged his readers to do: "We hope all who have subscribed will forward us their submissions at once. *Do so if you have to borrow the money.* [italics original] This will give you far less trouble than it will us to do without it."[16]

Legacies

In addition to many other responsibilities, Roberts remained active in real estate over the next several years, much to the benefit of the seminary and the Roberts family. In 1875, a major extension to the seminary building was added—a significant test of supporters' resources so soon after completing and furnishing the building.

In terms of property, Roberts finally sold the former Rumsey farmstead (minus that small two-acre plot owned by the seminary) on May 1, 1880, to Joseph Dibble for a staggering $22,000. On March 11 of the following year, Roberts sold a property on Goodman Street in downtown Rochester, that he had purchased sixteen years earlier, for an even $13,000! Since the original price was $3,612, this transaction marked an increase of 360 percent on his original investment. Just four weeks later, on April 15, 1881, Roberts bought the 186-acre Martindale farmstead on Black Creek in West Chili, straddling Chili-Riga Road, for $19,000. Taking only these real estate transactions into account, within one year Roberts had come into $35,000 and purchased a significant estate that would stay in the Roberts family until it was sold on March 17, 1917.

---

15. Ibid.
16. Ibid.

Chili Seminary 1878 (Moore family archives)

It was not surprising that little if any public notice had been made about the parent farm now being divorced from the school itself. Instead, although still holding to his original concept of the Rumsey farm as an important adjunct of the school, for about a decade Roberts quietly sought one or more partners to share its payments with him. In 1883, fate provided him with the single largest donation to date. As far back as 1866, Roberts had reached out to Abram Merritt (A. M.) Chesbrough to help buy the Rumsey farm. From a family of faithful early Free Methodists, and a cousin of Roberts's colleague, Reverend S. K. Chesbrough, A.M. Chesbrough was a wealthy railroad industrialist living in the Niagara region, whom Roberts had admired, calling him "a man of strict integrity, deep piety, great energy and force of character."[17]

In December of 1881, A. M. Chesbrough caught what seemed to be a bad cold, which manifested as badly congested lungs. His persistent coughing did not diminish, despite traveling to California to escape the harsh New York winter. With no surviving children, on December 6, 1882, the sixty-seven-year-old Chesbrough signed his will, in which he delineated twenty-three requests, dolling out numerous sums in support of ministers,

17. Roberts, "A. M. Chesbrough," 190.

widows, orphans, and the elderly. Item sixteen of these requests was by far the most extensive—$30,000 conditionally offered to Chili Seminary. One of the stipulations was that "so much of said bequest as may be necessary be used in the purchase of the farm now occupied by said corporation; that the balance be invested and that the income only of said farm and investment be used for the education in indigent scholars."[18]

> *Sixteenth:* I bequeath to the trustees of the Chili Seminary at Chili, near Rochester, New York, and to their successors the sum of thirty thousand dollars ($30,000), upon this condition and trust, that the Seminary is to take the name of the testator, and that so much of said bequest as may be necessary be used in the purchase of the farm now occupied by said corporation; that the balance be invested, and that the income only of said farm and investment be used for the education of indigent scholars.

Will of Abram Merritt Chesbrough
(Moore family archives)

In 2016 dollars, this donation represented close to $1,000,000. This certainly represents a generous sum, but it is especially noteworthy given that in the 1880s there were far fewer people with surplus capital in western New York than there are today.

---

18. Ibid.

Chesbrough died that fall, and presumably Roberts was notified soon thereafter. The Chili Seminary held a special trustee board meeting at the seminary building on December 4, 1884 and agreed to change the name of the institution to Chesbrough Seminary in honor of their largest benefactor to date. This was also one of the will's conditions, although it is not clear whether this was his unique request or whether it was suggested to him by supporters of the seminary. The Chili Seminary changed to A.M. Chesbrough Seminary by a simple trustee vote—and a $30,000 donation. Thirty-three days later, the New York State Board of Regents had entered the name change in their legers. The name remained Chesbrough Seminary for sixty years, until it was changed to Roberts Junior College for four years. For the last sixty-seven years, it has been known as Roberts Wesleyan College.

Incidentally, over the course of 1885 the value of Chesbrough's gift was paid out in different amounts (some as much as $5,000).

January 2, 1885 receipt for $5,000 from the A.M. Chesbrough estate
(Moore family archives)

The final $12,000 was received on November 21 in the form of 390 shares of stock in the Catarack Milling Company.

> Niagara Falls Nov 21st 1885
> Received of H. F. Evans, Executor of the
> estate of A. M. Chesbrough, deceased,
> Twelve thousand dollars, in two
> promissory notes, given by Chorley
> B. Gaskill, secured by an assignment
> of three hundred and ninety shares
> of stock of The Cataract Milling
> Company, being the balance unpaid
> of the legacy left by A. M. Chesbrough
> to Chili Seminary
>
> B. T. Roberts President
> of Trustees of A. M. Chesbrough, formerly
> Chili Seminary

November 21, 1885 receipt, shares of Catarack Milling Company
(Moore family archives)

By this point, the seminary had in its possession roughly the same amount of capital as was needed to purchase back the farmland, which the Trustees did on April 2, 1885. For the next five years, both Roberts's and the seminary's trajectory appeared healthy.

Unfortunately, about twenty years after its completion, on September 11, 1890, fire broke out at the seminary building. No cause was ever determined, but it seemed clearly accidental and started on the top floor near the cupola. The devastation must have been demoralizing for Roberts and the other witnesses, although a spirit of resilience ultimately prevailed.

> The A.M. Chesbrough Seminary building has done a great work so far, and though the buildings are in ruins, it has abundantly paid for every dollar that has been put into it. We want to rebuild at once.[19]

---

19. Roberts, "The A. M. Chesbrough Seminary," 192.

Adelaide Beers, whose husband had been an early seminary student, wrote, "While the sacred walls be blackened and ruined, some grand and glorious results remain, unscorched by fire, undimmed by smoke."[20] Efforts were begun almost immediately to revive the seminary's physical plant. For many months, the needed funding came only in small amounts.

In the December 1890 *Earnest Christian*, Roberts had asked the rhetorical question, "Where are the means coming from?" His answer for the funding started, "We cannot look for them from the proud. They choose to give to support pride. We must look for help to the humble few whose hearts God has touched."[21] He went on to ask for donations as small as a dollar. In September 1891, he was expressing thanks for subscriptions totaling $1,000 arising from a major week of camp meetings in Chili. This, he said, was pledged "towards erecting seminary buildings [plural]."[22] Incidentally, he expressed thanks at the same time for supporters from another camp at Suspension Bridge, New York: "Saturday a subscription of $500 was taken to help rebuild Chesbrough Seminary, several giving fifty cents a month, and some a dollar a month for a year."[23] Thus, from the earliest days of rebuilding, the plan of completing two new structures in tandem, as funds would allow, seems to have been the main thrust of Roberts's mission.

The December 1891 *Earnest Christian* announced the completion of a two-story addition to the Rumsey farmhouse, including "a dining room, a sitting room, a laundry, and rooms for fourteen students. Such a building is greatly needed for young children who are sent here to school."[24] Around this time, work had started on rebuilding what would later be dedicated as Roberts Hall: "The large building is going up rapidly and in a very substantial manner. The basement stone is up and the brick walls are being laid."[25] In the meantime, classes continued in the nearby Free Methodist church.

By 1892, Roberts had quietly started to inquire after major donors for another building, this one dedicated to academics and assemblies. During this period, while traveling, Roberts wrote to his wife that Edward P. Cox may be the benefactor for which they have been looking. Cox, a wealthy Buffalo resident, had been an early supporter of Roberts's and the two had worked closely together thirty years before in 1860, after Roberts's break from the Methodist Church. Cox was even entrusted to supervise the

20. Ibid.
21. Ibid.
22. Roberts, "Camp Meetings," 97.
23. Ibid., 98.
24. Roberts, "Seminary Buildings," 192.
25. Ibid.

operation of a large building on Thirteenth Street in Buffalo, which included one of the first "free" churches. Before the fall 1892 term, one that Roberts said "was never better attended," the Cox Hall building project was "being pushed rapidly" to finish in time for the incoming students.

> The Cox school building is being pushed on rapidly and is to be completed in time for occupation at the beginning of the school year. It is a convenient, well-planned school building 120 x 56 feet with a large assembly room, study and recitation rooms.[26]

According to Roberts, Cox "inquired about the cost, and when I told him about the $10,000, he said, 'that is not much.' He said he would pray over it." Cox ended up donating $8,000, a very large sum for a single donation.

Still, it was estimated that it would cost $1,500 to furnish the two buildings before the grand opening on September 14, 1892. The buildings were not completed by the start of the term, although it appears that the rooms were "fully furnished" and with "fine equipment." On that day, the official joint dedication took place.

Chili Seminary with the completed Cox Hall
(Moore family archives)

26. Roberts, "Chesbrough Seminary," 66.

The total cost of the vast building projects (including heating and grading of the grounds) totaled around $30,000 by this time. Thanks to overwhelming contributions, all but $5,000 was raised by the end of 1892. By the turn of the century, its basement and second floor were still unfinished. During the tenuous academic year beginning in 1892, three students from India, two from Japan, and one each from Mexico, Germany, and England attended, likely due to connections from the first generation of seminary students now serving in the mission field.

Needless to say, by the time Roberts died of a heart attack on February 27, 1893, Chesbrough Seminary had weathered some blistering financial issues and yet had managed to grow in some significant ways. Many challenges lay ahead, such as the struggle to complete the construction of Carpenter Hall during the Great Depression. Even so, by the end of the decade it was reported flatly for the first time that the institution was out of debt! When Roberts first purchased the Rumsey property in 1866, thirty-seven privately-funded and administered academies were in operation in western New York. By 1905 only six remained. The rest were either incorporated into the developing public education system or had withered away. The seminary had not only avoided the fates of similar institutions, but had started to thrive, due in part to diligent handling of real estate investments led by Roberts himself.

In 1886, Roberts wrote and published a book entitled *First Lessons on Money* in which he offered the following unadorned advice:

> Never go into debt for anything that will not stand as security for the debt, and which will not furnish you with means to pay it. Live within your income, no matter how small that may be . . . Avoid all mere speculations. Have nothing to do with stock gambling and dealing in margins. But it is proper, and often wise, to buy real estate if the income from it will pay interest and taxes, as it is altogether probable that it will rise in value.[27]

His own general formula for success seems to have consisted of various degrees of earnest prayer, diligence, opportunism, networking, calculated risk, and careful management; the exact proportion of those degrees remains up for debate. Clearly, though, something had worked, despite so many ways his debt could have ended in financial ruin for him and his family, not to mention the eradication of myriad opportunities for generations of students locally and around the world.

Had he not served in such charitable capacities, it seems clear that B. T. Roberts could have charted a lucrative career as an independent

27. Roberts, *First Lessons on Money*, 147–8.

businessman. So many Free Methodist writers have rightly touted Roberts's noble integrity, moral character, personal charisma, and religious dedication. While these characteristics should be noted and indeed serve to explain some of the driving forces behind his inspirational life and works, so many of these interpretations are mediated by subjective value judgments and only partially explain his success. Harvesting the copious details of his real estate investments (most of which likely still exist in public and private records) demonstrates an externalizing of those personal characteristics for which he is often lauded. In other words, without his fastidious business acumen, such intrepid religious convictions may not have materialized into any form resembling a seminary—or a church, for that matter. From this synergy of faith and work sprang the institution whose first 150 years we celebrate. This legacy is one that has been sustained at its core by earnest and steadfast self-sacrificial love.

Bibliography

Pfouts, Neil E. *A History of Roberts Wesleyan College*. North Chili, NY: Roberts Wesleyan College, 2000.
Roberts, Benjamin T. "A. M. Chesbrough." *Earnest Christian* (December 1883) 190–91.
———. "The A. M. Chesbrough Seminary." *Earnest Christian* (December 1890) 192.
———. "Camp Meetings." *Earnest Christian* (September 1891) 97–98.
———. "Chili School." *Earnest Christian* (October 1868) 125.
———. "Chili Seminary." *Earnest Christian* (February 1869) 66.
———. "Chili Seminary." *Earnest Christian* (July 1869) 33.
———. "Chesbrough Seminary." *Earnest Christian* (July 1869) 65–66.
———. *First Lessons on Money*. Rochester, NY: Roberts, 1886.
———. "Labor." *Earnest Christian* (November 1868) 160.
———. "Seminary Buildings." *Earnest Christian* (November 1868) 192.
Roberts, Benson H. *Benjamin Titus Roberts: A Biography*. North Chili, NY: The Earnest Christian Office, 1900.
Snyder, Howard A. *Populist Saints: B. T. and Ellen Roberts and the First Free Methodists*. Grand Rapids: Eerdmans, 2006.
Zahniser, Clarence H. *Earnest Christian: Life and Works of Benjamin Titus Roberts*. Published by the author, 1957.

5

Roberts and the Roots of Environmentalism

Contact and Divergence

—TIMOTHY R. VANDE BRAKE

B. T. Roberts was a contemporary of the founders of the modern environmental movement. As Henry David Thoreau was writing his pioneering essays on wilderness and conservation, Roberts was beginning his pastoral ministry in the Methodist Episcopal Church in western New York. As John Muir walked across California to encounter his beloved Yosemite Valley for the first time, Roberts was chartering a seminary in North Chili. And as Teddy Roosevelt was starting a political career in which he would persistently combat the abuses of big money and power, Roberts, in his final years, was urging the ordination of women. Of course, correspondences like these need not mean much. The United States was a large and rapidly expanding country, and Roberts's world was substantially different and more backward-looking than the worlds of each of these men. Yet there is good reason to posit a distant cousinship between them and Roberts, for Roberts was, in his own way, a champion of nature. And while his religious commitments would have divided him from the skeptical Thoreau, the mystical Muir, or the pugnacious Roosevelt, Roberts ultimately affirmed the same things these men did, if sometimes from different principles.

As we consider the evidence for classing Roberts with the first environmentalists, we must admit that it is mixed. Roberts sometimes seems an antagonist of what we would today call "creation care,"[1] as Howard A. Snyder attests:

> Roberts's [writings] reveal his Wesleyanism in his use of Scripture, reason, and experience in theological argumentation. Roberts put relatively less stress on the created order as a theological category, however. He did not for example lay the groundwork for an ethic of environmental stewardship, though the resources for that are available in Wesley. He did not put as much stress as did Wesley on salvation as the healing and restoration of the whole created order . . . Consequently, he did not bequeath to his Free Methodist progeny a broad biblical and theological basis for an ethic of the kingdom of God in all its dimensions.[2]

Snyder's judgment on this point carries considerable weight, not only because he has written a comprehensive biography of B. T. and Ellen Roberts, but also because he himself has sought throughout his career to ground just such an ethic.[3] In this essay I do not oppose Snyder's view of Roberts as a theologian. In fact, my own analysis of Roberts's published work corroborates his. Yet I do seek to establish that the beginnings of an environmental ethic may be found in Roberts if one views his life from the angle of action.

In many ways, Roberts led an exemplary life. Snyder's chronicling of this life in *Populist Saints* has already made possible a revaluation of Wesleyan political theology. In *Politics Strangely Warmed: Political Theology in the Wesleyan Spirit*, Gregory R. Coates points to Roberts as "a figure in Methodist history who represents the best of the Wesleyan tradition as it is lived out in the public sphere."[4] Coates argues that Roberts smooths out the inconsistencies in Wesley's political theology by enacting a more consistent (that is, populist) political ethic through his role in the founding of the Farmers' Alliance in the 1870s. Coates's response to Snyder's biography suggests that Roberts's most lasting contributions stem from his actions rather than from

---

1. "Creation care" (often capitalized) is a movement of the past several decades, primarily among evangelical Christians, to take seriously what Scripture says about human responsibility for God's world. Its advocates affirm that the earth belongs to God, not to us, though we have been given charge of it. Unlike some evangelicals, advocates of creation care are not hostile to science or to the scientific community; on the contrary, they collaborate with scientists to promote conservation of threatened species and ecosystems and to establish healthy and sustainable interaction between humans and the natural world.

2. Snyder, *Populist Saints*, 819–20.

3. His most thorough book on this subject, coauthored with Joel Scandrett, is *Salvation Means Creation Healed*.

4. Coates, *Politics Strangely Warmed*, xvii.

his writings. For though Roberts was a skillful rhetor who near the end of his life was editing two periodicals and writing books as occasions arose, his real genius was for bold, apt, and godly action. And since there was sometimes tension between his actions and his stated principles, a further aspect of his genius was his ability not to be paralyzed by the contradictions.

A prime example of this tension is Roberts's belief in *instantaneous* entire sanctification despite his devoting the second half of his life to creating and sustaining structures (periodicals, Chili Seminary, the Farmers' Alliance) that would nurture *gradual* entire sanctification.[5] Roberts's stance toward creation is similarly rich and ambivalent, for nature becomes a gentle and increasingly dominant theme in his life. To explore this theme, I will focus on three moments or habits in Roberts's career: first, his persistent use of outdoor camp meetings for evangelism, spiritual nurture, and revival; second, his founding of Chili Seminary as a manual labor institution—that is, simultaneously as a liberal arts school and a working farm; and third, his crucial role in founding the Farmers' Alliance, a grassroots movement to defend small farmers against corporate interests such as railroads and banks.

That Holy Grove

In a time of transition, B. T. Roberts was a Methodist of the old school. In the formation and practice of his faith, he looked back to figures like Francis Asbury rather than forward with the well-polished seminary graduates filling the urban pulpits in his own day. For Asbury, Methodism was an outdoor affair. As Mark Noll relates,

> In the course of one yearly circuit alone (1791–1792), Asbury left New York, passed through the large mid-Atlantic cities (Philadelphia, Wilmington, Baltimore), surveyed Virginia (Alexandria, Petersburg, Norfolk), touched down in North Carolina (Raleigh) and South Carolina (Charleston) and Georgia (Washington), came back through South Carolina and North Carolina, moved west across the mountains into Tennessee, pushed northward into Kentucky as far as Lexington, came back through Tennessee and proceeded north along the western slopes of the Alleghenies through Virginia to Uniontown in Pennsylvania, then traversed the mountains to reach Baltimore,

---

5. Snyder acknowledges this tension in early Free Methodism in his portrayal of the debates among clergy such as John Wesley Redfield, who advocated instantaneous entire sanctification, and Loren Stiles, who favored a gradualist approach. See Snyder, *Populist Saints*, 523–24.

circled back to New York City on the way up to Connecticut and seaboard Massachusetts, then went westward to Northampton, moved south over the Berkshires through Pittsfield and Albany, before returning to New York City eleven and one half months after departing.[6]

Though settled appointments had largely replaced circuit riding by the mid-nineteenth century, Roberts had a lot in common with his hardy precursors, including a fondness for the outdoors. Snyder comments regarding B. T. and Ellen's courtship, "as their writings make clear, they shared a deep love of nature."[7] This love fueled Roberts's devotion for camp meetings and for a particular old-growth grove that became known as the Bergen Camp Ground.

Camp meetings were protracted, counter-cultural worship gatherings in which male and female, young and old, rich and poor, rowdy and pious could assemble to hear sermon after sermon, to weep, to sing, and to exalt God in a place without walls. David Hempton traces their origins to practices of the Swedish army in Silesia in the early eighteenth century.[8] Other eighteenth-century precursors include the large outdoor meetings led by George Whitefield. Whitefield, a celebrated Anglican evangelist, came from England to tour colonies such as Georgia, Pennsylvania, and Massachusetts in the late 1730s and early 1740s.[9] During one tour he spoke to a gathering of nearly twenty thousand people on Boston Common, a crowd that George Marsden declares to be the largest in the history of the American colonies.[10]

In the early nineteenth century, camp meetings came of age. At Cane Ridge, Kentucky, in August of 1801, the Presbyterian minister Barton W. Stone organized a week-long gathering that drew between twenty and thirty thousand people. This meeting became legendary for stunning manifestations of the Holy Spirit: one participant recalled a roar like Niagara as hundreds of people were slain in the Spirit at one time.[11] Many of the early meetings were organized by Presbyterians, though they drew ecumenical audiences and soon became associated with the Methodists. As Michael K. Turner observes, "Ever pragmatic, the majority of the Methodists were willing to accept camp meetings as a legitimate work of God because the events

---

6. Noll, *America's God*, 196.
7. Snyder, *Populist Saints*, 147.
8. Hempton, *Methodism*, 46.
9. Marsden, *Jonathan Edwards*, 202–4.
10. Ibid., 205.
11. Turner, "Revivalism and Preaching," 127–28.

produced converts."[12] Asbury was an early supporter, viewing the meetings as a "battle ax and weapon of war" to "break down walls of wickedness, part of hell, superstition, false doctrine."[13] In the mid-nineteenth century, B. T. Roberts and his fellow evangelists wielded the meetings in this way to cleanse the Methodist Episcopal Church. But camp meetings were always more than a "battle ax" for Roberts; they were also a chance to meet God in a sacred space that only God could create.

Roberts likely first observed camp meetings in or near his hometown of Lodi, New York, as a child of eleven.[14] By the early years of his ministry, they had become his passion. In an 1852 editorial in the *Northern Christian Advocate,* he proclaimed, "Long live camp-meetings!"[15] In 1862, as the Civil War raged—and his own battles with the Methodist Episcopal Church smoldered—he attended six, from St. Charles, Illinois, to Union, New York.[16] One of these took place in a twenty-five acre grove of virgin forest northwest of Bergen, New York, on property that Roberts had helped purchase for the Methodists' Genesee Conference in 1856.[17] The 1862 meeting was the last assembly at Bergen of the "Nazarites,"[18] the band of pastors who had been expelled from the Methodist Episcopal Church a few years earlier and who had subsequently helped establish the Free Methodist Church.[19]

From the late 1850s to the early 1860s, the Bergen Camp Ground was the site of the largest camp meeting in western New York—an 1858 participant counted 104 well-filled cloth tents; in 1859 *The Brockport Republic* estimated up to 15,000 attendees.[20] And it was a rare and spectacular grove. In the early twentieth century, Baptist educator Galusha Anderson recalled attending as a youth:

> Within the bounds of the neighborhood was a beautiful primeval forest. There, in God's cathedral, whose pillars were the tall, straight trees, under the leafy arches of pendent limbs, the Methodists held in mid-summer their camp-meetings. Most of the people of the neighborhood, without respect to creed, attended them. Denominational walls for the time being were

12. Ibid., 130.
13. Quoted in Tucker, *American Methodist Worship,* 75.
14. Snyder, *Populist Saints,* 22–23.
15. Ibid., 212.
16. Ibid., 581.
17. Van Dussen, "The Bergen Camp Meeting," 78–79.
18. Ibid., 83.
19. Snyder, *Populist Saints,* 309–504.
20. Van Dussen, "Bergen Camp Meeting," 82–83.

broken down. Christians of different names preached and prayed together, and the forest rang with their songs of praise.

But there too, at times, were enacted the wildest extravagances. Men and women prayed at the top of their voices, and, as the excitement rose, a score at a time would pray, and each would utter his petitions with the full capacity of his lungs—and that capacity seemed marvelously great—until bedlam itself seemed to have broken loose. Sometimes persons fell to the ground, became pale and rigid, and were oblivious to all that was passing around them. Hours sometimes elapsed before they awoke to consciousness.[21]

This was the intense, authentic worship that Roberts loved. Indeed, if one can locate in Roberts an incipient environmentalism, its roots run through the Bergen Camp Ground.

Along with Loren Stiles, Roberts purchased the 25-acre grove from Asa Abell in 1856.[22] But in order to reflect the site's true ownership—money for the purchase was subsequently raised throughout the surrounding area[23]— and to provide a permanent structure for its governance, Roberts obtained a charter from the state legislature for a Genesee Camp-Ground Association, which was to elect trustees and function "under the jurisdiction of the Genesee Conference of the Methodist Episcopal Church."[24] Here, the legal acumen that was so often a boon for Roberts became a snag. For within a couple of years, Roberts and his fellow Nazarites had been expelled from their mother church. They were also eventually ejected from the association's board, though the charter did not necessitate such a step.[25] What is more, in the early 1860s the new board threatened the former Nazarites with lawsuits for meeting at the site they had originally purchased.[26]

The faceoff came in 1867 when the Free Methodists appointed a meeting at Bergen. This triggered the "Regency" trustees to get out an injunction. The Free Methodists "went to another ground,"[27] but were interrupted by the sheriff anyway.[28] When Roberts and his associates cleared themselves

21. Quoted in Snyder, *Populist Saints*, 348.
22. Van Dussen, "Bergen Camp Meeting," 78.
23. Snyder, *Populist Saints*, 349.
24. Van Dussen, "Bergen Camp Meeting," 78–79.
25. Roberts, *Why Another Sect*, 314.
26. Van Dussen, "Bergen Camp Meeting," 80.
27. Presumably this was a site close by, and perhaps one used by the Nazarites prior to 1856. See Snyder's discussion of the Bergen meeting's 1855 location in *Populist Saints*, 298.
28. Roberts, *Why Another Sect*, 315.

in court, the trustees appointed men to "[cut] wood on the camp ground, to sell, to pay the costs," even though felling healthy trees was specifically prohibited by the charter.[29] When Roberts got an injunction to stop the logging, the trustees testified that they were making ground safe by clearing it of "old," "unsound," and "more or less decayed" wood.[30] Roberts knew this was a lie: "We found eighty-seven green, sound, stumps—the wood was also sound and green"; even so, he did not prosecute.[31]

It is difficult to see in the actions of Roberts's opponents anything but malicious reprisal. Clear-cutting the Bergen grove seems an ugly and unnecessary coda to the Genesee Conference battles of 1858-9. Roberts could not call another meeting on the denuded site. For though he didn't voice it, the grove's destruction wounded him deeply. Even the Regency faction could not convene on the bare ground for long. In 1873, they moved their annual gatherings to Silver Lake, New York.[32] In his account of the affair, Roberts, with characteristic reserve, writes, "They beat us of course."[33] Beneath his reserve lurks a sorrow comparable to that expressed by Thoreau and Muir in their early essays on conservation.

In September of 1853, Thoreau traveled with his cousin George Thatcher to Maine to hunt moose.[34] With their Indian guide, they found they had to paddle far up the Penobscot and its tributaries to find game. When they finally came across a moose cow and calf, Thatcher shot immediately, wounding the cow and scaring away the panicked calf. Following the blood trail, they eventually found the moose dead and waterlogged in a creek. Thoreau's curiosity turned to disgust as their guide skinned her. Her milk streamed still warm from her "rent udder," and, after the guide had wrapped a few choice steaks in the hide, he left the carcass to rot.[35] Reflecting later on this incident and on the even more savage practices he had witnessed, Thoreau declared,

> I had had enough of moose-hunting . . . [T]his hunting of the moose merely for the satisfaction of killing him—not even for the sake of his hide—without making any extraordinary exertion or running any risk yourself, is too much like going out by night to some wood-side pasture and shooting your neighbor's

29. Ibid.
30. Ibid.
31. Ibid., 316.
32. Van Dussen, "Bergen Camp Meeting," 80-81.
33. Roberts, *Why Another Sect*, 316.
34. Richardson, *Henry Thoreau*, 300.
35. Thoreau, *The Maine* Woods, 156.

horses. These are God's own horses, poor, timid creatures, that will run fast enough as soon as they smell you, though they *are* nine feet high.[36]

Thoreau and Roberts both recognized a holiness in nature. Moose are "God's own horses," wrote Thoreau, and it is small-minded and vile to hunt them to extinction merely "to hang [your] hat on his horns."[37]

Roberts's muted anger over Bergen also finds a parallel in John Muir's freely expressed anger. Having witnessed decades of selfish and senseless destruction of old-growth forests throughout the nation, Muir wrote in 1901,

> Any fool can destroy trees. They cannot run away; and if they could, they would still be destroyed—chased and hunted down as long as fun or a dollar could be got out of their bark hides, branching horns, or magnificent bole backbones. Few that fell trees plant them; nor would planting avail much toward getting back anything like the noble primeval forests. During a man's life, only saplings can be grown, in the place of old trees—tens of centuries old—that have been destroyed.[38]

Like Thoreau and Muir, Roberts could lament the evil of exploiting nature for "fun or a dollar."

Yet to say that Roberts advocated "creation care" in our modern sense would be an overstatement. Just as he can be compared to Thoreau and Muir, he can as easily be contrasted with them: both men *voiced* their anger over nature's violation while Roberts never did. For Roberts, nonhuman nature did not merit the kinds of protections or exertions that human persons did. He could appreciate a lovely grove of trees and lament its destruction, but he would not go to court for it.

Roberts's attitudes toward nature are consistent with the long history of the church's devaluing of creation evident in its hymns. Shortly after the standoff over Bergen, Roberts saw through the press a book titled *Spiritual Songs and Hymns for Pilgrims*.[39] Through the next decade and a half, the volume went through several editions and revisions. In each printing, the book fits snugly in the hand or the pocket, and thus could have been used at

36. Ibid., 161.
37. Ibid., 118.
38. Muir, *The Wilderness World of John Muir*, 231.

39. The first edition of this book appeared in June of 1868. See Snyder, *Populist Saints* 709. Since none of the first edition appears to have survived, quotations are drawn from the 1869 printing, with the exception of "And let this feeble body fail." Here an 1878 edition is used, since Roberts Wesleyan College's Golisano Library's 1869 copy is missing this page.

a camp meeting. And while Roberts wrote none of the hymns, he compiled them. Consequently, they serve as a good place to view his kingdom theology. One of the songs begins, "We're bound for the land of the pure and holy," and has as its refrain: "O say, will you go to the Eden above?" One stanza is worth quoting in full:

> Nor fraud, nor deceit, not the hand of oppression,
>
> Can injure the dwellers in that holy grove;
>
> No wickedness there, not a shade of transgression,
>
> O say, will you go to the Eden above?

Many who bought this book had lived through the controversies over Bergen and must have resonated with these lines. They had felt the "hand of oppression" that had razed their "holy grove." Yet this hymn bids them not to protest but rather to lay their hopes in "the Eden above."

Another in the collection ("And Let This Feeble Body Fail") is even more telling:

> My soul shall quit the mournful vale,
>
> And soar to worlds on high:
>
> Shall join the disembodied saints,
>
> And find its long-sought rest[.]

Typical of nineteenth-century holiness theology, these verses imagine heaven as an ethereal realm of "disembodied saints." Earth, in contrast, is a "mournful vale" that weary, battle-scarred Christians want to escape. With such notions, why would "pilgrims" care about an embarrassingly material planet? In the twenty-first century, these attitudes are still so common that we are scarcely put off by them, even though the Apostles' Creed says, "I believe . . . in the resurrection of the *body*" and even though all four gospels record that Jesus Christ rose *bodily* from the grave. Yet in the past decade, theologians in the Free Methodist tradition—Richard Middleton and Howard Snyder, most prominently—have issued passionate correctives. Rethinking Scripture's metanarrative, Middleton argues for a kingdom theology that contrasts sharply with Roberts's *Songs and Hymns:*

> Humans, the Bible tells us, are cultural beings, defined not by our worship, for worship is what defines creation (all creatures are called to worship). But the human creature is made to worship God in a distinctive way: by interacting with the earth, using our God-given power to transform our earthly environment

into a complex world (a sociocultural world) that glorifies our creator.[40]

According to Middleton, humans' unique ability to protect or to cultivate the earth in ways that glorify God is their distinctive act of worship. Clear-cutting a magnificent grove out of spite would obviously not qualify. But neither would standing by to tolerate such a brutal act. If these eighty-seven trees had been one person, would Roberts have pursued justice to the end? Undoubtedly. As we read the hymns he sang, we understand why he let this case drop. His sorrow, however, he still had to deal with, and I like to think that this lingering unease was one thing that impelled him to more deliberate and forceful environmental action in the second half of his life.

A Steady Glow

Chili Seminary's founding was begun in 1866, a year before the clash over Bergen reached its end.[41] Roberts's plans for the new school were announced in the May 1866 issue of the *Earnest Christian*:

> A number of persons who are desirous of doing all the good in their power, have undertaken to establish a school, in which all shall be done that can be done, to train up youth in habits of piety, virtue, industry and economy, while they are acquiring the elements of a sound education. With this object in view, a farm has been purchased, of 145 acres. It is about ten miles west of Rochester, about one mile from Chili Station on the N.Y. Central Railroad. The farm is pronounced, by every one who has seen it, as one of the very best that can be found for this purpose . . . The design is to have all the scholars work from three to five hours every day. An accomplished farmer will teach the science and the practice of agriculture and horticulture. The cost of the farm is $17,000.00. Very liberal offers have already been made, by prominent men in the community, . . . to assist us in the erection of suitable buildings. We want to raise the money at once, to pay for the farm.[42]

In the years before its founding, Roberts had considered different models and locations for a seminary. Early on, he had thought of building on a

---

40. Middleton, *A New Heaven and a New Earth*, 41.

41. The site was purchased and classes were begun in 1866, though the seminary was not officially chartered until 1869. See *Catalogue of the Officers and Students of the Chili Seminary*.

42. Quoted in Snyder, *Populist Saints*, 614.

smaller piece of land within the city of Rochester, perhaps to provide for the sort of urban ministry that he and Ellen had shared in Buffalo.[43] But when he eventually purchased the farm in North Chili, his stated goals were essentially those of the manual labor movement.

This movement, an approach to education that paired farm work with the liberal arts, began in the early 1820s and quickly spread from Pennsylvania to Illinois and from Maine to Georgia.[44] Manual labor colleges allowed poor students to study for the ministry, but because they required large initial investments that could be recouped only slowly, if at all, they tended not to persist. In fact, the movement had largely played itself out by the mid-1830s.[45] It lasted, however, among evangelicals fanning out from the Finneyite revivals of the 1820s and 1830s. Their banner school was the Oneida Institute, founded in Whitesboro, New York, in 1827, and the movement's champion was Theodore Dwight Weld.[46]

In the history of American evangelicalism, few possess the intensity and focus of Weld. A convert of Charles Finney, he is perhaps best known as an abolitionist. And, historically, the manual labor movement may be most important as a bridge to abolitionism, for as it ennobled labor it broke down a key rationalization for slavery. But it was more than a bridge. In the hands of Weld and his companions at Oneida, the movement's goal became educating the whole person. Too often, ministers had emerged from rigorous seminary studies weak, debilitated, and unskilled in basic arts or crafts such as animal husbandry or carpentry. Weld himself had had to drop out of Andover Academy and Theological Seminary due to severe eyestrain some years earlier.[47] At Oneida, manual laborites such as Weld sought to "reunit[e] body and mind in healthful order,"[48] promoting a more biblical view of the human person and of creation. Daily farm work accomplished other goals too: for instance, it kept seminarians out of licentiousness and mischief, linked them directly to the people they would serve, and helped them avoid melancholy.[49] Lewis Tappan, an evangelical philanthropist from New York City, became the movement's crucial backer, creating in 1831 the Society for Manual Labor in Literary Institutions and appointing Weld as

---

43. Snyder, *Populist Saints*, 502–3, 612.

44. Goodman, "The Manual Labor Movement and the Origins of Abolitionism," 364.

45. Ibid.

46. Ibid., 355.

47. Abzug, *Passionate Liberator*, 24.

48. Ibid., 67.

49. Ibid., 67–68.

its first general agent.⁵⁰ Having been thrilled by Oneida, Tappan wrote, "I was delighted to see young men who a few hours previously were reaping, milking, etc come onto the platform before a large assembly and deliver their compositions in Latin and English—orations, poems, colloquys etc with ease and dignity."⁵¹ Something thrilling was afoot.

It seems unlikely that Roberts had direct contact with Weld.⁵² Twenty years Weld's junior, he benefitted from the abolitionist's writings and leadership just as other radical evangelicals did.⁵³ But the two men's faith journeys ultimately diverged: in the late 1860s as Roberts founded a school where the whole Bible was to be read each year by each student,⁵⁴ Weld was establishing near Boston a Unitarian congregation that would "serve the communal functions of a church while allowing the widest variety of religious expression among its members."⁵⁵ Weld's faith had blazed like a firebrand for a couple of decades, setting alight the social consciences of many, but it eventually burned out. Roberts's faith, in contrast, glowed steadily inside and outside the church to the end of his life.

Long before the 1860s, Roberts had nurtured sympathies for the labor movement's premises. At age twenty-one, while a top student at Genesee Wesleyan Seminary, he and Loren Stiles had gone into the woods to pray about whether to continue: "We had both intended to prosecute our studies farther . . . but seeing the formality of the Seminary professors, we were afraid to go farther for fear that we should lose our first love and become cold and formal."⁵⁶ In addition to a career-long distaste for religious formalism, one reads here Roberts's dread of losing contact with the common people and their work. By temperament, he loved such work. When he and Ellen, newly married, moved into a run-down parsonage in Pike, New York, Benjamin proved both handy and industrious: "If he only had the conveniences

50. Ibid., 66.

51. Quoted in Abzug, *Passionate Liberator*, 63–64.

52. He did, however, have several indirect ties to Weld. The most important of these was David F. Newton, who became Roberts's editorial partner when *The Golden Rule* merged with *The Earnest Christian* in 1862. See Snyder, *Populist Saints*, 557. As a co-editor, Newton worked with Roberts in the years leading up to the founding of Chili Seminary. Newton had been an early associate of Weld's, probably at Oneida before Weld turned to abolitionism. See Snyder, *Populist Saints*, 559.

53. Pamphlets Weld wrote or coauthored, such as *The Bible Against Slavery* (1837) and *Slavery as It Is* (1839), along with his gifts for organization and oratory and his loathing for any kind of hypocrisy make him "the greatest of the Evangelical abolitionists and reformers" (Dayton, *Discovering an Evangelical Heritage*, 27).

54. Snyder, *Populist Saints*, 620.

55. Abzug, *Passionate Liberator*, 291.

56. Snyder, *Populist Saints*, 40.

for working, I think he might make all the furniture we would need," Ellen wrote proudly to her Aunt Lydia.[57] Between these two incidents, while a student at Wesleyan University, Roberts wrote his father, "I am resolved to make the interests of my soul of first importance, my bodily health second, and the improvement of my mind third."[58]

Yet while Roberts's empathy with the labor movement ran deep, it vied with competing ministry goals as he looked to start a school. Except for passages such as the *Earnest Christian* article quoted above, this empathy seldom becomes explicit. One reason for this, as previously stated, was that Roberts was better at taking bold action than at articulating his reasons for it. Another may have been that he didn't want to jeopardize the funding of his school by drawing attention to the movement's failures: the Oneida Institute had closed its doors in the 1840s for lack of money, and Oberlin College had abandoned its manual labor program during the 1850s.[59] The fact that labor remained a crucial part of the educational program through 1960 at the school Roberts founded shows both that the school's farm could be largely self-sustaining and that farm work was deeply allied to the school's mission in other ways: chiefly, in its nurturance of a sound work ethic.[60]

Roberts's belated participation in the manual labor movement discloses a mature and many-faceted (though under-articulated) kingdom theology that is only in our time being recaptured. As Middleton writes in *A New Heaven and a New Earth*, the Bible calls all human beings to a "full-orbed bodily obedience" so that they may be fit, individually and communally, for their true and distinctive worship: interacting with the earth and transforming it to the glory of God.[61] Since we are currently immersed in a culture committed to "progress" but blind to its costs, we must be reminded what we have lost. Farmer and writer Wendell Berry does this with clarity and hope. Perhaps his best defense of manual labor's role in building community can be found in his stories and novels, where he chronicles his fictional town

57. Ibid., 177.
58. Ibid., 97.
59. Goodman, "Manual Labor Movement," 364.
60. Mendal Dick, in discussion with the author, July 28-30, 2015. Drawing from his own memories and from a conversation with Leo Mahnke, son of the last farm supervisor, Dale Mahnke, Dick related that farm operations at RWC ceased in 1960 for three reasons: 1.) the USDA stipulated that RWC had to sell its farm products to a distributor rather than directly to the College's cafeteria 2.) the USDA started paying farmers not to grow certain crops, and the College realized it could make more money by *not* farming 3.) the College needed a building for its maintenance department and so appropriated the Quonset hut that had replaced the campus's barn, which had burned in the late 1950s.
61. Middleton, *New Heaven*, 40-41.

of Port William, Kentucky. But his essays are eloquently persuasive as well. In his book, *What Are People For?* Berry argues that individuals' affectional engagement with manual labor is crucial for community:

> [T]he tobacco harvest in my own home country involves the hardest work that I have done in any quantity. In most of the years of my life, from early boyhood until now, I have taken part in the tobacco cutting. This work usually occurs between the last part of August and the first part of October. Usually the weather is hot; usually we are in a hurry. The work is extremely demanding, and often, because of the weather, it has the character of an emergency. Because all of the work still must be done by hand, this event has maintained much of its old character; it is very much the sort of thing the agriculture experts have had in mind when they have talked about freeing people from drudgery.
>
> That the tobacco cutting *can* be drudgery is obvious. If there is too much of it, if it goes on too long, if one has no interest in it, if one cannot reconcile oneself to the misery involved in it, if one does not like or enjoy the company of one's fellow workers, then drudgery would be the proper name for it.
>
> But for me, and I think for most of the men and women who have been my companions in this work, it has not been drudgery. None of us would say that we take pleasure in all of it all of the time, but we do take pleasure in it, and sometimes the pleasure can be intense and clear. Many of my dearest memories come from these times of hardest work.[62]

As Berry develops this theme, he notes that tobacco cutting assembles the whole community—young and old, male and female, neighbor and kin—and that one of its chief benefits is talk: "Some of the best talk I have ever listened to I have heard during these times, and I am especially moved to think of the care that is sometimes taken to speak well—that is, to speak fittingly—of the dead and the absent. The conversation, one feels, is ancient."[63]

Though Roberts belonged to a Christian tradition in which tobacco is a vice and Berry to a Christian tradition for which it has been a livelihood, both recognize the power of manual labor, and farm labor particularly, to bring people into conformity with the image of God. For just as God takes pleasure in his creation and his work, so we become more wakeful toward the creation's bounty and loveliness as we work it. We also become more jealous to protect it.[64] As Berry sums up,

62. Berry, *What Are People for?*, 141–42.
63. Ibid., 142.
64. Ibid., 138–39.

> Where is our comfort but in the free, uninvolved, finally mysterious beauty and grace of this world that we did not make, that has no price? Where is our sanity but there? Where is our pleasure but in working and resting kindly in the presence of this world?[65]

In founding Chili Seminary as a manual labor school, Roberts stepped into "creation care," although he and his successors at the school seldom articulated the kingdom theology they enacted, perhaps due to their devotion to the Holiness movement. If one longs to join the "disembodied saints" in a realm beyond, one cannot fully embrace transforming material culture as an expression of authentic worship. Roberts's commitment to Christian perfection anchored the seminary's orthodoxy against the tide of liberal theology in post-Civil-War America, but it also restricted how its members could interact with the world. At Chili Seminary, catalogs from the 1870s attest that students could be disciplined for laughing in their rooms, strolling on Sundays, or engaging in "any matched game of base-ball."[66] For smoking and chewing tobacco, among other "wicked" offenses, they could be expelled.[67] In these matters, Roberts and his fellow trustees were following Wesley, whose writings on scriptural holiness "left no room for levity or carelessness."[68] Farm labor provided a curious compromise, however: it allowed seminarians to indulge their bodies without breaching the code, since little is as physically satisfying as a hard day's work. It also cemented the seminary's populist ethos, clearing the way for Roberts's contribution to American politics.

Heart, Hands, Head

Gregory Coates has made a good case that Roberts is a prime example of Wesleyan political theology in action. Yet it shouldn't be missed that what Coates commends him for—helping to found the Farmers' Alliance—had broad environmental impacts as well. In giving a voice to small farmers, Roberts protected the land and livelihoods of thousands of families threatened by post-Civil-War industrialist greed. He also exemplifies how liberal learning can serve environmental ends. Like Teddy Roosevelt, Roberts

---

65. Ibid., 140.
66. *The Second Annual Catalog and Circular of the Chili Seminary*, 16.
67. Ibid., 15.
68. Hempton, *Methodism*, 59.

protected the common people, showing anger at injustice, reasoning carefully through problems, and acting with courage and speed.

In the 1860s, upstate New York, with its fertile soil and easy access to Manhattan by canal and river, boasted the country's most valuable farmland. But by the early 1870s, a new network of railroads had begun to knit the nation together, turning proximity to the coast into a disadvantage. For as larger and newer farms in the Midwest began to outpace the production of those in New York, railroads moved Midwestern goods to market reliably and cheaply. To the railroad owners, it became less profitable to service small upstate towns when they could run express lines all the way from major inland cities to the coast.[69] Banks compounded upstate farmers' woes, since towns were bonded to raise funds for railroad construction if most property owners voted in favor. In the postwar boom, small landowners often didn't understand the consequences of their votes, and they were regularly duped by agents who went door to door promising things their companies never meant to deliver.[70] These farmers often couldn't see that they were putting their livelihoods into the hands of corporations that cared only for profits.

As early as the 1860s, New York farmers began to organize against these threats. The National Grange (officially, the Patrons of Husbandry) was established in Washington, DC, in 1867, and the first permanent and active chapter appeared in Fredonia, New York, a year or so later.[71] Yet the Grange would not answer everyone's needs, for it was a secret society. Moreover, it had limited influence; a broader and more public movement was needed.

As frustration mounted, Roberts was uniquely poised to make a difference: he was a broad and incisive reader, an extensive traveler, an upstate farmer, and an articulate writer.[72] When he began to voice his opinions on the plight of small landholders, his anger brimmed over, as in this anonymous letter of January 1874 to the *New York Times*:

> I emphatically deny the right of any man or set of men to mortgage my farm in this way for the benefit of a grasping money-making, swindling corporation. These corporations well understand how to escape their part of the contract, how to cheat the towns out of the stock for which the bonds were

---

69. Snyder, *Populist Saints*, 747.
70. Ibid., 753–54.
71. Ibid., 748.
72. Ibid., 745–46.

issued. There is a far greater probability that they will do this than there is that the railroad will be built.[73]

Roberts recognized that greedy businessmen and unscrupulous politicians were driving small farmers to ruin in a hurry and that something had to be done. Accordingly, through the western New York Farmers' Club in early 1875 he issued a call to build a better organization. And between 1875 and 1877 in the Rochester courthouse, Roberts spearheaded the establishment of the New York State Farmers' Alliance.[74] Within a few years, this regional organization would spark a national movement that would, in turn, impel the founding of the Populist Party. And the Populists would place men in the U. S. Congress and would run in presidential elections.[75]

Because of its broad effects, helping found the Farmers' Alliance was one of Roberts's most important environmental acts. As we consider his previous ventures, though, we see a progression: first, his love of nature and camp meetings spurred him to purchase the Bergen Camp Ground and to grieve when it was desecrated; second, his love of farming moved him to found a seminary as a manual labor college; and finally, his anger at industrial greed prodded him to build an organization that would check the new elite and help small farmers to keep their land.

In this last accomplishment, Roberts resembles Teddy Roosevelt, who is increasingly recognized for his pathbreaking environmental advocacy, such as his protecting the Grand Canyon from damming and mining.[76] Less conspicuous, though no less important, was his signing of the Hepburn Bill. This bill, which became law in June of 1906, expanded the membership of the Interstate Commerce Commission (ICC) and gave it new powers to regulate the railroads.[77] Among other things, this bill granted the ICC the ability to set a maximum shipping rate and prohibited railroads from owning the goods they transported.[78]

Like Roosevelt, Roberts was practical but also devoted to the liberal arts—to pursuits such as the teaching and learning of Latin.[79] He felt that the mental discipline and judgment gained in such study could train one to be of use in the nitty-gritty of everyday life. Helping to establish the Farmers' Alliance required such judgment, if only because it went against the ex-

---

73. Quoted in Snyder, *Populist Saints*, 754.
74. Snyder, *Populist Saints*, 757–67.
75. Ibid., 778–86.
76. Burns, *The National Parks*.
77. Hawley, *Theodore Roosevelt*, 159–60.
78. Ibid., 160.
79. Snyder, *Populist Saints*, 615.

pansionist grain. As American industry picked up steam, Roberts narrowed rather than widened the gap between education and farming. Education begins with the head, but rightly ends with the hands and heart. Like Roosevelt, Roberts was extraordinary in his ability to bring his learning full circle for the benefit of others.

As we read Roberts's writings, we find things that put him at odds with contemporaries who viewed nature in a new way. But as we consider his actions, we note striking likenesses between Roberts and early environmentalists. He need not have read their writings to act in this way, for he knew the Scriptures, which declare, "The earth is the Lord's, and the fullness thereof; the world, and they that dwell therein" (Psalm 24:1). Roberts's environmental actions were ultimately a living out of his "full-orbed bodily obedience" to God in the world. Whether he was worshipping God beneath the tall hardwoods of the Bergen Camp Ground, teaching and farming on his North Chili campus, or speaking at the Rochester courthouse on behalf of a new association for farmers, he was acknowledging God's good gifts and fighting to preserve them. As we celebrate his life, we would do well to love the things he loved, keeping them before us however we can.

Bibliography

Abzug, Robert H. *Passionate Liberator: Theodore Dwight Weld and the Dilemma of Reform*. New York: Oxford University Press, 1980.
Berry, Wendell. *What Are People For?*. Berkeley, CA: Counterpoint, 2010.
Catalogue of the Officers and Students of the Chili Seminary. Rochester: Earnest Christian, 1879.
Coates, Gregory R. *Politics Strangely Warmed: Political Theology in the Wesleyan Spirit*. Eugene, OR: Wipf and Stock, 2015.
Dayton, Donald W. *Discovering an Evangelical Heritage*. Peabody, MA: Hendrickson, 1976.
Goodman, Paul. "The Manual Labor Movement and the Origins of Abolitionism." *Journal of the Early Republic* 13, no. 3 (1993) 355–88. http://www.jstor.org/stable/3124349.
Hawley, Joshua D. *Theodore Roosevelt: Preacher of Righteousness*. New Haven: Yale University Press, 2008.
Hempton, David. *Methodism: Empire of the Spirit*. New Haven: Yale University Press, 2005.
Marsden, George M. *Jonathan Edwards: A Life*. New Haven: Yale University Press, 2003.
Middleton, J. Richard. *A New Heaven and a New Earth: Reclaiming Biblical Eschatology*. Grand Rapids: Baker, 2014.
Muir, John. *The Wilderness World of John Muir: A Selection from His Collected Work*. 1954. Edited by Edwin W. Teale. Boston: Houghton Mifflin, 2001.
The National Parks: America's Best Idea. Directed by Ken Burns. Arlington, VA: PBS, 2009. DVD.

Noll, Mark A. *America's God: From Jonathan Edwards to Abraham Lincoln.* New York: Oxford University Press, 2002.

Richardson, Robert D., Jr. *Henry Thoreau: A Life of the Mind.* Berkeley: University of California Press, 1986.

Roberts, Benjamin T., compiler. *Spiritual Songs and Hymns for Pilgrims.* Revised edition. Rochester, NY: Roberts, 1869.

———. *Why Another Sect?* Rochester, NY: Earnest Christian, 1879.

The Second Annual Catalog and Circular of the Chili Seminary. Rochester, NY: Smith, 1871.

Snyder, Howard A. *Populist Saints: B. T. and Ellen Roberts and the First Free Methodists.* Grand Rapids: Eerdmans, 2006.

Snyder, Howard A., and Joel Scandrett. *Salvation Means Creation Healed: The Ecology of Sin and Grace: Overcoming the Divorce between Earth and Heaven.* Eugene, OR: Cascade, 2011.

Thoreau, Henry D. *The Maine Woods.* 1864. Repr., New York: Penguin, 1988.

Tucker, Karen B. Westerfield. *American Methodist Worship.* Oxford: Oxford University Press, 2001.

Turner, Michael K. "Revivalism and Preaching." *The Cambridge Companion to American Methodism,* edited by Jason E. Vickers, 119–37. Cambridge Companions to Religion. New York: Cambridge University Press, 2013.

Van Dussen, D. Gregory. "The Bergen Camp Meeting in the American Holiness Movement." *Methodist History* 21, no. 2 (1983) 69–89.

6

Religious Reform in Western New York

B. T. Roberts and Walter Rauschenbusch on Revival and Social Change

—JEFFREY A. MCPHERSON

Two of the most significant Christian figures to emerge from Rochester in the second half of the nineteenth century are Benjamin Titus Roberts (1823–1893) and Walter Rauschenbusch (1861–1918). B. T. Roberts is best known for his role in creating a new denomination, the Free Methodists, and for founding a school, Chili Seminary.[1] Rauschenbusch, undoubtedly the most famous theologian to come from Rochester, is best known for his part in creating and shaping the Social Gospel Movement. Roberts precedes Rauschenbusch by a generation. In fact, Roberts's arrival in Rochester coincides with Rauschenbusch's birth, and Roberts's death precedes Rauschenbusch's return to Rochester from New York City by four years. As far as we know, they did not know each other and there is no record of Rauschenbusch reading Roberts's published works. However, there is an interesting affinity in their thought that bears some analysis. Through this analysis we can see that Roberts and Rauschenbusch share a profound agreement that spiritual and social transformation necessarily go together. The traditions that follow from Roberts and Rauschenbusch and continue into the twentieth century tend to bifurcate the spiritual and social, revival

---

1. Chili Seminary is the forerunner of Roberts Wesleyan College.

and reformation. The conservative evangelical tradition of Free Methodism tends to emphasize the need for salvation at the personal level.[2] Religious revival is key to its spiritual narrative. The more liberal social gospel tradition of Rauschenbusch tends to emphasize the necessity of social reform. However, through this study we will see that in their own words, Roberts and Rauschenbusch affirm both revival and reformation; both are necessary in light of the coming Kingdom of God.

It is not surprising that Rochester provides the setting for this connection. Western New York in the nineteenth century, famously known as the "burned-over district" due to the variety and intensity of religious experience, boasted many religious and social movements.[3] The revivals of Charles Finney, the founding of the Church of Jesus Christ of Latter Day Saints by Joseph Smith, the Oneida Society, and the Spiritualist movement led by the Fox sisters are some of the religious movements from the vicinity of Rochester. Socially progressive movements include the suffrage movement led by Elizabeth Cady Stanton and Susan B. Anthony as well as the abolitionist movement with ties to Rochester through Frederick Douglas and the Underground Railroad. The birth of Free Methodism in 1860 is, perhaps, linked to this wider phenomenon of religious experience as a movement which capitalized on freedom for pursuing new religious ideas. The two themes of our analysis are clearly present in the social identity of Rochester in the nineteenth century. In light of the Rochester connection, there are two themes that emerge: the need for religious revival and the need for social transformation. It is easy to see that both are present in the history of Rochester and both issues take a central place in the respective thought of Roberts and Rauschenbusch.

This paper will begin with brief biographies of Roberts and Rauschenbusch to ground this study in the history of their connection to Rochester and western New York. Next we will examine some of the key social concerns that gripped Roberts and Rauschenbusch. For Roberts, we will focus on freedom and the responsibility of the church in relation to the poor. For Rauschenbusch, we will look at the degrading poverty of the industrial capitalistic system of the early twentieth century. We will examine the views of both men on Prohibition as an issue of mutual concern. Next we will consider the ways in which both Roberts and Rauschenbusch analyze these two aspects of salvation, personal and social transformation. Finally, we will draw some conclusions from our study.

---

2. While the Wesleyan foundation of Free Methodism mitigates this tendency due to its consistent engagement with social issues going back to the ministry of John Wesley, the North American Holiness movement and Evangelical tradition has, on the whole, emphasized personal conversion over against social transformation.

3. Cross, *The Burned-Over District*.

Biographies

Benjamin Titus Roberts was born on July 25, 1823 in western New York, not far from Buffalo. Roberts showed early promise as a scholar and in 1844, at age twenty-one, he attended Genesee Wesleyan Seminary in Lima, New York. This served as preparation for his formal education at Wesleyan University in Middletown, Connecticut from 1845 to 1848. While a student at Wesleyan University, Roberts experienced revival under the ministry of John Wesley Redfield, an itinerant preacher and revivalist who would later become a co-worker in the burgeoning Free Methodist denomination. After graduating from Wesleyan University in 1848, Roberts married Ellen Stowe in May of 1849 and began pastoring in the Methodist Episcopal Church throughout western New York. These ministry years were successful but marked with some controversy. When pastoring at the Niagara Street Church in Buffalo, Roberts urged the congregation to make the seats free but the congregation refused. This marked the beginning of Roberts's ongoing conflict with elements of the leadership within the Methodist Episcopal Church concerning the nature of holiness, the relationship of the church with secret societies, and most importantly the legitimacy of renting pews in church. Roberts published an article, "New School Methodism,"[4] that sharply criticized leadership for these practices in the church. This eventually led to his expulsion from the denomination in 1858. In 1860, after much prayer and consultation, Roberts led the formation of a new denomination at a meeting in Pekin, New York. Beginning in 1860, Roberts also established *The Earnest Christian*, a religious periodical that he would publish for the next thirty-three years. After the Civil War, Roberts purchased property in North Chili and founded the educational institution that would eventually become Roberts Wesleyan College. For the rest of his ministry, Roberts tirelessly worked to convert souls, promote holiness, and transform society for the sake of justice. Roberts passed away in February of 1893, five months shy of turning seventy years old.

Walter Rauschenbusch was born in Rochester, New York, in 1861. His father, August Rauschenbusch, held a position in the German Department of Rochester Theological Seminary. Earlier, August Rauschenbusch had a powerful Pietistic conversion experience that shaped much of his theological outlook. This Pietism was a significant influence on Walther Rauschenbusch's theological viewpoint throughout his life. Rauschenbusch grew up in Rochester although he spent significant time in Germany. He lived in Germany from 1865 to 1869 and studied at the Gymnasium in Gütersloh from 1879 to 1883. The German intellectual traditions impressed Rauschenbusch deeply. Upon his return from undergraduate studies in Germany

---

4. *Roberts*, "New School Methodism."

in 1883, he entered both the University of Rochester and the Rochester Theological School. Immediately after graduation in 1886, Rauschenbusch began as pastor of Second German Baptist Church in New York City, where he would pastor for the next eleven years. He married Pauline Rother in 1893. Rauschenbusch returned to Rochester from New York City in 1897 to teach at Rochester Theological Seminary. He was promoted to Professor of Church History in 1902. In addition to his best-known book *Christianity and the Social Crisis* (1907), Rauschenbusch also published *Christianizing the Social Order* (1912) and *A Theology for the Social Gospel* (1917), among many other works. During the early twentieth century, Rauschenbusch was avidly sought after as a speaker and well known throughout the country. Despite this popularity in America at times, his inability to cope with Germany's martial aggressiveness in the Great War cost him dearly, and his popularity waned with the onset of that war. Rauschenbusch passed away in 1918 at the age of fifty-six.

Social Issues

Roberts and Slavery

Central to Roberts's ministry was the issue of freedom. This comes as no surprise as Roberts is the founder of the Free *Methodist* Church. Two forms of freedom in the nineteenth century concerned him greatly. In the first place, Roberts believed that all persons should be free; that no person should be owned. Thus, Roberts was firmly and passionately against slavery and worked as an abolitionist throughout his ministerial career. In addition, freedom meant free churches. A common practice among urban Methodist Episcopal churches in the nineteenth century was selling or renting pews. The practical, if unintentional, result of this practice was the exclusion of the poor from church. In founding the Free Methodist Church, Roberts banned this practice from his new denomination. In fact, this was one of the central issues that drove the creation of this new denomination. "Thus it is accurate historically to say that the 'Free' in Free Methodist signifies freedom from slavery, oppression and racial discrimination, as well as free seats and freedom of the Spirit."[5]

Roberts held an anti-slavery position throughout his life. Howard Snyder discusses a "remarkable" poem that Roberts wrote to his sister Florilla in 1845, at twenty-two years of age. His poem begins with the abolitionist slogan "Am I not a woman and a sister?" and is accompanied by an abolitionist

---

5. Snyder, *Populist Saints*, 486.

coin with the same slogan. The poem ends with a moral injunction to repulse "that evil Spirit, the Genius of Slavery." The heart of the poem calls upon the *imago dei* of Genesis 1:26–7 as the key of abolitionist sentiment. In the voice of a slave he asks,

> Yet have I not that form divine
>
> Which God to all mankind hath given?
>
> Is not that soul immortal mine
>
> Which e'er must dwell in hell or Heaven?[6]

While this poem predates Roberts's Christian conversion, a biblical worldview, which asserts the inherent value of each individual, already shaped his thinking. From the beginning, his thought was shaped by the nineteenth-century revivalism that aimed for social reform alongside of Christian conversion.[7] Snyder comments that Roberts "must have accepted the revivalist-abolitionist consensus: just as Christian discipleship meant no compromise with sin of any form in society or church, so abolitionism meant no compromise with popular toleration of slavery. For the antislavery radicals—and no doubt for Roberts—abolitionism and revivalism were twin moral crusades."[8]

In February of 1861, Roberts published a biblical analysis of slavery and compared it to the slavery of America in the nineteenth century. Roberts argues that the biblical system is more like indentured servitude, because it does not treat the enslaved as chattel or property.[9] He argues that the providence of God stands against slavery and calls his readers to "remember them that are in bonds as bound with them."[10] In that same issue, Rev. A. A. Phelps, commenting on the mission of the Free Methodist Church, writes that "It is her mission to publish an unmutilated Gospel to others." This means preaching the whole gospel which necessarily excludes certain perspectives. Thus, to preach the whole gospel means to preach against slavery.

6. Ibid., 34.

7. Smith, *Revivalism and Social Reform*.

8. Snyder, *Populist Saints*, 35–36.

9. While this is true with regards to fellow Israelites, it is not true for foreigners. See Lev 25:44–46 (NRSV). "As for the male and female slaves whom you may have, it is from the nations around you that you may acquire male and female slaves. You may also acquire them from among the aliens residing with you, and from their families that are with you, who have been born in your land; and they may be your property. You may keep them as a possession for your children after you, for them to inherit as property. These you may treat as slaves, but as for your fellow Israelites, no one shall rule over the other with harshness."

10. Roberts, "Slavery," 57.

Phelps asks, "who will say that a Gospel which sides with oppression and apologizes for all the horrors of the 'peculiar institution' is a whit better than no Gospel at? In my opinion it is not half so good!"[11] To be the whole gospel, the message must be against oppression, for freedom, and preached to all, including the poor.

The first Free Methodist church was founded in St. Louis in 1859, one year before the inauguration of the denomination in 1860. Roberts travelled to St. Louis to help his friend and co-worker John Wesley Redfield found the church. This was the first time Roberts came face to face with the practice of slavery. While there was some debate among the new congregation as to whether slaveholders would be admitted into church membership, Roberts forbade this practice. The new church in St. Louis was Free. The first book of discipline of the Free Methodist Church in 1860 prohibited "The buying, selling, or holding of a human being as a slave."[12] As Howard Snyder writes, "Nonslaveholding as a test of membership was a specific prophetic stand against a political, social, economic, and moral evil in St. Louis on the eve of the Civil War."[13]

Rauschenbusch and Poverty

When Rauschenbusch began his ministry in Hell's Kitchen, he was stunned by the poverty that he discovered. He struggled to define the church's response to this great need for the majority of his career. "There among the working people my social education began."[14] It is no surprise, then, that poverty plays a central role in his writing. In *Christianity and the Social Crisis*, Rauschenbusch considers poverty in relation to the Old Testament prophets, especially Isaiah and Amos, as well as the ministry of Jesus. In reference to the Old Testament, Rauschenbusch examines the roots of poverty in ancient Israel and speculates regarding contemporary correlations. The key similarity between poverty in the ancient world and contemporary poverty is the lack of property among the poor. He notes that the prophets

11. Phelps, "Mission of the Free Methodist Churches," 48.
12. *Disciplines*, 29.
13. Snyder, *Populist Saints*, 486.
14. Hudson, *Walter Rauschenbusch: Selected Writings*, 10. See also Rauschenbusch's comment in his Introduction to *Christianity and the Social Crisis*, xxii. "For eleven years I was pastor among the working people on the West Side of New York City. I shared their life as well as I then knew, and used up the early strength of my life in their service . . . If this book in some far-off way helps to ease the pressure that bears them down and increases the forces that bear them up, I shall meet the Master of my life with better confidence."

show special concern for the widow, the orphan, and the stranger. These are people with no power, no influence, and no money leaving them with no central identity in the community. He compares them to "the proletarian immigrant of our cities, who also has no share in the modern means of production and no political power to protect his interests."[15] Rauschenbusch recounts, with admiration, the laws of the Old Testament that provide for the stability of agrarian culture. He is particularly interested in Sabbath years (Deuteronomy 16) and the year of Jubilee (Leviticus 25). He sees the prophetic defense of these institutions as a decisive insight into God's very nature. "It became one of the fundamental attributes of their God that he was the husband of the widow, the father of the orphan, and the protector of the stranger. . . . When the prophets conceived Jehovah as the special vindicator of these voiceless classes, it was another way of saying that it is the chief duty in religious morality to stand for the rights of the helpless."[16]

This perspective was repeated and reinforced for Rauschenbusch by the ministry of Jesus. "As with the Old Testament prophets, the fundamental sympathies of Jesus were with the poor and oppressed."[17] Rauschenbusch describes this fundamental position by referring to Jesus' inaugural sermon in Luke 4 and his comments in response to John's disciples in Matthew 11. In both passages "good news for the poor" is offered as proof of Jesus' messianic character. Subsequent scholarship has linked both passages to the year of Jubilee. Thus, Rauschenbusch's understanding of biblical Christianity hinges on the treatment of the poor. The same attitude is required of all who bear the name Christian, although the nature of the work will change depending on context.

Being a generation older that Roberts, Rauschenbusch is not as concerned with slavery as an institution. As Christopher Evans points out, Rauschenbusch's thoughts on race and racism are "tragically typical" for his era. When he does mention slavery, it is in part to lament that the church did not move more quickly and definitively to overcome this sinful institution. He does, however, offer modern abolitionism as evidence of the church exerting its moral weight to effect revolutionary social change.[18] In *A Theology for the Social Gospel*, he briefly mentions slavery as an example of the long-term effects of social sin in the Kingdom of Evil. "'The evils of one generation are caused by the wrongs of the generations that preceded, and will in turn condition the suffering and temptations of those who come

15. Rauschenbusch, *Christianity and the Social Crisis*, 9.
16. Ibid.
17. Ibid., 66.
18. Evans, *The Kingdom is Always but Coming*, 154.

after."[19] In this he recognizes the role of slavery in creating the conditions of oppression which exist in his day.

> When negroes are hunted from a Northern city like beasts, or when a Southern city degrades the whole nation by turning the savage inhumanity of a mob into a public festivity, we are continuing to sin because our fathers created the conditions of sin by the African slave trade and by the unearned wealth they gathered from slave labour for generations.[20]

In an article examining this issue, Rauschenbusch believed that the church could play a positive role in enhancing the social and economic situation of the African-American community that was mired in poverty.[21]

While not intended to be comprehensive and exhaustive, this section of the paper aims to show that both Roberts and Rauschenbusch were engaged in key social issues of their day. Moreover, their thinking on these issues is grounded biblically, especially in their reading of Jesus. Beyond slavery and poverty, though, both share a special concern for the effects of alcoholism and both are strong proponents of Prohibition. We turn now to this issue as a place of agreement between Roberts and Rauschenbusch.

Prohibition

Both abolition and temperance were key social concerns for B. T. Roberts throughout his life. After the Civil War and the Emancipation Proclamation, Roberts turned his attention from slavery to temperance as the key social concern. In March of 1884, Roberts penned an article for *The Earnest Christian* which outlined his case for Prohibition, which of course, goes much further than temperance.[22] While the temperance movement encouraged people to choose not to drink, the Prohibition movement sought to make the sale and trafficking of alcohol illegal. To begin, Roberts boldly asserts that the sale and trafficking of alcohol should be considered a crime because it is intrinsically wrong. To establish this case Roberts considers the devastating effects of alcoholism. Abuse of alcohol leads to such poor decision-making that many alcoholics lose all they own. In this way alcoholism is akin to robbery. It enslaves the will and leads to ruin. In addition, Roberts believes alcohol is the leading cause of crime. Without quoting his

19. Rauschenbusch, *A Theology for the Social Gospel*, 79.
20. Ibid.
21. Evans, *The Kingdom is Always but Coming*, 254.
22. Roberts, "Prohibition."

source, he claims that "It is a demonstrated fact that fully eighty per cent of the crime, and seventy-five per cent of the pauperism of the country are directly traceable to the use of strong drink."[23] Moreover, the sale and traffic of alcohol tends to corrupt business, such that those who deal in liquor cannot be trusted. The trade itself undermines the bonds of society.

Roberts also notes that the sale and consumption of alcohol is controlled in all countries. For example, it is already illegal to sell alcohol to people without the competence to know what they are doing, such as children, the insane, and those who are drunk. The question is not whether to restrict the sale of liquor or not, but whether the restrictions on the sale of liquor that already exist should be universalized.

Roberts also believes that the Bible is against the sale of alcohol.[24] He encourages his followers to act through moral persuasion and political action to get everyone to give up alcohol. He urges them to not be intimidated by the size of the industry or tempted by the lucrative taxes the industry generates. The money is tainted by its immoral source. Through his ministry Roberts knows the ill effects of alcohol abuse and is convinced that working to remove the temptation of alcohol from the community is the surest cure for this disease.

Through his work in Hell's Kitchen, Rauschenbusch witnessed the effects of alcohol abuse first hand. The temptation of alcohol is that in the face of great struggle, it offers the illusion of contentment. He recognizes that alcohol abuse is not only sinful, but it is a social disease.[25]

In *A Theology for the Social Gospel*, Rauschenbusch explains this idea by arguing that the sin of alcoholism comes from social customs and institutions. Alcohol has a social standing which makes it acceptable and even highly praised in society, unlike other addictive substances which are considered to be shameful. Thus, to overcome alcohol abuse the social standing of alcohol must change. The church has played a central role in this regard.

> The rapid progress in the expulsion of the liquor trade in America would have been impossible if the idealization of the drinking customs had not previously disappeared from public opinion. . . . The use of liquor is still common in America, but its social authority has been overcome. So far as I can see, this was done by the churches before either business or science lent much aid, and the decisive fact which set the voice of some of the denominations free was their refusal to tolerate in their

---

23. Ibid., 72.
24. See Hab 2:15.
25. Rauschenbusch, *Christianity and the Social Crisis*, 198–99.

membership persons financially interested in the liquor business, or to receive contributions from them. In the case of alcoholism, we can watch a gradual breaking down of the social authority of a great evil.[26]

Rauschenbusch remains concerned that social conditions could change to allow a recovery of the social status of alcohol. He is particularly concerned that college-age youth be kept from it. "The head of an important Eastern institution a few years ago proposed to introduce beer in the social gatherings of students in order to make them more sociable. . . . Even if the students of that institution should all stop drinking when they graduated, a lasting damage would be done to American college life if it became customary for the college community to pass into partial narcosis as a preparation for social enjoyment."[27] Prophetic words?

In fact, Rauschenbusch includes a prayer against alcoholism in his collection of *Prayers of the Social Awakening*. In this prayer, he calls upon God to remember those whose lives have been ruined by alcohol, both the alcoholics and those partners and children who have been affected. He calls upon the judgment of God for those who deal in the liquor trade and prays that they will have the strength to walk away from this career. He also prays against the political leaders who support this trade. He concludes,

> O God, bring nigh the day when all our men shall face their daily task with minds undrugged and with tempered passions; when the unseemly mirth of drink shall seem a shame to all who hear and see; when the trade that debauches men shall be loathed like the trade that debauches women; and when all this black remnant of savagery shall haunt the memory of a new generation but as an evil dream of the night. For this accept our vows, O Lord, and grant thine aid.[28]

While prohibition is no longer an issue that concerns us, and we have certainly come to recognize the strong genetic influence on alcoholic disposition, we still feel the sting of alcoholism in our culture and mourn its damage. While we may not agree with the strong stance that both Roberts and Rauschenbusch take on this topic, we can see that, for both men, faith must inform social conviction. Both see a crucial role for the church in creating the environment in which this sin is eradicated. For both, prohibition is an issue of holiness.

---

26. Rauschenbusch, *A Theology for the Social Gospel*, 64.
27. Rauschenbusch, *Christianity and the Social Crisis*, 305.
28. Rauschenbusch, *Prayers of the Social Awakening*, 100.

Economics

The most obvious connection between Roberts and Rauschenbusch with regard to social concern is their mutual support for the economics of Henry George and Richard Ely. Henry George was a prominent nineteenth century economist whose principle work, *Progress and Poverty* (1879), struck a chord with reform-minded individuals. George was especially concerned with the large, and increasing, economic gulf between rich and poor. It also troubled him that huge profits resulted from concentrated wealth rather than merit. In response, he proposed "the single tax," that was essentially a property tax on landowners whose proceeds would be used to benefit the poor. Rauschenbusch supported George's candidacy for mayor of New York in 1886 and says in *Christianizing the Social Order* that he owes his "first awakening to the world of social problems to the agitation of Henry George in 1886."[29] Roberts also admired Henry George for his dedication to economic justice. Roberts published an excerpt from George on "The Single Tax" in *The Free Methodist*.[30] While interested in the proposals of Henry George, Roberts's argument in *First Lessons on Money* was influenced by the economic analysis of Richard Ely, another important nineteenth-century American economist.[31] According to Evans, Rauschenbusch, in 1885, devoured Ely's books.[32] Both Roberts and Rauschenbusch learned from George and Ely that the ideas of Jesus have practical implications for the real world. They also learned that Jesus' ideas and priorities can be helpfully applied to contemporary economic problems.

The Gospel and Social Transformation

Roberts

We have already seen that Roberts is deeply concerned about the wholistic well-being of all people. The issues surrounding free churches, freedom from slavery, and prohibition shape Roberts's social understanding. To engage these issues faithfully, Roberts develops a radical understanding of Christianity that required a whole-hearted commitment to God. The radicalism of the Bible and the radical nature of faith consists in their ability to define the root of the human predicament and prescribe the solution. The

---

29. Quoted in Evans, *The Kingdom is Always but Coming*, 64.
30. See Snyder, *Populist Saints*, 719, 778.
31. Snyder, *Populist Saints*, 719.
32. Evans, *The Kingdom Is Always But Coming*, 65.

human predicament is sin and the radical nature of Christianity requires a clean break with sin. In describing this break, however, Roberts shows that he understands sin to manifest itself individually and personally as well as socially, in slavery and alcohol.

> Sin may be deeply planted in the nature, confirmed by indulgence, and strengthened by Legislative enactments. God shows it no quarter. Slavery struck its roots deep in the virgin soil of our country; but God overthrew it. Intemperance has the high sanctions of law for its support; but itself and the laws by which it is sustained are placed under the ban of the Higher Law.[33]

The transformation of the heart leads to the transformation of society. These two aspects of salvation are intricately linked in Roberts's theology.

We can see this connection in the inaugural issue of *The Earnest Christian*. Here Roberts introduces the new periodical with an article on "Free Churches."[34] In this article, Roberts explains his reasoning for the necessity of free Churches. It becomes clear in this article that Roberts shares John Wesley's concern for salvation that impacts life in this world.[35] Roberts begins his article by affirming the radical difference that Christianity means to this present world. He states that if Christianity were universally present, the cause of evil would be removed, the current state of sin would be reversed, and "it would bring Paradise back to earth."[36]

In making an argument for the necessity of free pews in churches, Roberts discusses the place of the poor in the church. He directly and powerfully affirms the necessity of the church's ministry to the poor. Quoting from Jesus' exchange with John's disciples in Matthew 11:5, Roberts notes that the crowning evidence of Jesus' status as Messiah is that the gospel is preached to the poor. As noted above, this passage is generally regarded as a Jubilee passage. Thus, freedom from slavery and the gospel for the poor are intractably linked in this passage.

There are several places in *The Earnest Christian* where this connection between personal salvation and social reform is made plain. One such

---

33. Roberts, "Radicalism of the Bible," 37.

34. Roberts, "Free Churches."

35. In his article *The Scripture Way of Salvation*, Wesley insists that salvation is not merely "going to heaven" but that its benefits are experienced now. "It is not a blessing which lies on the other side of death; or as we usually speak, in the other world. . . . It is not something at a distance; it is a present thing, a blessing which through the free mercy of God, ye are now in possession of."

36. Roberts, "Free Churches," 6.

article, titled "Reformation" distinguishes between revivals and reformations.[37] Revival has Latin etymological roots and means "to live again". Thus, the goal of a revival is to bring souls that are dead in sin back to life in God. Reformation, with similar roots, means to re-create or re-shape. A reformation calls for a change for the better in life and manners. These two ideas are always linked in Christianity.

> A revival of Christianity, if genuine, is always attended with a reformation. The subjects of it are made better outwardly as well as inwardly. There is a marked and visible improvement in their conduct generally. There is more happiness in the family and peace in the neighborhood. The state of things in the community is improved. Men become more honest and trust-worthy."[38]

In this way, holiness accompanies revival. Sanctification is a necessary element of spiritual change and it leads to transformation and renewal in society.

Roberts refers to this transformation as a radical change. A transformed heart leads to a transformed society. Roberts describes this transformation in a short article from *The Earnest Christian* titled "A Great Want." Practical holiness is the key to change in society. That is, there is a profound need for people who will live with honesty and integrity as a function of holiness.

> The great want of the times is men and women in every neighborhood who, in every-day life, year in and year out, manifest before the world, practical holiness.... Such persons are needed to keep alive in the minds of the people, the true idea of what it is to be a Christian. They are needed to comfort the afflicted and relieve the distressed. They are needed as friends to be consulted by those in trouble. They are needed to keep before the world examples of holy living. They are needed to point out the way to those who are really in earnest to go to heaven.[39]

The holiness of Christianity manifests itself in the day to day lives of its adherents. Their practical holiness manifests itself in plain sight. This has the long-term effect of softening the hearts of others. This action, in part, contains the gospel message.

Christianity has led to momentous social transformation. But, as Roberts understands this process, Christianity never aimed at social transformation. How did the Good News of Christianity bring out profound social

---

37. Roberts, "Reformation."
38. Ibid., 161.
39. Roberts, "A Great Want," 190.

change? Not by attempting to do so, but "by curing man of his inhumanity to man."[40] Roberts continues,

> The Gospel softened the hardened hearts of mankind, as the sun melts icebergs—by shining upon them. As a tree puts off the dead leaves that cling to it despite the winds of winter, as new leaves come, so society put away its inhuman customs and debasing practices, when the hearts of its members thrilled and glowed by the newly felt pulsations of love to God and love to man. Darkness was dissipated by bringing in the light. Cold was banished by the incoming of heat.[41]

Christianity is not aimed at securing a future otherworldly existence. Salvation profoundly affects life here and now. "It insists upon the faithful performance of all the duties we owe to others in every relation of life."[42] Salvation, precisely because of a transformed heart, leads to a renewed, transformed life. Snyder explains it well:

> For Roberts, reformation was most fundamentally based on the righteousness and justice of God, and on God's requirement of righteousness on earth. Outer righteousness, and therefore the promotion of righteousness and justice in society, was part of inner holiness.[43]

Rauschenbusch

Rauschenbusch's best known work, *Christianity and the Social Crisis*, makes the case that "the essential purpose of Christianity was to transform human society into the kingdom of God by regenerating all human relations and reconstituting them in accordance with the will of God."[44] Through a historical study of the prophetic message in the Old Testament, the nature of the kingdom of God in the preaching of Jesus, and the history of the church, Rauschenbusch preaches "an eloquent revivalist sermon meant to reclaim the sinner."[45] For Rauschenbusch the sinner is the one who does not understand his own complicity in the social sin of his generation. At a basic

---

40. Roberts, "Gospel Reforms," 134.
41. Ibid.
42. Roberts, *First Lessons on Money*, 143.
43. Snyder, *Populist Saints*, 741.
44. Rauschenbusch, *Christianity and the Social Crisis*, xxi. Quoted in Stanley Hauerwas, "Walter Rauschenbusch and the Saving of America," 82.
45. Hauerwas, *A Better Hope*, 81.

level Rauschenbusch sees sin as selfishness. "[Humanity's] sin consisted in a selfish attitude, in which he was at the centre of the universe, and God and all his fellowmen were means to serve his pleasures, increase his wealth and set off his egoisms."[46] Salvation, which is personal, "would consist in an attitude of love in which he would freely co-ordinate his life with the life of his fellows in obedience to the loving impulses of the spirit of God, thus taking his part in a divine organism of mutual service."[47] In this way, "The social gospel is the old message of salvation, but enlarged and intensified."[48] Thus salvation comes with a new awareness of the depth and complicity of sin as well as a transformation. The requisite transformation must take place on three levels: individually, in the church, and in society as a whole. "A saved church is the beginning of the salvation of the nation. Or, better put, for Rauschenbusch the saving of the nation and the saving of the church are one inseparable whole."[49]

Winthrop Hudson notes that Rauschenbusch's good friend and colleague Leighton Williams responded to *Christianity and the Social Crisis* with an article on "The Reign of the New Humanity," published in the periodical *The Kingdom*.[50] While Williams is generally positive about the book, for example he praises it for its systematic approach, he also criticizes Rauschenbusch for focusing too much on the human side of this social project and not giving full credit to the divine gospel. He writes, "The heart of our movement is a deep, personal experience, mystical in its nature, which forever makes us different men from what we were before we received it, and puts a gulf between us and the world that has it not."[51] Williams goes on to clearly state that "the evangelical experience [is] the basis of its social propaganda."[52]

While Rauschenbusch never formally responded to Williams's criticism, Hudson notes that there are comments in *Christianizing the Social Order* which take Williams's comments into account.

> Spiritual regeneration is the most important fact of any life history. A living experience of God is the crowning knowledge

---

46. Rauschenbusch, *A Theology for the Social Gospel*, 97–98.
47. Ibid., 98.
48. Ibid., 5.
49. Hauerwas, *A Better Hope*, 82.
50. Hudson, *Rauschenbusch: Selected Writings*, 37–40.
51. Ibid., 38.
52. Ibid., 39. In this quotation Williams is referring to the *Brotherhood of the Kingdom*. The Brotherhood was a small religious society dedicated to the interaction of the church with social issues.

attainable to a human mind. Each one of us needs the redemptive power of religion for his own sake, for on the tiny stage of the human soul all the vast world tragedy of good and evil is re-enacted . . . No material comfort and plenty can satisfy the restless soul in us and give us peace with ourselves. All who have made the test of it agree that religion alone holds the key to the ultimate meaning of life, and each of us must find his way into the inner mysteries alone.[53]

And in words that Roberts would affirm, Rauschenbusch also claims, "It is not this thing or that thing our nation needs, but a new mind and heart . . . We want a revolution both inside and outside."[54]

While Rauschenbusch spent his career working and arguing for social change, especially in support of the poor he did not think of himself as merely an academic liberal theologian. Nor did he think of himself as a social worker. This may be surprising to some, but Rauschenbusch primarily thought of himself as an evangelist.

Stanley Hauerwas, quoting from a biography of Rauschenbusch by Dores Sharpe, tells the story of an encounter between Sharpe and Rauschenbusch.

> There on the beach, as the water lapped at our feet, we had our meal. For me it was an hour of holy communion. We talked of spiritual values and things pertaining to the Kingdom of God. Rather abruptly he turned his steady, penetrating gaze on me and asked: "How do you think of me and my work?" My reply was: "I think of you as an evangelist and of your work as evangelism of the truest sort." The effect was electric, for he threw his arms around me and, with deep emotion, said, "I have always wanted to be thought of in that way. Your testimony gives me new fighting power." That he considered himself such may be adjudged from his own words: "I have always regarded my public work as a form of evangelism, which called for a deeper repentance and a new experience of God's salvation."[55]

This characterization fits that nature of his writing which resembles revivalist sermons for social change.

In an early article, titled, "The New Evangelism," Rauschenbusch argues for a new definition of what evangelism entails. Rauschenbusch begins the article by relativizing historical appropriations of the gospel. The pure

---

53. Hudson, *Rauschenbusch: Selected Writings*, 39–40.
54. Ibid., 40.
55. Hauerwas, *A Better Hope*, 71–72.

gospel is always greater than our current understanding such that the fullness of the gospel has never been entirely grasped by any generation. "It is a lack of Christian humility to assume that our gospel and *the Gospel* are identical."[56] While this humility isn't surprising, Rauschenbusch does make some claims that are consistent with a liberal perspective. "The gospel, to have power over an age, must be the highest expression of the moral and religious truths held by that age."[57] Thus, in Rauschenbusch's understanding, the gospel must always speak to the current generation.

Rauschenbusch defines two fundamentally different types of evangelization. On the one hand, evangelism can proclaim new truths. This happens rarely in Christianity, and is limited to Jesus, Paul, and perhaps the reformers depending on your theological perspective. On the other hand, evangelism can be a call "to live and act according to the truth which the church has previously instilled . . . and which [has been] accepted as true."[58] An evangelistic call of this type must present a vision of true reality which convicts the current generation of sin. But it must also summon them to something which powerfully seizes their hearts.

Rauschenbusch draws an important distinction between the traditional message of the church, which focuses on salvation as otherworldly, and morality as personal piety. This focus results in a limited vision: "The morality of the church is not much more than what prudence, respectability and good breeding also demand."[59] Rather, Rauschenbusch calls upon the church to consider more broadly its voice and message in relation to public life, especially the realms of business and politics. In particular, Rauschenbusch is concerned about the way in which certain segments of society are alienated from public life. Rauschenbusch's foci in this regard are the industrial wage-workers of the early twentieth century. In his day, Rauschenbusch diagnoses the main problem of the church as social division. The church, insofar as it is the church of the commercial and professional classes, alienates the working class. As the church identifies itself with a particular class, it loses its voice to speak in response to social ills.

In response to this diagnosis, Rauschenbusch calls for a new evangel that responds to contemporary social ills with the wisdom of the church. This new message relies on two essential influences: the spirit of Jesus, as he is presented in Scripture with a focus on the Kingdom of God, and a clear vision of our own time.

56. Hudson, *Rauschenbusch: Selected Writings*, 137.
57. Ibid.
58. Ibid., 139.
59. Ibid., 141.

During this time, which defined much of his eventual theology, Rauschenbusch came across the important nineteenth-century work, *The Tongue of Fire*, by William Arthur. The influence of this work can be seen in some of Rauschenbusch's writing from this period. In a short piece written for a New York periodical, *For the Right*, Rauschenbusch describes how he affirms both social reform and personal regeneration. This demonstrates that Christian conversion is essential to the goal of Rauschenbusch's system. He writes,

> One of the peculiarities which distinguishes *"For the Right"* from many other papers akin to it, is that it stands for a combination of personal regeneration and social reform. Most of the social reformers claim that if only poverty and the fear of poverty could be abolished, men would cease to be grasping, selfish, overbearing, and sensual. We do not see it so . . . On the other hand, we differ from many Christian men and women in our insistence on good institutions. They believe that if only men are personally converted wrong and injustice will gradually disappear from the construction of society. It does not appear so to us. Revivals in the South were not directly followed by a general freeing of slaves . . .[60]

Following this introduction Rauschenbusch includes a long quotation from *The Tongue of Fire* that emphasizes this both/and position. Rauschenbusch refers to this book as "one of the finest and most notable books on spiritual religion."[61]

The quotation from *The Tongue of Fire* discusses both sides of this equation in turn. First Arthur considers personal regeneration as essential for the good of society. Political instruments are unable to affect this change and good institutions are subject to people in control of them. Arthur concludes,

> The only way to the effectual regeneration of society is the regeneration of individuals: make the tree good, and the fruit will be good; make good men, and you will easily found and sustain good institutions. Here is the fault of statesmen—they forget the heart of the individual.[62]

While many more conservative Christians might end the discussion at this point, Arthur continues. Personal regeneration is not a guarantee, he claims, for social transformation. There is not a spontaneous development of good

60. Ibid., 60.
61. Ibid., 61.
62. Ibid.

institutions from Christian principles implanted in the minds of people. Evil practices can, and do, prevail in Christian society.

> The most disgusting slave-system, base usages fostering intemperance, alienation of class from class in feeling and interest, systematic frauds in commerce, neglect of workmen by masters, neglect of children by their own parents, whole classes living by sin; usages checking marriage and encouraging licentiousness; human dwellings which make the idea of home odious and the existence of modesty impossible, are but specimens of the evils which may be left age after age, cursing a people among whom Christianity is the recognized standard of society.[63]

Indifference to these pressing moral concerns is plainly not Christian. Rather, Arthur calls upon his readers to spread practical holiness and transform the institutions of our society.

> The most dangerous perversion of the gospel, viewed as affecting individuals, is, when it is looked upon as a salvation for the soul after it leaves the body, but no salvation from sin while here. The most dangerous perversion of it, viewed as affecting the community, is, when it is looked upon as a means of forming a holy community in the world to come, but never in this. Nothing short of the general renewal of society ought to satisfy any soldier of Christ; and all who aim at that triumph should draw much inspiration from the King's own words: "All power is given unto me in heaven and in earth." Much as Satan glories in his power over an individual, how much greater must be his glorying over a nation embodying, in its laws and usages, disobedience to God, wrong to man, and contamination to morals! To destroy all national holds of evil; to root sin out of institutions; to hold up to view the gospel ideal of a righteous nation; to confront all unwholesome public usages with mild, genial, and ardent advocacy of what is purer, is one of the first duties of those whose position or mode of thought gives them an influence on general questions."[64]

This reference to William Arthur is significant. Arthur is a Methodist author from the nineteenth century and this book was very popular. Winthrop Hudson comments that this "holiness volume [was] reprinted constantly throughout the remaining decades of the nineteenth and the early decades

---

63. Ibid.
64. Ibid., 62–63.

of the twentieth century."⁶⁵ Roberts began a printing business to help him publish *The Earnest Christian* along with significant theological works that would help the people of his denomination. He moved the print shop to North Chili in 1883 and expanded its capabilities. In August 1886, William Arthurs's *The Tongue of Fire* is listed as one of the books available for sale from the press. This gives some indication of its value in Free Methodist circles.⁶⁶ In addition, *The Tongue of Fire* is quoted favorably twice in *The Earnest Christian* for its insight into spiritual matters.⁶⁷ Both articles refer to Arthur's work as an authority on spiritual renewal and divine power.

Conclusion

In the final analysis, this passage from William Arthur perfectly summarizes the perspective of both Roberts and Rauschenbusch regarding the essential connection between revival and reformation. The modern stereotype of evangelical/conservative and liberal/modern church tradition pits the former as narrowly concerned with person spiritual regeneration and the later as so concerned with social issues that church becomes indistinguishable from a social club. This paper demonstrates a profound departure from this stereotype in the theology of B. T. Roberts and Walter Rauschenbusch. Both are thoroughly socially and evangelically engaged theologians. With regards to social issues, Roberts focuses his attention on slavery while Rauschenbusch focuses on poverty. Both focus on prohibition and reformed economics as well. Moreover, both acknowledge the need of conversion and evangelism as a necessary precursor to social change. Christ's gospel requires both: revival and reformation. The lives and writing of Roberts and Rauschenbusch affirm this truth. And insofar as we can discern this truth in their writing, their twin concerns should help us shape our thinking on these important issues today.

Bibliography

Arthur, William. *The Tongue of Fire, or The True Power of Christianity*. Ithaca: Cornell University Press, 1950. London: Hamilton, 1858.

Cross, Whitney R. *The Burned-over District: The Social and Intellectual History of Enthusiastic Religion in Western New York, 1800–1850*. Ithaca: Cornell University Press, 1950.

65. Ibid., 59.
66. Snyder, *Populist Saints*, 687.
67. See Roberts, "Endued with Power," and S. K. Wheatlake, "Power from on High."

The Doctrines and Disciplines of the Free Methodist Church Adopted August 23, 1860. Buffalo, NY: B. T. Roberts for the Free Methodist Church, 1860.

Evans, Christopher H. *The Kingdom Is Always but Coming: A Life of Walter Rauschenbusch.* Grand Rapids: Eerdmans, 2004.

George, Henry. *Progress and Poverty: An Inquiry into the Cause of Industrial Depressions and of Increase of Want with Increase of Wealth—The Remedy.* 50th anniv. ed. New York: Schalkenbach Foundation, 1935.

Hauerwas, Stanley. "Walter Rauschenbusch and the Saving of America." In *A Better Hope: Resources for a Church Confronting Capitalism, Democracy, and Postmodernity,* 71–107. Grand Rapids: Brazos, 2000.

Hudson, Winthrop S., ed. *Walter Rauschenbusch: Selected Writings.* New York: Paulist, 1984.

Phelps, A.A. "Mission of the Free Methodist Churches." *The Earnest Christian* (February 1861) 47–49.

Rauschenbusch, Walter. *Christianity and the Social Crisis in the 21st Century.* Edited by Paul Rauschenbusch. 1920. Repr., New York: HarperCollins, 2007.

———. *Christianizing the Social Order.* New York: Macmillan, 1912.

———. *For God and the People: Prayers of the Social Awakening.* New York: Pilgrim, 1910.

———. *A Theology for the Social Gospel.* Louisville: Westminster John Knox, 1997.

Roberts, B. T. "Endued with Power." *The Earnest Christian* (May 1874) 153–54.

———. *First Lessons on Money.* North Chili, NY: Roberts, 1886.

———. "Free Churches." *The Earnest Christian* (January 1860) 6–10.

———. "Gospel Reforms." *The Earnest Christian* (May 1890) 133–36.

———. "A Great Want." *The Earnest Christian* (December 1883) 190.

———. "New School Methodism." In *Benjamin Titus Roberts: A Biography,* edited by Benson H. Roberts, 112–26. Rochester, NY: Earnest Christian, 1879.

———. "Prohibition." *The Earnest Christian* (March 1884) 69–76.

———. "Radicalism of the Bible." *The Earnest Christian and Golden Rule* (February 1869) 37–9.

———. "Reformation." *The Earnest Christian and Golden Rule* (November 1881) 161.

———. "Slavery." *The Earnest Christian* (February 1861) 53–57.

Smith, Timothy L. *Revivalism and Social Reform: American Protestantism on the Eve of the Civil War.* Baltimore: John Hopkins University Press, 1980.

Snyder, Howard A. *Populist Saints: B. T. and Ellen Roberts and the First Free Methodists.* Grand Rapids: Eerdmans, 2006.

Wheatlake, S. K. "Power from on High." *The Earnest Christian* (January 1889) 10–11.

Section II
Every Relation of Life

7

From Primal Harmony to a Broken World

Distinguishing God's Intent for Life from the Encroachment of Death in Genesis 2–3

—J. Richard Middleton

There are few texts in the Bible as important as Genesis 2–3. The seemingly simple story of the garden, the first couple, and the original disobedience, constitutes a profound articulation of God's intent for human life (Genesis 2) and how things have gone terribly wrong (Genesis 3). Yet this seemingly simple story is actually a highly complex piece of literature, containing a structured plot, nuanced rhetorical patterns, and Hebrew puns or wordplays that make theological points. Plus, the text is laced with a variety of lacunae or gaps that cry out for explanation.

The placement of Genesis 2–3 at the outset of the larger biblical story that stretches from Genesis to revelation suggests it is paradigmatic for understanding human life, both in its ideal state and in its present, distorted reality. Yet this text has often been interpreted in ways that constrict human life and that are at odds with what it actually says. For example, Christians (both past and present) have often understood Genesis 2–3 to teach the God-ordained subordination of women to men, the essentially fallen nature of work, and a generally pessimistic view of the human condition, where a "sin nature" is thought to be genetically passed on to every person born in the world.[1] Yet none of these notions can be supported from a careful reading of the text.

A partial explanation for such misreadings might include the deceptive simplicity of the story, along with the fact that later Scripture does not provide much guidance for understanding its meaning. Yet, by far the most significant explanation is that interpreters have brought extraneous cultural assumptions and paradigms to the text and then made the text conform to these assumptions. One of the things that unites many of these assumptions is the tendency to merge *creation* (God's original purpose for life) with *fall* (the distortions that presently pervade human life).[2]

As far back as 1891, B. T. Roberts published a booklet in favor of the ordination of women, where he addressed one of the historic misreadings of Genesis 2–3 in a particularly prescient way.[3] In the course of responding to objections to women's ordination based on what the Old Testament supposedly teaches, Roberts effectively refuted in brief compass the idea that Genesis 2–3 supports the subordination of women. His attention to nuances in the text and especially to the fundamental distinction between God's intent (Genesis 2) and the subsequent corruption of that intent (Genesis 3) is a model of theologically informed biblical interpretation.[4]

1. This interpretation, known as "original sin," is usually thought to originate with Augustine, and has decisively influenced both Roman Catholic and Protestant Christianity. See especially Augustine, *City of God*, book 14. This is not the view of the Eastern fathers, who were able to affirm the reality of sin without postulating an inherited "sin nature."

2. It may be objected that the very idea of reading the garden story as a narrative about the "Fall" is an extraneous assumption that interpreters have brought to the text. Although the text does not use the metaphor of a "Fall" to describe the primal sin, I have no problem with the term so long as we do not allow this metaphor to control our reading of Genesis 3. While a "Fall" might be an appropriate metaphor to describe the Orphic myth of the soul's descent from heaven and entombment in a body, Genesis 3 portrays the primal sin more in terms of a *transgression* or *fracture*—a relational *falling out*.

3. Roberts, *Ordaining Women*, 33–36.

4. B. T. Roberts proposed a formal resolution for the ordination of women to the pastoral office as early as 1890 at the General Conference of the Free Methodist Church (which he helped found in 1860), but it was defeated by a mere four votes (37 to 41). The denomination granted various levels of authority and ordination to women in pastoral ministry throughout the years, from serving as lay delegates to the General Conference in 1890, to becoming Evangelists or lay preachers in 1894, then ordination as Deacons with authority to pastor in 1911 (though this excluded serving as senior pastor of a congregation). It was not until 1974 that the General Conference unanimously passed a resolution for the full ordination of women as Elders (with the possibility of serving as senior pastor). For more details, see the "FMC Statement on Women in Ministry," adopted by the 1995 General Conference; see also Winslow, "Wesleyan Perspectives on Women in Ministry."

This essay will build on Roberts's brief insights through a careful literary and theological reading of Genesis 2–3 as a coherent, though complex, narrative. Focusing initially on the two embedded subplots of Genesis 2 (reinforced by two parallel sets of Hebrew wordplays), this essay will clarify the Creator's normative intent for flourishing in two fundamental human relationships, namely, the relationship of human and earth (*ādām* and *ădāmâ*), which is relevant for understanding the dignity of work, and the relationship of man and woman (*'îš* and *'iššâ*), which is relevant for understanding male-female equality.

Then the essay will sketch the larger plot traversing Genesis 2–3, which begins with the prohibition of the tree of the knowledge of good and evil (chapter 2) and climaxes with human overreaching to grasp this knowledge illegitimately, with disastrous consequences (chapter 3). These consequences include distortions of both sets of relationships elucidated in Genesis 2, which sets up another narrative tension, since human life does *not* reflect God's purposes for flourishing by the end of Genesis 3.

In light of the vision of earthly flourishing portrayed in Genesis 2 (which begins to be distorted in Genesis 3), the larger canonical story of Scripture can be seen as aimed at the restoration of God's creational intent, which involves the equality of men and women, the dignity of work and stewardship of the earth, and the renewal of the image of God in humanity—all of which are dimensions of what B. T. Roberts (following John Wesley) would call *social holiness*.[5]

God's Intent for Flourishing: The Two Major Plotlines of Genesis 2

It is well recognized by biblical scholars that there are two plotlines in Genesis 2, each organized around a tension or lack followed by a two-fold resolution. The first plotline is centered on *the ground*, which lacks vegetation and a human to work it (Gen 2:4–15), while the second is centered on *the human*, who lacks a companion or "helper" (Gen 2:18–25).[6] Each of these lacks is signified by the presence of negations in the text at 2:5 and 2:18 (the words "no" and "not" in English translations represent various Hebrew ways

---

5. Wesley is famous for the following words (published in 1739) in critique of the solitariness of desert monasticism: "The gospel of Christ knows no religion, but social; no holiness but social holiness." Wesley, "Preface," 321.

6. My analysis of the two plotlines in Genesis 2 is indebted to the classic study by Trible, "A Love Story Gone Awry," in her *God and the Rhetoric of Sexuality*, 72–143 (see esp. 75–105).

of expressing negation). These lacks can be understood as articulating plot tension that requires resolution.

Each of these plotlines constitutes a subplot in the larger, overall garden narrative of Genesis 2–3, and each subplot comes to resolution with the portrayal of an ideal relationship of primal harmony that embodies YHWH God's intentions from the beginning.[7] So if we want to understand the Creator's desire for human flourishing we need to attend carefully to these two plotlines that articulate how YHWH God resolved the narrative tensions in two fundamental human relationships—the relationship of humans and the earth and inter-human relationships (especially that between men and women).

The Dignity of Work in God's World (Genesis 2:4–15)

After an introduction or heading in Genesis 2:4a ("These are the generations [*tôlĕdôt*] of the heavens and the earth when they were created"), the narrative proper begins in 2:4b.[8] Then comes the first subplot. In a complex sentence that builds up then thwarts the reader's expectations, the narrator begins by signaling the initial lack, which thus functions as a narrative tension (Gen 2:5). The earth or ground had no vegetation whatsoever (it did not yet have anything growing) because God had not yet sent rain to water the ground and because there was no human (*ādām*) to work it.[9]

---

7. Whereas the opening creation story (Gen 1:1—2:3) consistently uses the word "God" (*ĕlohîm*) for the Creator, and the narrative from Gen 4:1 onwards uses the covenantal divine name YHWH (usually thought to be pronounced Yahweh), the narrative of Gen 2:4—3:24 uses the compound name YHWH *ĕlohîm* for the deity. There will come a time when a *different* name is used in the garden story (but not by the narrator), and that difference will be significant.

8. The book of Genesis is divided into ten units, each of which is introduced by a heading that uses the term "generations" (*tôlĕdôt*). Except for the first heading (2:4a), all the rest name a person and focus on their descendants (in the sense of what was "generated" from—or came of—that person; we might think of translating *tôlĕdôt* as "developments"). These ten units consist either of a genealogy or a narrative about one or more of the descendants (though some include both a genealogy and a narrative). The headings occur at Gen 2:4a; 5:1; 6:9; 10:1; 11:10; 11:27; 25:12; 25:19; 36:1 (and 9); 37:2. The first *tôlĕdôt* heading (2:4a) introduces a narrative that describes what developed from (or came of) "the heavens and the earth," which God created.

9. This analysis suggests a translation of Gen 2:4b–5 as follows: "In the day that the LORD God made the earth and the heavens, when no plant of the field was yet in the earth and no herb of the field had yet sprung up—for the LORD God had not caused it to rain upon the earth, and there was no one to till the ground—" (NRSV adapted). Translations of the Bible will usually be from the NRSV. I will, however, will sometimes give my own, more literal, rendering. All italics in biblical quotations are my own emphases.

While it makes sense to delay the origin of plants until there is a water source, the second requirement (a human worker) may initially seem counter-intuitive. This is probably because we are thinking of what we would call "nature" (vegetation in the wild), which does not require human presence. That the ground needed someone to work it suggests that what the Creator had in mind was not "nature" pure and simple, but a garden that needed human care. The garden that YHWH God intended was thus an *agricultural project*.[10]

Having set up the first plot tension in Genesis 2:5, the narrative then moves to the first stage of resolution of this tension, as water is supplied. A stream or mist[11] rises from the ground (instead of the expected rain from the sky) and begins to provide water (Gen 2:6). Thus, we have a partial fulfillment or resolution of the plot.

Subject	Tension/Lack (*Negations*)	Attempt At Resolution/ Fulfillment	Resolution/ Fulfillment	Wordplay/ Resonance
The ground	*No* plants or grass—because *no* rain and *no* human to work the ground (2:5)	A stream/mist to water the ground (2:6) [*partial fulfillment*]	YHWH God formed the human—from the dust of the ground (2:7)—to work and protect the ground/garden (2:15)	Ground (*ădāmâ*) Human (*ădām*)

Figure 1: The Subplot of Human and Ground in Genesis 2

Then comes the second (and climactic) stage of plot resolution (Gen 2:7), when *also* from the ground (technically, from the *dust* of the ground) YHWH God forms "the human being." Not only is *ādām* the generic word for "human" and not the word for "man" as male (that will follow, in a later stage of the narrative), but this word is given with the definite article, thus "the human" (*ha'ādām*). This is not yet the name Adam (for that we must wait until Genesis 4 or even Genesis 5).[12]

---

10. As we shall soon see, this is more than an agricultural project. But it is *at least* that.

11. This latter is the meaning of the term *ēd* in its only other biblical occurrence, Job 36:27 (there we are told that God distills rain from the mist up in the sky).

12. There are four places in the narrative of Genesis 2–3 where *ādām* appears without the definite article, but none of these is a proper name. According to 2:5, "there was no-one [lit. no *ādām*] to till the ground." In Gen 2:20, 3:37, and 3:21 we have *lĕ'ādām*

Having formed the human from the dust of the ground, YHWH God breathes into the human's nostrils the breath of life, with the result that the human becomes a living being (*nepeš ḥayyāh*)—the King James Version says that the human becomes a "living soul." We should pause to note the text's understanding of being human.

First, instead of *having a* "soul" (as later Christian tradition came to claim, under the influence of Platonism), here a human *is* a "living soul" or organism (the identical phrase *nepeš ḥayyāh* is used for animals in Gen 2:19).[13]

The second point of note is that to be human is to be created *mortal*; this is the import of being made from the "dust" of the ground (note that Gen 3:19 speaks of returning to the ground, "for out of it you were taken; you are dust, and to dust you shall return").[14]

So, having provided for the two primary needs of the ground, namely a water source and a human worker, YHWH God then "planted a garden in Eden" (Gen 2:8). The Creator is thus portrayed as the first gardener; he initiates the first cultural project, which turns out to be an *agricultural* project, which the human (as God's image) will continue.

There is much that could be said about the garden, including its being well-watered by a river (did this derive from the primordial stream or mist?), which then divides into four rivers (literally, four "heads," in the

---

(to/for the human); here the preposition *lĕ* (*to* or *for*) is appended to *'ādām* without the vowel change that usually indicates a definite article (*lā'ādām*). However, in the first case (2:20), the same verse also uses *hā'ādām* (the human); and it should be remembered that there would have been no distinction in the original Hebrew consonantal text (so the vowel pointing that the Masorites introduced, which we have in our current Hebrew Bibles, may be idiosyncratic). Gen 4:25 is the first clear use of *'ādām* without the definite article ("Adam knew his wife again"). Yet Gen 4:2, which first mentions the man knowing his wife, has *hā'ādām*. In Gen 5:1, which begins a genealogy, we finally have the proper name *Adam* clearly intended.

13. The phrase *nepeš ḥayyāh* is used for animals also in Gen 1:20, 24, and 30. Both the NIV and he NRSV translate *nepeš ḥayyāh* as "living being" in Gen 2:7 and as "living creature" in Gen 1: 20, 24; and 2:19 (in Gen 1:30 *nepeš ḥayyāh* is translated as "breath of life"). To use "living" (*ḥayyāh*) with *nepeš* is not redundant, since a dead *nepeš* refers to a corpse (an organism after the life has left it; as in Num 5:2; 6:6; 9:6–7).

14. The poignant reference to human mortality in Ps 103:14 uses the very words "formed" and "dust" found in Gen 2:7. Paul also calls Adam a "man of dust," referring to his having been created mortal, in 1 Cor 15:42–49. Even John Calvin understood that the first humans were created mortal. Commenting on "you are dust, and to dust you shall return" (Gen 3:19), he notes that "what God here declares belongs to man's *nature*, not to his *crime* or *fault*" (emphases in original). For Calvin (who believed in an immortal soul, something never taught in Scripture), the punishment meant that we do not directly proceed from death to eternal blessedness, but experience the violent sundering of soul and body. See Calvin, *Commentaries on the First Book of Moses*, 1:180.

sense of headwaters). Whereas two of the rivers (the Tigris and the Euphrates) are well known and thus locate Eden in the geographic region of Mesopotamia (part of the Fertile Crescent), two of them (the Pishon and the Gihon) are unknown, and serve to *disassociate* Eden from any recognizable geography.[15]

We are also told that gold and onyx stone are found in one of the lands that the first river (the Pishon) flows around (Gen 2:10–14).[16] While the presence of rivers suggests a potential for irrigation agriculture (and possibly river travel), the presence of gold and onyx suggests the potential for mining, with accompanying technology, and perhaps even decorative art. Such potentials for human development cohere with this being a *garden* that YHWH God planted, and not "nature" pure and simple. The world of Genesis 2 is thus a cultural reality, requiring cultivation through human agency.

But this world is also sacred space. This garden, with its trees, rivers, and mention of precious and semiprecious stones, is reminiscent of a royal garden or sacred grove in the ancient Near East, a locale fraught with divine presence.[17] Such gardens would include a river or stream, landscaped terraces, a fruit orchard or arboretum, and a variety of animals (possibly even some exotic ones, in effect, a miniature zoo). These gardens were typically attached to the royal residence (the palace), where the king lived (in this case, the king is YHWH God, and humans will be tending his garden).

Whereas Genesis 1 draws on the conceptuality of heaven and earth as a cosmic temple, with humanity as God's "image" or cult statue in the temple, meant to mediate God's presence and rule from heaven to earth (heaven functioning as the cosmic Holy of Holies), the garden in Genesis 2 is the locus of divine presence on earth, where YHWH God "walks" in proximity to humanity.[18]

---

15. The name Gihon does show up in 2 Chr 32:30 for a spring near Jerusalem. But this is nowhere near Mesopotamia (where the Tigris and Euphrates are located), and it may be an attempt to echo the sacred character of Jerusalem, associating it with Eden.

16. We are told that the Pishon "flows around the whole land of Havilah" (Gen 2:11) and the Gihon "flows around the whole land of Cush" (Gen 2:13). While Havilah is unknown, the name Cush occurs in the Old Testament, suggesting a known geographical region, though it refers to Nubia, not Ethiopia, as is often thought. See Yamauchi, *Africa and the Bible*, chap. 6: "Why the Ethiopian Eunuch Was Not from Ethiopia" (161–81). Yet the legendary quality of the description is suggested by the fact that rivers don't actually flow *around* geographical areas. The desire to make the text sound more realistic leads some translations (like the NIV) to render "flow around" as "wind through." But the Hebrew verb used in Gen 2:11 and 13 clearly means to "surround."

17. See Wenham, "Sanctuary Symbolism in the Garden of Eden Story."

18. On the motif of the cosmos as temple, see Middleton, "The Role of Human Beings in the Cosmic Temple."

It is also significant that a sacred grove beside a primeval river is the typical setting for the *mïs pî* (mouth washing) or *pït pî* (mouth opening) ritual, known from Mesopotamian texts. This was the ritual process through which a humanly constructed cult image was vivified and transformed ("transubstantiated," says one scholar[19]) from an inert wooden statue into a living breathing "image" of a god.[20] So when YHWH God forms the human being from the dust of the ground and breathes into the earth creature the breath of life (Gen 2:7), the text narrates God's consecration of humanity to bear the divine image, or—more forcefully put—to become the cult-image of YHWH God on earth, a distinctive site of divine presence.[21]

And, indeed, having planted a lush, rich garden (Gen 2:10-14), YHWH God places the human there in order to *work* it and to *protect/guard* it (Gen 2:15).[22] The human is thus granted the vocation of continuing the creative task that the divine gardener had begun. The continuity between YHWH God's original planting of the garden and the human's ensuing vocation vis-à-vis the garden is an echo of the *imago Dei* theme that is explicit and prominent in Genesis 1:26-28.[23] It suggests that humanity is granted a sacred task, a vocation of great dignity, that reflects or images something of the Creator's own work.

The sacredness of human work (including agricultural labor) is further communicated by the connotations of the Hebrew verbs for "work" (*'ābad*) and "protect" or "guard" (*šāmar*). Whereas *'ābad* is used elsewhere for priests *serving* YHWH in the tabernacle and temple, *šāmar* is the verb the used for *keeping* (that is, obeying) the Torah (and we might also think of the priestly task of *guarding* the sanctity of the temple). However, we should not think that the text means for us to "serve" or "obey" the ground.

---

19. For "transubstantiation," see Jacobsen, "The Graven Image." For the application of Jacobsen's analysis of the Mesopotamian ritual to Genesis 1, see Herring, "A 'Transubstatiated' Humanity."

20. For a detailed study of Genesis 2-3 and the Mesopotamian (and equivalent Egyptian) ritual, see McDowell, *The Image of God in the Garden of Eden*.

21. Note that Genesis 1 and 2 thus convey the same theological idea (humans as God's image) through quite different literary motifs.

22. Whereas Gen 2:5 had said that there was no human to work the *ground*, in Gen 2:15 the human is put in the *garden* to work it (and also to protect it). We should not, however, make an absolute distinction between the ground and the garden. In fact, the "it" in the phrase "to work *it* and protect *it*" is feminine singular, which therefore refers back to the feminine singular word for "ground" and not the masculine singular word for "garden." Working the garden (which YHWH God planted) is working the *prepared* ground.

23. For a thorough discussion of humanity created as image of God (*imago Dei*), see Middleton, *The Liberating Image*; for a summary, see Middleton, *A New Heaven and a New Earth*, chap. 2: "Why Are We Here?"

That would be a non sequitur, since 'ābad can simply mean to "work" (the cognate noun 'ăbôdâ means "work" or "labor") and šāmar can simply mean "protect" or "watch over."[24]

The use of these two verbs together to describe the human task in the garden suggests what we might call sustainable agriculture, as we both *develop* (work) and *conserve* (guard/protect) our earthly environment. And since this earthly realm is also God's temple, the cultic or religious *connotations* of 'ābad and šāmar carry over into their use in Genesis 2:15, allowing the reader to overhear distinct echoes of sacredness in the vocation granted humans at creation.[25]

What happens when humans work the primitive landscape of a garden throughout history? The implication would be that as the human race faithfully tended this garden or cultivated the earth, the garden would spread, until the entire earthly realm would be transformed into a fit habitation for humanity—and also for God. Based on this original commission, humans will, indeed, go on to develop complex cultures (the beginnings of cultural development are recorded in Genesis 4), until we find the redeemed urban reality of the New Jerusalem, the holy city (Revelation 21–22), portrayed as the culmination of history. The description of this city is intertwined with aspects of Eden, such as the tree of life (Rev 22:2) and a river, designated the "water of life," flowing from God's throne, which is in the midst of the city (Rev 21:6; 22:1).[26]

This first subplot of Genesis 2 thus conveys (prior to the origin of sin) the God-intended relationship of humans to the ground from which we are taken. It is fundamentally a relationship of *work* (humanity's contribution) and *sustenance* (the ground's contribution); human and ground are made for each other. In God's ideal world, humans are interdependent with their earthly environment.

This mutual relationship is signaled by a wordplay or pun in Hebrew between the word for human ('ādām) and the word for ground or soil ('ădāmâ). Biblical scholars have suggested various equivalent English puns, such as the *groundling* from the *ground*, the *earth creature* from the *earth*,

---

24. The noun 'ăbôdâ is used for ordinary human labor in Ps 104:14 and the verb šāmar is used for God protecting or guarding the psalmist from danger in Ps 121:7–8.

25. Overhearing the *connotations* of other uses of these two verbs is not the same as what James Barr called "illegitimate totality transfer," which would import the *meanings* of these verbs from their cultic or religious usage. See Barr, *Semantics of Biblical Language*, 218.

26. The fulfillment of Eden in the New Jerusalem is discussed in Middleton, *A New Heaven and a New Earth*, chap. 3: "The Plot of the Biblical Story," and chap. 8: "The Redemption of All Things."

the *human* from the *humus*.²⁷ The point is that the aural resonance (the similarity of sounds) of *ādām* and *ădāmâ* suggests a primal ontological resonance (a shared reality) between the human and the ground.²⁸ Not only is the *ādām* taken from the *ădāmâ* (a matter of derivation or origin), but the very purpose of the *ādām* is to work (and protect) the *ădāmâ* (a matter of calling or vocation).²⁹ This suggests the high dignity of human work, even of agricultural labor, upon which all of complex human society and culture depends.

The Equality of Men and Women (Genesis 2:18–25)

The second subplot of the garden story begins in Genesis 2:18, when YHWH God affirms that it is "not good" for the human to be alone, and so proposes to make "a helper as his partner." Here, as before, the negation ("not") signals plot tension (things are *not yet* as God intended).³⁰

As is well known to students of Hebrew, the term "help"/"helper" (*'ēzer* in this case; but often the participle *'ozer*) is typically used in the Old Testament for someone with superior power or status who comes to the aid of an inferior (Ps 22:11 [MT 22:12]; 72:12; 107:12; Isa 31:3; 63:5; Jer 47:7; Lam 1:7; Dan 11:34, 45). Thus, God is regarded as the helper (= savior) of Israel (see Ps 30:10 [MT 30:11]; 54:5).³¹

In Genesis 2:18 and 20 the word "helper" is immediately followed by *kĕnegdô*, a compound word meaning "as his partner" or "as his counterpart" or possibly "as one suitable for him."³² This word *kĕnegdô* qualifies "helper"

---

27. See Brown, *Seven Pillars of Creation*, 81–88.

28. For a fuller exploration of the centrality of the *ādām–ădāmâ* connection not only in Genesis 2–3, but throughout the Primeval History (Genesis 1–11), see Miller, *Genesis 1–11*, chap. 3: "The *ădāmāh* Motif" (37–42; nn49–50).

29. Whereas the human was initially to *work* the ground (Gen 2:5), once YHWH God planted the garden the human task is expanded to include *guarding* the garden (Gen 2:15). While working the ground could certainly lead to the development of a garden, the fact that humans were given a head start, so to speak, by the Creator means that their task now includes *protecting* what he started.

30. Although no further explanation is given at this point, we may surmise that the human needed not only companionship but also help in the vocation of working and guarding the garden.

31. The use of MT with biblical references stands for the Masoretic Text (the Hebrew Bible used by Jews), which sometimes has different versification from that found in Christian Bibles.

32. The core of the compound word *kĕnegdô* is *neged*, which means "before," "opposite," "corresponding to," or "in front of." The word conveys the sense of being face-to-face with an equal.

so it will not be taken as a superior helper, but rather (in this particular case) as *an equal*.[33]

Subject	Tension/Lack (*Negations*)	Attempt At Resolution/ Fulfillment	Resolution/ Fulfillment	Wordplay/ Resonance
The human	*Not* good to be alone—needs a helper as his counterpart (2:18)	Animals brought to the human—he named them, but found *no* helper as his counterpart (2:19–20) [*continuing lack*]	YHWH God built the woman—from the rib/side of the human (2:21–22)—to be a helper as his counterpart (cf. 2:18)	Man (*'iš*) Woman (*'iššâ*)

Figure 2: The Subplot of Woman and Man in Genesis 2

As with the previous subplot of human and ground, the resolution of this new plot tension proceeds in two stages. The first step towards resolution occurs when YHWH God forms animals from the ground (from which the human was also formed) and brings them to the human "to see what he would name them" (Gen 2:19). The fact that YHWH God does not bring the animals to the human *to see if any of them would be a suitable helper* suggests that this is not trial-and-error on the Creator's part, as commentators sometimes suggest. YHWH God is aware that the animals will not fulfill the basic human need specified in Genesis 2:18. But it is not enough for the Creator to know this; *the human* needs to recognize this for himself. The text thus suggests that humans need to be active participants in our own flourishing (even though such flourishing is ultimately a gift from beyond ourselves)—such is the dignity of the human creature in relation to our Creator.

The dignity of the human creature is also signaled by the statement: "whatever he called each living creature that was its name" (Gen 2:19). In other words, YHWH God simply allows every name the human comes up with to stand (without correction or prodding); the human's choices are respected.

An interesting detail is that whereas the Creator brings two categories of animals (in Gen 2:19) to the human, namely, "birds of the sky" and

33. This, of course, is almost the opposite of the common misreading of the woman as subordinate to the man. The woman's subordination is sometimes tied to her being the man's "helpmate" (meaning something like a *sidekick*). "Helpmate" is here a bastardization of the phrasing of the KJV, which has "an help meet for him" (where the older English "meet" means "suitable" or "appropriate").

"beasts of the field" (this latter is a term for wild animals), the narrator notes that "the human gave names to *all the livestock*, the birds of the sky, and all the beasts of the field" (Gen 2:20). Where did *livestock* come from?

It is fascinating that *prior* to naming, there were only *wild* land animals. But naming is coincident with a category of *domesticated* land animals. This change (the introduction of the category of *livestock*, through the act of naming) adds something significant to the original human vocation to work the ground. The human task in the world has been expanded. And, indeed, in Genesis 4 we find, in the second generation, Cain working the ground (horticulture) and Abel keeping flocks (animal husbandry), in fulfillment of this new dimension of the human task in the world.[34]

So not only does YHWH God desire the human to participate in the decision-making process, by deciding whether the animals could be helpers suitable for him and what their names will be, but human naming has now effected a significant transformation in the human vocation; it has introduced a new *relationship* of humans to animals, thus resulting in an entirely new *category* of animals.

The text also notes that although the human named the animals, he could not find a helper as his partner (Gen 2:20). This negation (the continued use of "not") signals that the narrative lack continues.

It is important to understand the logic of the disjunction between naming and partnership. Naming is predicated on an asymmetry of power, an inequality between the one named and the one doing the naming. We name animals (pets, some farm animals), inanimate objects (boats, buildings), and newborn children. But once our children are grown into adults and become equal to us in status, we no longer have the authority to change their names at our whim (I don't envy any parent trying that!). By contrast, oppressors and slave masters often re-name those they subjugate, which expresses an unequal power differential between them. In all cases, whether naming is legitimate (as with children) or illegitimate (as with slaves), naming is incompatible with finding an *equal* helper.

The fact that the human named the animals thus functions as evidence that they did not qualify as the appropriate "helper" that God had intended. So, the narrative lack continues; the human is still fundamentally alone.

---

34. This addition of *livestock* is evident also in the contrast between the initial description of the snake as more shrewd than any of the wild animals that YHWH God made (Gen 3:1) and the later statement that the snake is cursed beyond any of the livestock and wild animals (Gen 3:14). In the narrative world of Genesis 2-3 YHWH God did not technically *create* any livestock. Some wild animals (which YHWH God created) *became* livestock when the human domesticated them.

Then YHWH God acts a second time, to bring about resolution to the second subplot. He puts the human into a deep sleep[35] and takes one of the ribs (or sides) of the human, from which he makes (literally, "builds") a woman (Gen 2:21–22).

This term for "rib" (*ṣēlāʿ*) is not an anatomical term in Hebrew. It is an architectural term (hence the appropriateness of God "building" the woman). Since *ṣēlāʿ* tends to be used for one of two *sides* of a structure (a building, a cabinet, or the altar), it is entirely possible that the text is saying that YHWH God split the (previously un-gendered) human in half, with the result that the human now becomes a man (*ʾîš*) for the first time. However, it may be that "the human" was always male and only came to gender *awareness* when confronted by his appropriate partner.[36]

However, if we follow the text carefully, the narrator continues to refer to the human as *haʾādām*, with some exceptions. It is in *the human's own speech* (when YHWH God brings the woman to him) that we find the first use of the term *ʾîš*, the Hebrew term for man as male. In other words, the term for man as male (*ʾîš*) occurs in the human's *self-recognition* when confronted with his *neged*, his vis-à-vis, the one in whom he sees himself, yet with a difference.[37]

In this first speech attributed to a human being in the Bible (which is in Hebrew poetry), *haʾādām* exclaims:

> This at last is bone of my bones
>
> and flesh of my flesh;
>
> this one shall be called Woman [*ʾiššâ*],
>
> for out of Man [*ʾîš*] this one was taken. (Gen 2:23)

---

35. The Hebrew word for "deep sleep" (*tardēmâ*) is often associated with visionary experiences in the Old Testament, as in the revelation given to Abram in Gen 15:12. It is, therefore, possible that we should understand what comes next as something revealed to the human in a vision. See Walton, *Lost World of Adam and Eve*, 80.

36. Even if we do not think that *haʾādām* prior to the creation of the woman was meant to be understood as generically human (either pre-gendered or androgynous), everything said up to this point about "the human" (*haʾādām*) applies to *both* men and women. All people are mortal, all are living organisms, all have the God-given vocation to work in God's world, all need companionship, etc. This is why Walton (*Lost World of Adam and Eve*, 80, 200), suggests that *haʾādām* should be understood not only as an individual but also as an archetype of all people (after all, this person's name is later given in Gen 5:1 as "Human" [=*Adam*]).

37. In contrast to YHWH God bringing the animals to the human *to see what he would name them*; no purpose is explicitly stated for bringing the woman in Gen 2:22. The bringing is thus open ended; what will the human's response be?

Here we have the second Hebrew pun or wordplay in Genesis 2. The man recognizes the woman that YHWH God has brought to him as one similar-yet-different from himself. This is indicated both by the resonant pun he makes (*'iššâ* taken out of *'îš*) and by his description of her as "bone of my bone and flesh of my flesh" (this is kinship terminology, as 2 Sam 5:1 makes clear). The man recognizes his true soul- and body-mate (2:23). This *at last* is his equal.[38]

Now, it might be objected that verse 23 is an example of naming, so it suggests an asymmetry of power (the subordination of the woman to the man). However, "woman" is not her name (the name *Eve* will come later). Prior to the man's use of the term, the narrator (in 2:22) noted that YHWH God made the *ṣēlāʿ* into a woman (*iššâ*), which is clearly not intended as a name.

Beyond this, the man's *recognition* of this other as "woman" deviates from the common pattern of naming in the narratives of Genesis. In Genesis naming is typically indicated by the use of the verb *qārā'* (to call) and the noun *šēm* (name); both *qārā'* and *šēm* are used in the naming of the animals in Genesis 2:20 (literally, he *called* their *name*). Here, however, we have the verb *qārā'* without the noun *šēm*. Beyond this, the text uses the passive (the Niphal stem) of *qārā'* ("this one *shall be called* [or *is called*] woman"), which further suggests recognition of her character, rather than naming *per se*.[39]

As in the case of the wordplay between the *'ādām* and the *'ădāmâ*, the aural resonance of *'iššâ* with *'îš* suggests a deep ontological resonance between the man and the woman—a primal harmony of being. Just as the *'ādām* is taken *from* the dust of the *'ădāmâ* and is made *for* the *'ădāmâ*, so the *'iššâ* is taken *from* the side of the *'îš* and is made *for* the *'îš*. These two sets of wordplays suggest that primal resonance or harmony is God's original intent for human life.

---

38. The phrase "flesh of my flesh" might also serve to support the view that *ṣēlāʿ* is not "rib" but "side," in that the woman is created both from the bone *and the flesh* of the human. And then later we are told that in marriage the two become "one flesh" again (Gen 2:24). But perhaps that is thinking too literally about the matter.

39. I have counted some seventy-three uses of *qārā'* in naming formulas in the book of Genesis, in which sixty-five occur with *šēm*. Of the eight that occur without *šēm*, three are used in reference to naming places (Gen 16:14; 21:31; 25:7), while five occur in Genesis 1, where God names realms of creation—*day, night, heaven, earth,* and *seas* (Gen 1:5, 8, 10). It would be too tedious to list the seventy-three occurrences of *qārā'* with *šēm*; suffice it to say that nowhere in Genesis is any person named with just the use of *qārā'*.

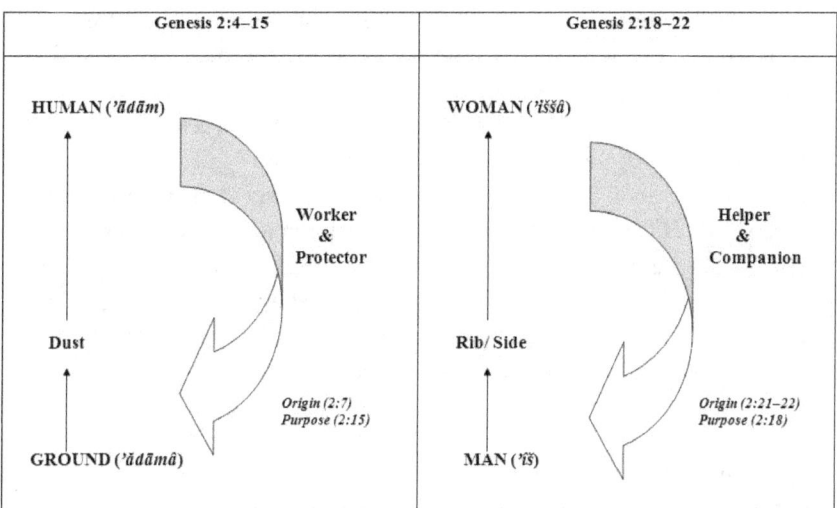

Figure 3: Parallels between the Creation of Human and Woman in Genesis 2

The very pattern of the text works against the notion of the superiority of men or the subordination of women. Here we simply need to look at the formal parallel between *the human taken from the ground* and *the woman taken from the man*. Given the pattern of derivation and purpose in both cases, we have three choices. If we claim that the woman is subordinate to the man, then humans must be subordinate to the ground. If, on the other hand, we start with the western bias of thinking that humans are superior to the earth, this would imply that women are superior to men. However, perhaps Genesis 2–3 is not advocating superiority at all—in any direction. Rather, the text affirms nothing less than *mutuality*; just as humanity and the earth are made for each other and need each other, so it is with women and men. That is how creation was meant to function—in mutual harmony and shalom.

The trouble is that this harmony doesn't last.

The Overarching Plot of Genesis 2–3: From Creation to Fall

Beginning in Genesis 3 the narrative shifts precipitously towards the complex process of temptation and resulting disobedience—an episode involving the woman and the man, the snake (a new character in the story, introduced in 3:1), and "the tree of the knowledge of good and evil" (which had been mentioned by the narrator in Gen 2:9).[40] This unusual tree becomes the central topic of conversation between the woman and the snake in Genesis 3:1–5.

Back when YHWH God planted the garden, two specific trees in the midst of the garden were singled out—"the tree of life" and "the tree of the knowledge of good and evil" (Gen 2:9). The latter tree is mentioned again, when YHWH God places the human in the garden with the commission to tend it. The human is given permission to eat from any tree in the garden (Gen 2:16), with a single exception, accompanied by a dire warning—"but of the tree of the knowledge of good and evil you shall *not* eat, for in the day that you eat of it you shall [surely] die" (Gen 2:17).[41]

The Two Trees and the Choice of Life or Death (Genesis 2:9, 16–17)

What is the meaning of the two trees and the warning about death?[42] Here it is important to note that in both the Torah (especially Leviticus and Deuteronomy) and the wisdom literature of the Old Testament (especially Proverbs), two covenantal paths are set before Israel (and all humanity)—the paths of life and death, also described as the ways of blessing and curse.[43] In these texts *life* refers to fruitfulness, flourishing, security, and blessedness in the land (we might call this *abundant life*; see John 10:10), while *death* refers to living a life constricted by danger, anxiety, violence, and exile from the land.[44] These divergent paths are linked in the Torah to obedience to God versus disobedience, and in Proverbs they are further connected to wisdom versus folly. Life or blessing is the outcome of wisely choosing to obey God (which is equivalent to going with the grain of the universe), whereas death or curse flows from the folly of disobedience (going against the grain).[45]

---

40. Given the characterization of the snake as one of the wild animals that YHWH God made (thus one of the animals the man named), I have avoided the more mythical sounding "serpent."

41. I have added the word "surely" to the NRSV translation. The Hebrew for "you shall *surely* die" in Gen 2:17 is a distinctive verbal formulation that repeats the verbal root in an infinitive followed by a finite form of the verb ("to die you will die"). The result is emphatic. Thus, Robert Alter translates it as "doomed to die" (Alter, *Genesis*, 8).

42. For a fuller discussion than I can give here, see Middleton, "Reading Genesis 3," esp. the sections entitled "The Tree of Life and the Warning about Death" and "The Tree of the Knowledge of Good and Evil."

43. The two contrasting paths are summarized in Deut 30:15–20 and Prov 2:20–22.

44. A series of covenantal blessings and curses linked to obedience and disobedience can be found in Leviticus 26 and in Deuteronomy 28.

45. The significance of the two covenantal paths is explored in more detail in

This begins to help us understand the warning about death in Genesis 2:17. Death should not be understood here as the introduction of human mortality (as if humans were previously immortal); this is a traditional interpretation in the history of Christian thought, but we have already seen that humanity was created mortal ("from the dust") in Genesis 2:7. The warning could, conceivably, be taken to mean that the moment the fruit of the forbidden tree was eaten, the eater would drop down dead (something that does *not* happen). But if we take seriously the Old Testament background of the divergent paths of life and death, blessing and curse, it makes more sense to see the consequence of disobedience as the gradual diminishing of the fullness of life (death will have begun to encroach on life). Thus, at the end of the garden narrative humanity is exiled from the garden, with access to the tree of life blocked (Gen 3:24).

So much for the tree of *life* and the warning about *death*; but what does "the tree of the knowledge of good and evil" represent, and why is its fruit prohibited? Biblical interpreters have proposed various interpretations of this tree, including sexual "knowledge" (since in Gen 4:1 the man "knows" his wife and she conceives) or the attempt to grasp total knowledge of all things (where the phrase "good and evil" is understood to mean *everything*, whether it is good or evil).[46] However, the most obvious meaning comes from examining the entire phrase "knowledge of good and evil" (*or* "knowing good and evil") in the rest of the Old Testament. The phrase is primarily used to describe the normal human ability to make ethical decisions (Deut 1:39; 1 Kgs 3:9; Isa 7:15).[47] This usage suggests that the tree of the knowledge of good and evil represents a normative and valuable human trait. So why would it be prohibited?[48]

Middleton, *A New Heaven and a New Earth*, chap. 5: "Earthly Flourishing in Law, Wisdom, and Prophecy."

46. "Good and evil" is thus understood as a merism or *merismus*, the use of two extremes to signify not only the extremes but also everything in-between, as in the exhortation to "do good or do evil" (Isa 41:23), which means *Do something, anything!*

47. In one case the phrase refers to the ability to discriminate between "good and bad" with the senses, which has diminished in old age (2 Sam 19:35 [MT 19:36]). The Hebrew words "good" and "evil/bad" have a wide range of meaning, and can refer to any sort of valuation.

48. We should note that there is a negation ("not") used in the prohibition against eating from this tree, which is reflected in the proliferation of negations in the conversation the snake and the woman have about the tree (Gen 3:1–5) and also in YHWH God's later mention of the tree (Gen 3:11, 17). When read with the two other sets of negations (about the *lack* of vegetation on the land; the *lack* of a companion for the human), we might think that this negation about eating from the tree likewise indicates a lack *that should be remedied*. And some interpreters have, indeed, read the story as a Fall "upwards" or "forwards," into maturity, as if the humans *needed* to eat from this

This question becomes especially pointed when we consider Proverbs 3, which states: "Blessed is the person (*ʾādām*) who finds wisdom, / and the person (*ʾādām*) who gets understanding; / . . . She [wisdom] is a *tree of life* to those who lay hold of her; / those who hold her fast are called blessed" (Prov 3:13, 18).[49]

To call wisdom "a tree of life" clearly has bearing on Genesis 2. Proverbs 3 is making the point that the consistent choosing of wisdom (*holding fast* to her) results in a blessed and full life. We could even say that a pattern of wise choices grows into a tree, the fruit of which is life in its fullness. Yet, strangely, in Genesis 2 the tree of *life* is separated from the tree of *the knowledge of good and evil* (which is equivalent to choosing wisdom).

This is because the first humans do not yet have enough experience to be able to make *wise* ethical decisions for themselves. They are like children, who initially need to trust their parent (in this case, YHWH God) about what is good and evil. We don't allow young children to have the option of taking hard drugs or to make the choice between abstinence and sexual promiscuity. Once they have sufficiently internalized what is good by living according to their parents' direction, they will have their character formed in the direction of virtue. At that point, ethical decision-making can begin. The Eastern Orthodox tradition (along with C. S. Lewis, in his novel *Perelandra*) has therefore understood that the tree of the knowledge of good and evil was only *temporarily* forbidden; it was not permanently off-limits.[50] There would come a time when the first humans would be equipped to make their own ethical decisions (they would be allowed to eat of this tree). But to allow this too early would sear their conscience and result in disastrous consequences for themselves and for others (which is exactly what happens in Genesis 3 and following).

---

tree in order to attain their full potential as adults. This is a tempting reading, but it is contradicted by the tragic outcome of the eating, where human life becomes diminished and constricted; this diminishing of life confirms that the prohibition should have been respected.

49. This is my own translation (many modern translations have "happy" instead of "blessed," which misconstrues the force of the Hebrew). The "she" in verse 18 is a reference to "wisdom," which in Hebrew is a feminine noun (the Hebrew for "understanding" is a masculine noun).

50. In *Perelandra*, spending the night on the Fixed Land is Lewis's equivalent to eating of the tree of the knowledge of good and evil in Genesis 2–3. After the period of testing, the Perelandrian equivalent of Adam and Eve are given the Fixed Land as their permanent home.

The Process of Temptation and Sin (Genesis 3:1–6)

The fascinating episode of temptation and sin deserves an extended exposition in its own right. But given the parameters (and length requirements) of this essay, I need to forgo a full discussion here, so that we can move to the consequences of disobedience—the effects of the Fall on the two originally harmonious relationships that YHWH God established.[51]

For our purposes, it is sufficient to note some of the ways the woman's discussion with the snake constitutes a profound study in the phenomenology of temptation. For a start, both the snake and the woman refer to the Creator merely as *God* (*ĕlohîm*) rather than as *YHWH God* (they consistently avoid the unique covenant name that the narrator uses, perhaps as a distancing tactic). Beyond that, the prohibition against the forbidden tree is softened from a *command* (Gen 2:16) to simply what God *said* (this change is introduced by the snake in Gen 3:1 and followed by the woman in Gen 3:3); and then the prohibition against *eating* from the forbidden tree is made more onerous than it originally was, when the woman adds "nor shall you *touch* it" (Gen 3:3). Finally, the woman softens the warning that YHWH God had given concerning the consequences of disobedience. The original warning was that *in the day* you eat the fruit of the forbidden tree you will *surely die* (Gen 2:17). But the woman omits reference to *in the day* (which suggested immediate consequences) and describes the consequence simply as "you shall die" (Gen 3:3).[52]

From initially questioning the woman about whether eating of any of the trees in the garden was permitted (Gen 3:1), the snake finally denies outright that they will die, while trying to make the Creator seem stingy, "for God knows that when you eat of it your eyes will be opened, and you will be like God, knowing good and evil" (Gen 3:5). And the woman buys it. She becomes convinced that the forbidden fruit is desirable for gaining wisdom (which it is, though the timing is wrong); so, she eats, as does the man "who was with her" but said nary a word (Gen 3:6).

---

51. One important dimension of the temptation narrative is the Hebrew pun or wordplay between the word for "shrewd" or "crafty" or "intelligent" (applied to the snake) and "naked" (applied to the man and woman). Like the negation about the forbidden tree, which differs from the negations that introduce the two subplots about the human and the ground and the man and the woman, this wordplay is different from the puns that designate primal harmony between humans and ground and between men and women. For an extended discussion of the temptation narrative, including the wordplay concerning the snake, see Middleton, "Reading Genesis 3," esp. the sections on "The Snake" and "The Process of Temptation and Sin."

52. Thus, omitting the Hebrew construction that indicated the certainty or seriousness of the consequence (see earlier note).

Consequences of the Fall: From Life to Death

True to the warning that YHWH God had given, death begins its incursion into life, diminishing and inhibiting human flourishing. This is portrayed most clearly in the formal judgments YHWH God pronounces (Gen 3:14–19); but life begins to be constricted even before these pronouncements.

The Beginning of Death's Encroachment (Genesis 3:7–13)

The result of their disobedience is an immediate existential change in the man and woman (which fulfills the warning about "in the day" they eat of it). The man and the woman become aware of their nakedness and—in contrast to their previous lack of shame (Gen 2:25)—they make clothing to cover themselves (Gen 3:7), thus providing protection from exposure to each other (there is no-one else around). Nakedness (with its implied vulnerability) is no longer safe; and from here on in the Bible nakedness is portrayed negatively ("uncovering" someone's nakedness symbolizes exposure to being violated).

Beyond this immediate sense of shame, the text reports their newfound fear of YHWH God, evident in their hiding when they hear him walking in the garden (Gen 3:8), something the man admits to when questioned (Gen 3:10). So, even prior to the formal passing of judgment, the transgression generates (via nakedness, with its vulnerability) both shame and fear, which distances the transgressors not only from each other, but also from their Creator.

When YHWH God questions the man about whether he ate from the prohibited tree (Gen 3:11), he blames the woman "whom you gave to be with me" (Gen 3:12), who in turn blames the snake for deceiving her (Gen 3:13). This refusal to take blame for one's actions is a further aspect of the phenomenology of sin that reads true to life in the fallen world we know. And this finger pointing generates a formal declaration of judgment on the snake, the woman, and the man—in reverse order of those blamed.

These declarations of judgment are not technically punishments (in a legal sense), but rather the natural *consequences* of human evil. Nor are they normative; they do not *prescribe* what *must* be. Rather, the judgments *describe* ways in which life becomes distorted from what God originally intended. Further, these distortions are consequences of the Fall that men and women *usually* experience. These consequences not only admit of exceptions (as we shall see), but they are culturally conditioned, describing what is typical in the ancient agricultural social order that Israel was part of (we could easily think of further consequences that apply more specifically to current western society). Finally, although these judgments have often been thought of as a series of "curses," neither the man nor woman is technically "cursed"—that word is used only of the snake and the ground in Genesis 3.

Diminishing of Life for the Woman (Genesis 3:16, 20)

The typical consequences for the woman are twofold (Gen 3:16).[53] First, YHWH God declares: "I will greatly increase your pangs in childbearing; / in pain you shall bring forth children." If we follow most modern translations, which take these two lines of Hebrew poetry to be saying essentially the same thing, there will be an increase of pain in childbirth; that this is an *increase* of pain and not pain's origin suggests that the text understands pain as a normal response of living organisms (it does not originate with sin). But the incursion of death into human life means that childbirth (a normal part of most women's lives) will become more difficult.

This is a solid interpretation of the second line, which clearly refers to bringing forth (*yālad*) children. However, a good case can be made for taking the word rendered "pangs" (*'iṣābôn*) in the first line to mean "sorrow" (as the KJV does); it can refer to emotional (and not just physical) pain. Likewise, the word for "childbearing" (*hērôn*) more usually refers in the Old Testament to "conception," the first stage of the childbearing process. To have women's "sorrow in conception" (or possibly "sorrowful conception") multiplied would thus be a reference to the emotional grief many women have over infertility (the inability to conceive) or possibly miscarriage (line 1), in addition to the physical pain of bringing forth children (line 2). And if we read on in Genesis, the emotional pain of "barrenness" is, indeed, a problem for many of the women (such as Sarah, Rebekah, and Rachel) whose stories are recounted there.[54]

The second consequence for the woman is that the man will rule her, despite her desire for him (Gen 3:16). This could mean that her yearning for intimacy (which is part of the good order of creation) will not be reciprocated. But the woman's "desire" might be linked to the previous line about

---

53. Given the scope of this essay (with its focus on how sin has affected the human-ground relationship and the woman-man relationship), I will need to pass over the judgment on the snake. For that, see Middleton, "Reading Genesis 3," esp. the section on "The Formal Declaration of Judgment."

54. A persuasive argument for this translation (and interpretation) of the consequences for women is given by Curley and Peterson, "Eve's Curse Revisited." I would not, however, refer to this consequence as either a punishment or a "curse" (as the authors do), since this language is not used in Genesis 3.

"sorrow in conception"; in that case, it could refer to the sort of desperate yearning for children exhibited later in Genesis by women (such as Leah, Tamar, and Lot's daughters) who sought to become pregnant by men, by any means necessary (some of these stories are particularly tragic).[55] Whether "desire" is viewed positively or negatively, the original mutuality between the woman and the man (signified by the wordplay between 'iššâ and 'îš) will now be replaced by an asymmetry of power between them, as men begin to rule women; primal resonance has become dissonance.[56]

When the narrative resumes (after the formal proclamations of judgment), the first thing the man does is to *name* the woman, thus exhibiting his rule over her; the name he gives her is *Eve* "because she was the mother of all living" (Gen 3:20). Although the wordplay between "Eve" (ḥavvâ) and "living" (ḥai) suggests something beautiful and even tender, this initially positive point is contradicted by the fact of naming, which enacts an asymmetry of power (he had previously named the animals, thus proving that animals were not equal partners).

Do all women experience great difficulty (with accompanying grief or pain) in conception and childbirth? Do all men dominate women? The answer to these questions is clearly *no*. These are *typical* human experiences in a fallen world, but they admit of exceptions. And, like all consequences of the Fall (ways in which death has encroached on flourishing), they should be resisted, with remedial measures, where possible. Indeed, Christ has come to set right all human relationships that are out of whack with God's original intentions. The tragedy is that so many in the Christian tradition have read the fallen reality of male superiority (or even domination) as if it were God's normative intent from the beginning.

Diminishing of Life for the Human/Man (Genesis 3:17–19)

Following the judgment on the woman, God pronounces consequences for the man. Although the text does not use the word for man as male ('îš), but the word for human ('ādām), the 'ādām is treated as male in Genesis 3:17 (he listened to the woman). Nevertheless, everything said here is relevant to both men and women.[57]

---

55. For an analysis of these examples in Genesis, see Curley and Peterson, "Eve's Curse Revisited," 168–70.

56. This contrasts with the mutuality of rule granted to *both* male and female in Gen 1:26–28; there the only divinely authorized human rule was *over the non-human*.

57. It is curious that even after the creation of the woman the narrative continues to use the word 'ādām both for the man (Gen 2:22, 23, 25; 3:8–9, 12, 17, 20–21) and for humanity generally (Gen 3:22–24).

Due to the sin of the ʾādām, the ʾădāmâ is "cursed," and the relationship of the ʾādām with the ʾădāmâ becomes difficult (Gen 3:17–19). There is mention of "thorns and thistles" and "sweat"; and what was earlier described as "work" (ʿābad) is redescribed as painful "toil" (ʿiṣābôn). The Hebrew word for "toil" was already used for the woman's "pain" in conception and/or childbearing; here we might follow the KJV and also translate it as "sorrow," in the sense of the emotional pain that will accompany the physical difficulty of farming the land (for example, when crops fail). And if we read on in Genesis, we will see that famine is a particularly recurring problem for Abraham and his family, which leads to two separate migrations (of Abraham, then of Jacob and his sons) to Egypt in search of food.[58] The point is that the harmonious relationship of human and ground (which was God's original intent for work) has been disrupted; primal resonance has become dissonance.[59]

Given that this encroachment of death into ordinary human work (which renders it toilsome and sorrowful) applies to both men and women (women were certainly involved in agricultural labor in the ancient world), we are justified in treating this as a consequence of the Fall for all people generally (hinted at by the continued use of ʾādām), and not just for men. Just as everything said of haʾādām prior to the creation of the woman is true for all people (all are mortal, all are living organisms, all have the God-given vocation to work in God's world, all need companionship), so it makes sense to think that this consequence is meant to apply to the human race generally.

This sorrow and toil is applicable, beyond agricultural labor, to all forms of work. We may think of the working conditions of factory workers in the Third World or even the exploitation of cheap labor in the service sector in the First World (with wages that often make it impossible to survive, much less to raise a family). It is relevant to top down management styles that give workers little voice, and to the workaholism of many who are well-paid in the financial and tech sectors, which often leads to the breakdown of families.

Nevertheless, while work in a post-Fall world is often burdensome and even oppressive, work is not simply an evil to be endured. It is part of the

---

58. Note the parallel between the barrenness of the land (addressed to the man) and the barrenness of the womb (addressed to the woman). Both themes are picked up in the narrative of Genesis. For this interpretation, see Curley and Peterson, "Eve's Curse Revisited," 170.

59. Interestingly, it is not only humans who suffer the consequences of the transgression; God is also affected. Because the human heart has become evil (Gen 6:5) God is "grieved" or "pained" in his heart (Gen 6:6); the verb here is yāṣab, from which the noun ʿiṣābôn ("pain" or "toil" or "sorrow") is derived.

Creator's good purpose for humanity, and it is thus subject to the renewal that Christ brings.

Finally, we are told that the 'ādām will ultimately return to the dust of the 'ădāmâ from which he was taken (Gen 3:19). This raises the question of why returning to the dust of the 'ădāmâ is mentioned as a consequence of sin if humans were created mortal in the first place (and so would be expected to have a finite life span). This leads us to consider the conclusion of the story narrated in Genesis 2–3, which contains an important clue to a further meaning of the tree of life.

Brokenness and Grace Outside the Garden (Genesis 3:21–24; Genesis 4–6)

The final consequence of the Fall, narrated at the end of Genesis 3, is that ha'ādām is exiled from the garden (Gen 3:23), something clearly meant to apply to both the man and the woman. The reason YHWH God exiles them from the garden is to prevent them eating from the tree of life and thus *living forever* (Gen 3:22). This means that while eating from the tree of life initially symbolized human flourishing in God's world (living life to the fullest), at some point the Creator would have made this flourishing permanent (perhaps continual eating from this tree was necessary to live forever). Human disobedience, however, intervened and prevented them from reaching this goal. So, humans *continue* in their mortality.[60]

Just as God graciously clothes the naked humans with skins (Gen 3:21), even though this required the death of animals, so exiling them from the garden is not purely tragic; it is a remedial act of grace, which prevents the sinful human state from becoming permanent.[61] God's grace is further evident in his accompanying the exiled humans outside the garden, helping Eve to bring forth a child (Gen 4:1) and conversing with Cain—even putting a mark of protection on him (Gen 4:9–15).[62]

---

60. The Eastern Orthodox tradition (along with C. S. Lewis, in his novel *Perelandra*) has seen that there would have been a movement from initial mortality to immortality if the original humans had not sinned. Given the reality of sin, which has corrupted and distorted human life, we needed the intervention of God in Christ to lift the burden of sin and death ("the sting of death is sin"; 1 Cor 15:56) by the introduction of resurrection life (see 1 Cor 15:42–57).

61. The idea of sinful immortals might remind us of the character of Q in *Star Trek: The Next Generation*. A member of the Q Continuum (a group of immortal beings), with no sense of innate morality, Q toys with mere mortals (especially Captain Picard) for his own amusement and intellectual stimulation (to alleviate his boredom).

62. The fact that God speaks to Cain after the Fall suggests that the often-heard

Whereas *ha'ādām* was originally created to work (*'ābad*) and guard (*šāmar*) the garden (Gen 2:15), the human role is now limited to working (*'ābad*) the ground *outside* the garden (Gen 2:23). This is a significant diminution of the original human task, which was never actually portrayed as fulfilled in the narrative of Genesis 2–3 (an episode describing that would need to be inserted between chapters two and three). Beyond that diminution, it is tragic that YHWH God must station cherubim with flaming sword to guard (*šāmar*) the garden—specifically the tree of life—*from* humans (Gen 3:24), who were its original guardians.

While life outside the garden is clearly difficult (the human-earth *relationship* has been somehow disrupted), the text does not say that "nature" was changed because of the Fall. The realism of the "thorns and thistles" (Gen 3:18) would simply be the world outside the garden; and this fits well what we know of the world in its natural state.

Nor does human nature suffer any sort of immediate and radical corruption, as the classical doctrine of "original sin" might suggest. The only change specifically mentioned at the end of Genesis 3 is that *ha'ādām* "has become like one of us, knowing good and evil" (Gen 3:22), which is a fulfillment of what the snake had promised (Gen 3:5). Yet, according to Genesis 1 humans were *created* in God's image (Gen 1:26–27). They were *already* like God; it was not something they needed to attain (as the snake suggested). And this God-likeness was not connected to their knowing good and evil, but rather to their being granted dominion over the earth.[63]

So, when YHWH God affirms the truth of the snake's claim, that God-likeness has resulted from eating the forbidden fruit (Gen. 3:22), it has an ironic sense. They have indeed become like God, but in an inappropriate way—which will not be good for them. And their eyes were indeed opened, with the result that they knew they were naked and so they tried to cover their nakedness (Gen 3:7).[64]

Here it is helpful to counterbalance the classical notion of original sin (which assumes that all post-Fall humans come into the world enslaved to sin, by a quasi-genetic inheritance) with the actual narration of the development of sin in Genesis 4, and later in Genesis 6. The initial transgression

---

Christian definition of sin as *separation from God* is overly simplistic. It does not fit the narrative of Genesis (or the rest of Scripture, where God is often present to people despite their sin).

63. For an analysis of the relationship of human dominion over the earth and being created in God's image, see Middleton, *The Liberating Image*, esp. chap. 2: "The Symbolic World of Genesis 1."

64. The sort of knowledge of good and evil they acquired was: naked = *bad*; covered = *good*.

(the "originating sin"[65]) by the parents develops in the next generation into murder (Cain kills Abel). But this is not a necessary progression; the narrative portrays Cain's struggle with anger and even depression (Gen 4:5) leading up to the murder, including God's claim that he can "do well" and that although "sin is lurking at the door" he "must master it" (Gen 4:7). God's words to Cain suggest that *sin* (the first use of this word in Genesis) is not inevitable for human beings; it can (initially, at least) be resisted.

It turns out that part of the problem with the classical notion of original sin (which assumes that everyone is born with a "sin nature") is that Augustine misunderstood Paul's point in Romans 5:12. Augustine rightly understood that "sin came into the world through one man, and death came through sin"; fair enough—this fits Genesis. But Augustine used an Old Latin translation of the New Testament (which shows up later in the Latin Vulgate); this translation goes on to say "and so death spread to all, *in whom* all have sinned" (where *in whom* means *in Adam*).[66] Augustine thought that because we (somehow) sinned *in Adam*, we genetically inherit a sinful nature from our parents. And many Christians since Augustine have followed his lead in thinking that everyone born after Adam is automatically a sinner, which often leads to a pessimistic view of human nature.

However, the NRSV better represents the original Greek of Paul's formulation when it translates the contested phrase as "*because* all have sinned." (Rom 5:12). The point is not that all humanity mysteriously sinned *in Adam*, but simply that we have all sinned, which is an empirical fact.

Indeed, rather than an immediate change in human nature, the narrative of Genesis portrays a *process* by which humans come more and more under the sway of sin. After Cain's murder, we find Lamech's revenge killing of a young man who injured him, a killing that he boasts about to his wives (Gen 4:23). Yet even here the growth of sin is intertwined with positive cultural innovation, such as the building of cities, the invention of new forms of livestock tending, musical instruments, and metal tools (Gen 4:17, 20–22). But sin continues to grow and infect the human race, until every "inclination of the thoughts of [the human heart] was only evil continually" (Gen 6:5), and the earth was destroyed or ruined ($š\bar{a}ḥat$) by the violence with which humans had filled it (Gen 6:11).

Here we finally have something as pervasive as "original sin" in the later theological sense of the term—that is, a situation of communal and systemic evil we are all born into (but this is a historical progression and

---

65. This is Fretheim's term for what happens in Genesis 3; see Fretheim, *God and World in the Old Testament*, 70–76.

66. Augustine's use of the Old Latin for Rom 5:12 is clear in his *On the Merits and Forgiveness of Sin* 1.10–11.

not a genetic inheritance). Such a developmental (and communal/systemic) view of sin as narrated in Genesis is true to human experience.

The Restoration of Flourishing through Jesus Christ

Contrary, then, to how many Christians have interpreted Genesis 2–3, the text does not teach the subordination of women to men or the essentially fallen nature of work. Rather, it affirms the original equality of men and women and the dignity and value of work in God's world. Human sin has, indeed, corrupted and distorted the mutuality of male-female relationships that God intended; and it has inhibited the ability of people to find meaning and sustenance from engaging the world with their gifts and abilities, which was God's original purpose.

Indeed, sin has so permeated our world that we are all born into a social order that indelibly bears its marks (and our families of origin are not exempt either); the result is that sin becomes a lived, empirical reality for all people. And yet humans do not thereby lose the image or likeness of God, as Genesis 5:1 and 9:6 make clear by applying these terms to post-Fall human beings. A proper balance of human dignity (in God's image) and human brokenness is necessary to understand the biblical picture of life in the contemporary world.

A beautiful articulation of this balance is found in C. S. Lewis's *Prince Caspian*: "You come of the Lord Adam and the Lady Eve," said Aslan. "And that is both honour enough to erect the head of the poorest beggar, and shame enough to bow the shoulders of the greatest emperor on earth."[67]

But beyond distinguishing between God's *creational* intent for the flourishing of human beings (the path of life and blessing) and the *fallen* reality of human brokenness (the path of death and curse), we also need to grasp the amazing *redemption* that is possible through Christ, a redemption that is applicable to every dimension of our lives that has been touched by sin.

In the words of the Christmas carol "Joy to the World," "He comes to make his blessings known far as the curse is found."[68] Perhaps this is why Paul is so excited in 2 Corinthians 5:17 that he leaves out a verb: "If anyone is in Christ—new creation! The old has passed away; behold, the new has come!"[69] And that "new creation" affects all relationships. As Paul says in Galatians

---

67. Lewis, *Prince Caspian*, 211–12.
68. "Joy to the World," lyrics by Isaac Watts (1719).
69. This is my own literal translation.

3:28, "There is no longer Jew or Greek, there is no longer slave or free, there is no longer male and female; for all of you are one in Christ Jesus."

Indeed, this new creation extends beyond human beings to the earth itself, and ultimately to all God has made. So, Colossians 1 tells us that that through Christ "God was pleased to reconcile to himself all things, whether on earth or in heaven, by making peace through the blood of his cross" (Col 1:20). And the apostle Peter (in a sermon in Jerusalem) connects Christ's second coming with "the time of universal restoration that God announced long ago through his holy prophets" (Acts 3:21). This leads to the Bible's expectation of nothing less than "a new heaven and a new earth" (Rev 21:1), a world "where righteousness is at home" (2 Pet 3:10).[70]

Beyond reading Genesis 2–3 in light of this vision of God's intent for flourishing, it is even more important that we *live towards* this vision, seeking to incarnate God's purposes for flourishing in every dimension of life—including our treatment of others (whether male or female) and our work and creative engagement with God's world. Then we will be on the road to manifesting B. T. Roberts's vision of social holiness.

Bibliography

Alter, Robert. *Genesis: Translation and Commentary*. New York: Norton, 1996.
Barr, James. *The Semantics of Biblical Language*. London: Oxford University Press, 1961.
Brown, William P. *The Seven Pillars of Creation: The Bible, Science, and the Ecology of Wonder*. Oxford: Oxford University Press, 2010.
Calvin, John. *Commentaries on the First Book of Moses, Called Genesis*. Vol. 1. Translated by John King. Grand Rapids: Eerdmans, 1948.
Curley, Christine, and Brian Peterson. "Eve's Curse Revisited: An Increase of 'Sorrowful Conceptions.'" *Bulletin for Biblical Research* 26, no. 2 (2016) 157–72.
Fretheim, Terence E. *God and World in the Old Testament: A Relational Theology of Creation*. Nashville: Abingdon, 2005.
General Conference of the Free Methodist Church. "FMC Statement on Women in Ministry." http://fmcusa.org/blog/1995/08/01/fmc-statement-on-women-in-ministry/. Accessed March 22, 2017.
Herring, Stephen L. "A 'Transubstatiated' Humanity: The Relationship between Divine Image and the Presence of God in Genesis i 26f." *Vetus Testamentum* 58 (2008) 480–94.
Jacobsen, Thorkild. "The Graven Image." In *Ancient Israelite Religion: Essays in Honor of Frank Moore Cross*, edited by Patrick D. Miller Jr. et al., 15–32. Philadelphia: Fortress, 1987.
Lewis, C. S. *Perelandra*. London: Bodley Head, 1943.
———. *Prince Caspian: The Return to Narnia*. New York: Macmillian, 1951.

---

70. For more on the theme of the renewal of creation, see Middleton, *A New Heaven and a New Earth*, esp. chap. 8: "The Redemption of All Things."

McDowell, Catherine L. *The Image of God in the Garden of Eden: The Creation of Humankind in Genesis 2:5—3:4 in Light of mīs pî pīt pî and wpt-r Rituals of Mesopotamia and Ancient Egypt*. Siphrut: Literature and Theology of the Hebrew Scriptures 15. Winona Lake, IN: Eisenbrauns, 2015.

Middleton, J. Richard. *The Liberating Image: The* Imago Dei *in Genesis 1*. Grand Rapids: Brazos, 2005.

———. *A New Heaven and a New Earth: Reclaiming Biblical Eschatology*. Grand Rapids: Baker Academic, 2014.

———. "Reading Genesis 3 Attentive to Human Evolution: Beyond Concordism and Non-Overlapping Magisteria." Chap. 4 in *Evolution and the Fall*, edited by William T. Cavanaugh and James K. A. Smith, 67–97. Grand Rapids: Eerdmans, 2017.

———. "The Role of Human Beings in the Cosmic Temple: The Intersection of Worldviews in Psalms 8 and 104." *Canadian Theological Review* 2, no. 1 (2013) 44–58.

Miller Jr., Patrick D. *Genesis 1–11: Studies in Structure and Theme*. Sheffield: JSOT Press, 1978.

Roberts, Benjamin. T. *Ordaining Women*. Rochester, NY: Earnest Christian, 1891.

Trible, Phyllis. *God and the Rhetoric of Sexuality*. Philadelphia: Fortress, 1978.

Walton, John H. *The Lost World of Adam and Eve: Genesis 2–3 and the Human Origins Debate*. Downers Grove, IL: IVP Academic, 2015.

Wenham, Gordon J. "Sanctuary Symbolism in the Garden of Eden Story." In *I Studied Inscriptions from before the Flood: Ancient Near Eastern, Literary, and Linguistic Approaches to Genesis 1–11*, edited by Richard S. Hess and David Toshio Tsumura, 399–404. Sources for Biblical and Theological Study 4. Winona Lake, IN: Eisenbrauns, 1994.

Wesley, John. "Preface" to *Hymns and Sacred Poems* (1739). Vol. 14 of *The Works of John Wesley*. 3rd ed. Peabody, MA: Hendrickson, 1991.

Winslow, Karen Strand. "Wesleyan Perspectives on Women in Ministry." http://fmcusa.org/blog/2005/07/01/wesleyan-perspectives-on-women-in-ministry/

Yamauchi, Edwin M. *Africa and the Bible*. Grand Rapids: Baker, 2005.

8

Christian Belief and the Challenge of Threats and Inducements

—Andrew C. Koehl

I arrived to teach at the school established by B. T. Roberts knowing little of its founder and the Free Methodist tradition. I have since been grafted into this singular heritage of devotion, evangelism, and justice. My professional background is in religious epistemology, and this chapter is an exploration of the warrant and justification of Christian belief in light of the possible influence of scriptural threats and inducements. While I find Roberts's focus to be on a faithful Christian life in church and society, he does not shy away from teaching on the reality of hell and the urgent need to avoid it.

There are various views of hell among Christians, and Roberts endorses one that is particularly frightening, the view that at some point the opportunity for salvation will expire, and if one has not made proper choices by that moment, he or she will be permanently consigned to an eternity of torture. I call this the "eternal abandonment view" of hell, and the threat of such a hell is profoundly troubling to Christians, seekers, and skeptics alike. How should one think about the impact of the fear of hell (or the desire for scriptural rewards) on the epistemic status of Christian belief, and should a Christian epistemologist like myself be wary of the unabashed endorsement of the eternal abandonment view of hell by B. T. Roberts?

I begin with a summary of Roberts's teaching on how choices influence the experience of God and how the desire to avoid hell might prepare one for belief. I then apply tools of the analytic, epistemological tradition in which I am trained to an exploration of whether Christian beliefs are epistemically suspect when influenced by the warnings (and enticements) of the gospel. I also consider similar challenges to atheistic belief. In addition to epistemic conclusions about Christian and atheistic belief, I end with some reflections on this part of the tradition of B. T. Roberts.

B. T. Roberts on the Experience of God and the Fear of Hell

Contemporary Christian philosophers who have explored the role of experience in producing Christian knowledge include William Alston, who argues in *Perceiving God* that Christian belief can count as knowledge when it issues from the reliable, socially-established, and self-supporting belief-forming process he calls Christian Mystical Practice.[1] Alvin Plantinga argues that Christian belief can be justified and warranted when it is produced by properly-functioning cognitive faculties operating on a wide variety of common human experiences.[2] For Plantinga and Alston, as well as for other Christian thinkers, elements such as one's background beliefs and attitudes have a profound impact on the nature of one's current religious experiences and whether they can rationally justify Christian belief. This author, for instance, has laid out eleven factors that influence whether one's basic Christian belief is warranted, including one's virtues and vices, background beliefs, personality, and various motivations.[3]

For B. T. Roberts, authentic encounters with God are crucial to the formation and maintenance of saving faith, and the essential *motivational* preparation for such experiences involves conscious choices. Coming to know God is not a mere intellectual exercise; it involves the transformation of the will.

> The believing must be with the heart, the affections, THE WILL, and not merely with the head—the Intellect. Believing in this way brings one into righteousness, into the principle of right, into the determination and the power to do right.[4]

---

1. Alston, *Perceiving God*.
2. Plantinga, *Warranted Christian Belief*.
3. Koehl, "On Blanket Statements."
4. Roberts, *Pungent Truths*, 15.

> God speaks generally to the soul in a still, small voice. You must live near him to hear that voice.[5]

Roberts quotes the General Rules of Methodism when he insists that God's Spirit "writes on truly awakened hearts."[6] Among the attitudes that open one to the experience of God are willingness to trust,[7] committing to spiritual disciplines such as quietness, prayer and reading Scripture,[8] and living in humility, repentance, gentleness and forgiveness.[9] Attitudes that mitigate against experience of God include cowardice,[10] impatience,[11] self-deception,[12] "unbounded admiration" of oneself,[13] comparing oneself to others instead of to biblical standards,[14] a lack of willingness to confess one's sins,[15] seeking peace and ease instead of the will of God,[16] dissension and lack of forgiveness,[17] and moral faults such as being "covetous and stingy."[18] In short, "All sin is blinding in its nature."[19] How one lives, the habits one establishes and ingrains, will put one in a better or worse state for knowing God.

> Conviction may be deep and overwhelming; but it is never irresistible. Those who will can always resist the Holy Ghost. St. Stephen told his hearers that they always resisted the Holy Ghost. Yet they would not own that they were doing it. Perhaps they did not know it. The habit of resisting the Spirit had become second nature to them. If you are ever expecting to get right with God, yield now to the gentle drawings from above. They will probably never be stronger. But every time you resist them the power of resistance is greatly strengthened.[20]

5. Ibid., 306.
6. Ibid., 5.
7. Ibid., 89.
8. Ibid., 72, 249–50.
9. Ibid., 54, 108.
10. Ibid., 62.
11. Ibid., 271.
12. Ibid., 60, 302–3.
13. Ibid., 9, 239–40.
14. Ibid.
15. Ibid., 11.
16. Ibid., 9.
17. Ibid., 263–4.
18. Ibid., 9, 274–76, 303–4.
19. Ibid., 92.
20. Ibid., 62.

Given the motivational influences on belief-formation, in particular the sort of stubbornness that can arise from resisting the Holy Spirit, Roberts insists that preachers reflect on the threat of damnation and communicate this danger to the congregation:

> The preachers at a camp meeting should feel a deep concern for the salvation of souls. The wretched, dangerous condition of the unsaved should rest as a heavy burden upon them ... The more preachers have of this feeling, the deeper anxiety will God's people feel for the lost. A spirit of awakening will rest upon the congregation, and sinners will be converted to God.[21]

> The Bible teaches future punishment just as plainly as it does future rewards. It declares that there is a hell as emphatically as it does that there is a Heaven ... You will also find that we are warned against going to hell as earnestly as we are persuaded to go to Heaven. The New Testament, especially, abounds in vehement exhortations to *flee from the wrath to come*.[22]

The Epistemic Problem for Christian Belief

From The Fear of Hell

One important role for the preacher, then, is to communicate the reality of hell and the urgency of avoiding it.

> But do you deliver God's message in God's own words? Stand in fear of hell; but do not be afraid to say hell! If you are a messenger of God, you have warnings from God. Do not fail to deliver them faithfully. The salvation of your own soul, as well as that of your hearers, is at stake.[23]

According to Roberts, the "desire to flee from the wrath to come" is an important disposition in the person who will come to believe in God and continue in that faith; this is emphasized by many Christian preachers today as well.

Whatever the value of warnings about hell in bringing people to faith, don't such appeals create a problem for the epistemic status of Christian belief? We generally think that a belief is evidentially tainted if one is

---

21. Ibid., 17.
22. Ibid., 248–49.
23. Ibid., 315.

intimidated into holding it. The "appeal to force" fallacy occurs when threats are used to compel belief instead of evidence. How is Christian belief *not* the result of a bald "appeal to force" when arrived at in the way that Roberts and many other Christians recommend? Might the plausibility of Christianity to a particular believer be unduly influenced by a deep-seated fear of hell?

If humans are ever psychologically influenced to form a belief apart from proper evidence, it would be one that they feel they must hold to avoid infinite, everlasting suffering. A Christian might reference historical arguments, the appearance of design in the universe, the cosmological argument, or experience of God as evidence for her beliefs. In some cases, however, these evidences may not have been enough to warrant Christian belief for her apart from the influence of a fear of damnation. One might think that such beliefs could fail to be warranted, not because of anything the believer did wrong, but because of an influence that she might not and perhaps cannot recognize.

From Positive Inducements

Note that a similar challenge to the warrant of Christian belief arises from positive incentives offered for it, such as the promise of eternal life or the offer of love, peace, forgiveness, and strength in this one. Roberts reminds us that "the arms of infinite love will embrace [us]"[24] when we pursue God.

> Man is made for eternity. The longest earthly existence is too short for his immortal longings. Its pleasures are unsatisfying, its honors empty and short-lived . . . Reader, lay hold on eternal life![25]

> God's grace, like the sun, shines everywhere. To those who welcome the light which God sends to the soul, and have courage to walk in it, the light shines with increasing brightness.[26]

Such extolling of the benefits of following God is, of course, common among Christians. The fruits of faith are naturally attractive to many of us, and they would seem to have some influence on our coming to believe in Christ. A similar epistemic concern, then, arises from the rewards promised to the faithful as emerges from the fear of damnation: How can one's Christian beliefs be rationally respectable if they arise not (merely) from evidence and

---

24. Ibid., 347.
25. Ibid., 150.
26. Ibid.

argumentation, but from powerful desires for significant benefits? Are we unduly bribed into belief?

The Epistemic Argument of this Chapter and Notes on Terminology

The question of this chapter, then, is whether threats (and promises of rewards) compromise Christian believing. I compare this challenge to a difficulty arising from Freud's concept of wishful thinking, and conclude that a response by Alvin Plantinga is useful in dealing with the challenge of threats and inducements. I argue that Christian beliefs can be warranted and justified even if they are influenced by the dread of damnation or the desire for divinely promised benefits. Since atheistic beliefs are susceptible to a similar challenge, they are due scrutiny as well. I find that atheistic views can sometimes remain justified when exposed to the possibility of fears and enticements, but they cannot be *warranted*.

Below I use "positive epistemic status" to reference a panoply of terms (such as "rationality," "reasonability," "justification," and "warrant") used by epistemologists to characterize propositions well-fitted for acceptance by those who desire to believe truly. The term "justified" is defined *internalistically*; it describes a proposition that is well-believed from the internal perspective of the believer. A belief is justified in this sense if, given her evidence, the believer should expect that her belief is likely to be true.

I follow Plantinga in defining "warrant" as "that, whatever precisely it is, which together with truth makes the difference between knowledge and mere true belief."[27] It used to be thought that if one's true belief were *justified*, it would count as knowledge. Gettier's famous cases have shown that justification, when conceived of internalistically, is not enough to produce knowledge.[28] One's beliefs can be true, and one can be justifiably convinced that they are, and yet one might still fail to have knowledge because of factors not recognizable from one's perspective. For instance, one might possess an unrecognized intellectual defect, lack crucial information, or be in misleading circumstances. Warrant, therefore, is now generally thought to include factors external to the perspective of the believer, facts of which she cannot be directly aware. These might include the belief being actually indefeasible,[29] reliably formed, produced by properly-functioning faculties,

27. Plantinga, *Warrant: The Current Debate*, 3.
28. Gettier, "Is Justified True Belief Knowledge?"
29. A belief is defeasible if there is other information such that, if the believer had it, her belief would lose its justification. See Annis, "Knowledge and Defeasibility."

or generated in a non-misleading environment. These sorts of criteria are external in the sense that whether they obtain cannot be directly observed by the believer.

Wish-Fulfillment as a Challenge to the Warrant of Christian Belief

How might a Christian respond to the epistemic challenge that arises from the fear of hell and the desire for divine benefits? Plantinga addresses a similar concern arising from Freud's contention that religious belief is the result of wish-fulfillment. Freud presents wish-fulfillment as a random, non-truth-tracking cause of belief in God.

> As we already know, the terrifying impressions of helplessness in childhood aroused the need for protection—for protection through love—which was provided by the father; and the recognition that this helplessness lasts throughout life made it necessary to cling to the existence of a father, but this time a more powerful one. Thus, the benevolent rule of a divine Providence allays our fear of the dangers of life; the establishment of a moral world-order ensures the fulfillment of the demands of justice . . . and the prolongation of earthly existence in a future life provides the local and temporal framework in which these wish-fulfillments shall take place.[30]

Freud cannot prove in a particular case (or in *any* instance for that matter) that desires and fears of this sort have created belief in God. Let's suppose, however, that wish-fulfillment *is* the determining cause of some people's theistic beliefs. Should we conclude that those beliefs are unwarranted?

Plantinga argues that we shouldn't. According to Plantinga's *proper functionalism*, a belief is warranted *if and only if* it is produced by properly-functioning cognitive faculties successfully aimed at truth in an appropriate environment. (Proper function is understood in terms of a cognitive design plan that could have come from God or from naturalistic evolution.) For a belief to be warranted, it must be generated by properly-functioning cognitive faculties, the purpose of which *in that instance* is the production of true belief. The question, then, is whether wish-fulfillment would be a cognitive process *aimed at true belief.*

Sometimes thought processes are aimed at goals other than truth, such as psychological well-being or survival. Suppose that upon hearing

---

30. Freud, *The Future of an Illusion*, 30.

that I have a cancer that only five percent of patients survive, I come to be convinced that I will recover, despite the odds. This belief is not well supported by the evidence, but through it I gain the psychological benefit of a more peaceful existence, as well as a slightly elevated chance of survival. My belief-forming faculties *may be operating perfectly* in generating the belief that I will survive; in this instance, however, the purpose of this thought process is psychological well-being and survival, not truth. Freud suggests that wish-fulfillment is a process of this sort; it aims not at producing *true* beliefs, but *comforting* ones.

Note, however, that even if all theistic beliefs *are* the result of wish-fulfillment, and wish-fulfillment *is* designed to produce comfort, it still does not follow that theistic beliefs are unwarranted. There is often more than one purpose for a given belief-forming process, and warrant requires only that *one* of those purposes be the production of true belief. If God, and not merely evolution, is the designer of our cognitive faculties, then the purpose of wish-fulfillment in the formation of theistic belief could be *both* to produce psychological comfort *and* to produce true beliefs about God. If wish-fulfillment in some instances does produce theistic beliefs, then these beliefs, having issued from properly functioning cognitive faculties successfully aimed at truth, would be warranted. (There may even be a further purpose of this cognitive faculty of wish-fulfillment. If Freud is right that confidence in ultimate justice is one of the results of wish-fulfillment, such assurance could be intended by God to help Christians persevere in the pursuit of goodness and the Kingdom of God.) The general lesson here is that motivational factors such as fears and desires can indeed be among the proper inputs to belief-forming processes that issue in warranted beliefs such as those associated with the gospel.

Application to the Challenge from Threats and Inducements

It does seem plausible that some people come to believe in Christ as a psychological protection against the worst of all punishments. We can now see, however, that it doesn't follow from this that Christian belief in such cases is unwarranted. As Plantinga points out, cognitive faculties can be aimed at truth in addition to other ends such as psychological well-being and survival. If God has a profound influence on the sorts of fears and desires we experience, it certainly could be the case that trepidation about damnation can serve as an appropriate input to a properly functioning cognitive process that issues in Christian belief. If we have a divinely appointed cognitive design plan, part of that design could be for fear of hell to sometimes produce true belief in God. Rational fears *often* influence the production of true beliefs. Facing a real danger can cause fear that rightly impacts beliefs on the subject. The purpose of fear-engendered belief-formation processes is often survival, well-being, *and* the formation of true beliefs. If God does exist, then God might have intended the fear of hell to be among the inputs of thought processes that issue in true beliefs about God.

Is Fear of Hell Rational?

In short, a worldview that envisions a divine and providential creator accommodates well the possibility that God could have designed us to be drawn to him through fears and desires as well as by rational reflections. Even so, there are concerns with this line of response. One might contend that while *rational* fears can be part of truth-conducive cognitive processes, the fear of hell is not rational. Is this the case?

Presumably the rationality or irrationality of this fear will depend in part on one's background information. The dread of damnation may not fit well with the totality of an atheist's beliefs and experiences. If God does not exist, it is very unlikely that there is a hell, so it seems that trepidation regarding judgment would not be rational for atheists. What about theists? Is the fear of hell rational for them? For many it might not be. Many theisms, Christianity included, hold that God is good and loving. Against that background information, belief in the sort of hell in which one could be infinitely tortured for eternity with no chance of escape might seem irrational. If the belief in such a hell is irrational, presumably the fear would be as well.

Remembering our Pascal, however, we should realize that the prospect of hell is so terrible that even if the chance of experiencing it is small, the possibility might rightly remain troubling. Even if it seems extremely unlikely that a perfectly good God would have such a hell, the experiencing of it (if real) would be so horrible that fearing it might be rational. Not only might the fear of hell be rational for theists, it could be rational for anyone, including atheists. Even if one's background beliefs do not cohere with the existence of God, let alone with an unending hell, given the limitations of human understanding, it is possible that one is mistaken. The infinitesimal odds of there being a hell would be offset by the infinite nature of the threat, making at least some level of fear reasonable. Trepidation about damnation, then, can be rational for both theists and atheists.

Even if the fear of hell for some people *is* irrational, however, this still need not remove warrant from a belief influenced by it. There is no reason to think that a fear must always be rational to be an input to a properly functioning thought process aimed at truth. A good cognitive design plan will be adaptable to new circumstances. While it is natural to suppose that rational fears will lead to true beliefs about the feared event, if humans come to be permanently mired in various sorts of irrational fears, an excellent design plan could at least sometimes turn this tendency towards the production of important true beliefs as well. This would be even more likely if God, and not merely evolution, is the author of our cognitive design plan. While some thought processes, might be designed to have among their inputs rational fears, others might operate successfully on irrational fears. Whether the fear of hell is rational or irrational, it could conceivably serve among the inputs to a truth-conducive theistic belief-forming process.

Is a Fear-Based Process for Christian Belief-Formation Ethical?

Isn't it unethical or unfitting for God to design us so that intimidation is used to produce Christian belief in us? Wouldn't it be more admirable for a perfect God to appeal to us through reason and love? Let me advance two responses to this charge. First, my argument does not require that the fear of infinite torture and permanent abandonment be part of God's original cognitive design plan. It is possible that this view of hell was not revealed by God but came from the fertile imagination of human minds. God might not desire for humans to be subjected to this terrifying threat. Maybe the genesis of this concept falls into the category of evils made possible by God allowing humans to think for themselves and exercise free will. God could have adapted his design plan to accommodate the emergence of a regrettable fear that he never intended humans to grapple with. Given that humans *would* be subject to this terror, God may have chosen to sometimes incorporate it into a belief-forming process aimed at the production of true Christian belief.

Alternatively, perhaps God *did* design us so that the aversion to hell is operative in the Christian belief-forming processes of at least some of us. Suppose God's primary plan is to influence us through rational argument and love, not to threaten us with permanent torment. Most would hopefully respond with love when so entreated. On the other hand, as Roberts writes, "Every day a man lives in sin he is becoming hardened in sin, and the probability of his ever becoming converted is lessened."[31] We can become so hardhearted that "the habit of resisting the Spirit [becomes] second nature."[32]

---

31. Roberts, *Pungent Truths*, 8.
32. Ibid., 62.

The contemptuous and incorrigible among us might not be susceptible to tender and winsome theistic-belief-forming processes. For the proudly impenitent, unalloyed gentleness might serve only as a perpetual context for manipulation, narcissism, and unrepentance. The lone idea strong enough to constrain such persons to humility and repentance might be the threat of unending torture at the behest of someone infinitely more powerful than they are. They might respond only to a bigger bully, and God can be that bully to them. The availability of a fear-based belief-forming process, perhaps as a last resort, could thus be literally a Godsend for those of us in such a condition. In the wisdom and mercy of God, using the fear of permanent abandonment and torture may be a way in which God becomes "all things to all people" that he might "by all means save some."[33]

In conclusion, it might be that the fear of perpetual, unrelenting torment was never intended by God as part of our cognitive design plan. Given the prevalence of this fear, however, God makes grudging but effective use of it. Alternatively, God might have originally intended the incorrigible among us to experience the fear of hell and for that fear to contribute to the formation of Christian belief. Either way, using the dread of damnation in these ways to influence Christian belief-formation is not incompatible with God's nature as a loving being who respects our rationality and freedom.

What About the Justification of Christian Belief?

So far I have argued that aversion to damnation need not deprive a Christian belief of warrant. What about the *justification* of those beliefs, however? We like to think of ourselves as objective evaluators beyond the possibility of manipulation, but if there is anything capable of making a cheat out of an honest person it is the threat of hell. Does the possibility that one's Christian belief is engendered (at least in part) by a deep-seated fear of damnation serve as a defeater for the justification of those beliefs? Could it be that one finds theism so convincing because of a fear of hell, and not because of the evidence? Once a believer is made aware of this possibility, what should be her epistemic response? Should she try to withhold her belief or to believe less firmly? Should she disavow her belief, even though it still seems true to her?

Given the variety of believers and their situations, there is not just one kind of epistemic impact for all Christians who reflect on the possible influence of fears and inducements. Some may lose justification or confidence; others may not. I have argued elsewhere that when an exclusivistic believer

---

33. 1 Cor 9:22 (NSRV)

(one who believes in the unique truth of her religion) encounters religious diversity, there are numerous factors that influence the epistemic status of her beliefs and the responses appropriate for her.

> Religious diversity will and should have a profound impact on many exclusivists and the epistemic status of their beliefs. Many exclusivists are epistemically impoverished, and thus the epistemic status of their exclusive beliefs may well be lessened or defeated by religious diversity. Many exclusivists should find diversity troubling, and many should try to hold their beliefs tentatively, or to give them up altogether . . . Others will have a suitable implicit sense of their epistemic wealth as they form their exclusive beliefs and live in accordance with them . . . Ultimately, the effects of religious diversity are on individuals and their particular beliefs, and have to be assessed case by case.[34]

These conclusions also apply to the believer who becomes aware of the possible influence of the fear of hell on her Christian beliefs. The proper epistemic response will depend on factors such as her level of virtue, her degree of spiritual insight, her personality, the nature of her religious experiences, the self-support and social establishment of her belief system, the strength of the arguments for her beliefs, the nature of other defeaters for her belief and her available resources for dealing with them, her understanding of the cognitive design plan (including insights gained from reading this and other papers), her degree of conviction, and the particular beliefs she has about hell and the nature of God.[35] If she is well-situated with regards to these factors, her beliefs need not lose justification, and there may be no epistemically obligatory actions for her to take. If she is not well-positioned, then she and her beliefs may indeed be impacted.

The *Particular* Epistemic Impact of the *Eternal Abandonment View* of Hell

Among influential epistemic factors, one's views on the nature of hell are particularly pertinent to our topic. Some theists hold that there is a one-time judgment after death that consigns one without appeal to an eternity of either bliss or torture. Some theists don't believe in hell at all, and others hold that the punishment of the damned is that they cease to exist. Others

---

34. Koehl, "On Blanket Statements," 411.

35. See Koehl, "On Blanket Statements," 398–403, for a detailed description of these epistemic factors.

believe, as C.S. Lewis famously wrote, that "the doors of hell are locked on the inside,"[36] that God is ever willing to save from hell those who seek God's assistance.[37] Note how much more terrifying the eternal abandonment view of hell is, because in a moment one could die and find oneself in excruciating, unending pain, with no God there to love them and no possibility of escape. This fear is, in a sense, *infinitely* more terrifying than the fear of mere death or a hell like that embraced by C. S. Lewis. The person who believes in the eternal abandonment view of hell, then, has a much stronger defeater for the justification of her beliefs than does one who embraces a view of hell that allows for God's continued entreaties.

For a theist who departs from the eternal abandonment view, hell would still be a serious affair, but one intimately overseen by a loving God who is committed to mercy and reconciliation, and who will not let any particular deadline get in the way of his redemptive purposes. If a theist rejects the eternal abandonment view of hell, she should naturally be less troubled by the possibility that she has been unduly influenced by the prospect of hell, and her appropriate epistemic response would arguably be less dramatic. A believer in the eternal abandonment view of hell, then, has at least an *epistemic* reason to consider whether this is indeed the teaching of Scripture, since the warrant and justification of her beliefs is seriously (though perhaps not irreparably) impugned by this doctrine.

Similar Defeaters for Atheistic Beliefs

Of course, theists aren't the only ones vulnerable to psychological influences on belief-formation. Atheists are people too, and as such they are likewise susceptible to fears and enticements. Some might arrive at atheistic belief through a desire to be accepted by atheist peers or to separate themselves from their parents, out of anger or disappointment, to gain a sense of autonomy or to avoid religious proscriptions, or out of resentment that they might have to give account for their misdeeds or lack of compassion.

While one might assume that the only belief that *the fear of hell* could engender is belief in God, epistemic reactions to fear are manifold. While one reaction to fear of hell is to mitigate the fear by forming belief in God, one could also react with anger to the threat of damnation and even resentment and hatred for any God who would resort to such intimidation. This

---

36. Lewis, *The Problem of Pain*, 115.

37. This is sometimes called the "restorationist" view of hell. See Gregg, *All You Want to Know*, for representative arguments regarding the annihilationist, restorationist, and eternal torment (or abandonment) views of hell.

outrage and enmity could engender atheistic belief. Likewise, fear of life in a godless world might influence some to believe in God while others respond by embracing atheistic existentialism to shore up their insecurities. Similar things can be said regarding the positive enticements that might impact beliefs about the existence or non-existence of God.

How well does atheistic belief hold up to the epistemic challenge of fears and hopes? With regards to warrant, it does not fare as well as theistic belief. If God does *not* exist and our design plan comes through naturalistic evolution, atheistic beliefs caused by most fears and inducements are created by processes the purpose of which is not truth but mere psychological benefit. If there *is* a God who has designed our cognitive faculties, then again thought processes turning fears and enticements into atheistic beliefs would either be forms of cognitive malfunction or processes aimed merely at psychological benefits. In neither case would this atheistic belief be warranted. The atheist should reflect on the fact that if fears and hopes have undue influence on her being an atheist, there is no way that her atheistic belief can be warranted. There is no God (on her view) who could have designed her cognitive faculties to profitably employ such motivations towards the production of true belief.

With regards to justification, the outlook for some (though not all) of our angry or resentful atheist friends is more sanguine. Suppose the atheist is confronted with the possibility that her atheism has been produced not primarily by rational reflection, but by her ire and indignation towards the notion of hell, or by one of the perceived psychological benefits of atheism listed above. What is her proper epistemic response in this case? As with the theist, it is possible that she need not be troubled and that she need not make any epistemic adjustments. For instance, if she is very reflective as to her motivations and can see no evidence of undue influence, and if she is a sophisticated atheist with direct access to strong support for her position, then her justification may not be impugned. If these things are not true of her, then her justification may well be undermined. As with theists, awareness of possible psychological influence including fears and enticements will defeat the justification of the beliefs of some atheists, but not all.

Conclusion

The Epistemic Impact of Fears and Inducements

Plantinga's counter to Freud provides a helpful line of response to the epistemic challenge to Christian belief from psychological influences. B.

T. Roberts and others who encourage us to be emotionally influenced by the promises of salvation and the possibilities of damnation are not doing anything that need remove the justification or warrant of Christian belief. A Christian's beliefs can be warranted even when influenced by the fear of hell and the desire for rewards, and they can also remain justified when she reflects on these possibilities. While some poorly-situated believers may suffer epistemic consequences when they consider the possible influences of intimidation or inducement, this need not be so for other theists.

The atheist is confronted by similar challenges to the warrant and justification of her beliefs. Where, perhaps unbeknownst to her, her forming of atheistic beliefs is unduly influenced by worries or enticements, her beliefs will fail to be warranted. The good news for the atheist is that, as with the theist, she can still be justified in maintaining her atheistic beliefs if she is epistemically well-situated. For theists and atheists alike, we have no way of knowing to what degree our belief-forming practices are influenced by fears and desires. It may be that in most cases they are not. If they are, however, this does not necessarily mean that those beliefs are unwarranted or unjustified. In either case, each believer should look to strengthen her epistemic situation and to move forward with humility.

A Reflection on the Eternal Abandonment View of Hell

I argued above that while the beliefs of an epistemically well-situated Christian can remain warranted and justified even if she is influenced by the fear of hell, it is more difficult (though not impossible) for a Christian who embraces the *eternal abandonment* view of hell to be epistemically well-situated. Concerning this view of hell, however, I also suggested that some malevolent souls might be reachable only through this ultimate of threats. Thus, it could be fitting for a loving God to employ a fear of such a hell in his cognitive design plan for some of us. (B. T. Roberts is committed to the teaching not for this reason, but because he believes it to be clearly taught in Scripture.) On the other hand, many sensitive souls may have their vision of the Divine marred by this doctrine. I do suspect that it has a negative personal, ethical, and epistemic influence on many. Some recoil from the image of God formed in them as they encounter the threat of unending abandonment and torture. This is especially true of people who have been abused and others who are victims of the misuse of power—the very ones whom Roberts so deeply loved, and for whom he spent his life advocating.

This is a pastoral issue, and as such, I know it is one that would weigh heavily on B. T. Roberts. I am reminded of Roberts's entry in *The Earnest Christian* when his second youngest son died:

> We expected that he would live and preach the Gospel when we were gone. It never occurred to us that there was any danger of his dying. But he has gone. God has taken him. His ways are far above our ways. We bow submissive to His will, and kiss the hand that has so sorely smitten us. We beg our friends to pray for us in this our heavy sorrow.[38]

Roberts here expresses anguish and compassion for his lost son as well as submission to God even when God's purposes are not understood. I do not doubt, then, that Roberts would feel deeply the anguish not only of those who have lost a child in death, but the infinitely worse sorrow that would accompany the belief that a loved one who has passed was currently experiencing excruciating torture without end. In the above entry, Roberts kisses "the hand that has so sorely smitten us." Given his conviction that the eternal abandonment view of hell is clearly taught in Scripture, I take it that he would kiss that same hand when it is delivering (or allowing) this infinitely worse state of affairs.

Such submission and humility may be admirable and required of us, but given how this particular view of hell is in such deep tension with other biblical themes, especially the love and mercy of God, we must struggle with whether this is indeed the teaching of Scripture, or whether perhaps regarding to this doctrine Roberts fell into the error he warned his readers about: "We cannot by our zeal for one class of Scriptures atone for our neglect of other Scriptures of equal importance."[39]

If the eternal abandonment view is indeed the teaching of Scripture, then we must, like Roberts, submit, and the pastoral response is to keep teaching the doctrine, to serve those seekers in love, and to trust the Holy Spirit, whose job it is to "convince the world of sin and righteousness and judgment." (John 16:8) It is essential, however, that we explore this doctrine carefully and wrestle pastorally with the impact of various doctrines of hell on believers and seekers alike, for the vision of God is essential to both personal and societal transformation. It is as we behold God in our hearts and minds that we become transformed.

> And we all, with unveiled face, beholding the glory of the Lord, are being changed into his likeness from one degree of glory to

---

38. Roberts, "In Deep Affliction," 63.
39. Roberts, *Pungent Truths*, 364.

> another; for this comes from the Lord who is the Spirit. (2 Cor 3:18)

The vision of God we have is strongly influenced by doctrine, and in a tradition rooted in the desire for right relationships in the home, in the church, and in society, we must be fastidious in seeking understanding of the most foundational relationship of all, that between God and God's people. How God disciplines us, and whether God could abandon us (for how long, and under what terms), are not ancillary issues; they are core to the nature of our relationship with God.

Sometimes I think that ambiguity regarding the eternal abandonment view of hell in the Christian tradition may serve (whether by divine design or divine opportunism) to draw both the tender-hearted and the incorrigible towards God. At other times I am concerned that the harm of this ambiguity is far greater than any good that might come of it. Of course, the truth of the matter is the primary concern, and whatever the truth may be, we need to proceed with boldness, openness, and humility, while in good conscience reflecting on Scripture, tradition, reason, and experience.

Social Transformation and Knowledge

I want to end with an important codicil to the epistemic argument of this chapter. I emphasized near the beginning, as B. T. Roberts taught, that various kinds of choices—because they influence our desires, emotions, and fears—prepare us well or poorly for coming to know God. I could have given the impression that knowledge of God is primarily individualistic. This could not be further from the truth. We are social beings. An important conclusion of my article, "Reformed Epistemology and Diversity," is that helping seekers come to warranted belief about Christ is not primarily about argument. Instead, it is about the transformation of culture.

> Because of his concern for goodness, God has created us so that character and intellect influence one another, and because of the importance of love and God's desire to transform all of human life and culture, he has created us with an emphasis on relationship and community, making our knowledge, especially in those crucial areas of how we should treat one another and how we should interact with him, to a large degree dependent on our relationships and our environment.[40]

---

40. Koehl, "Reformed Epistemology and Diversity," 181.

As we transform culture, more people are enabled to come to Christ, and as more of us come to Christ and walk in the holiness towards which B. T. Roberts was always impelling his readers and hearers, society will be more deeply transformed. I have profound respect for the character of B. T. Roberts and his indefatigable promotion of holiness and societal transformation. As he taught, these two go hand in hand, and as an epistemologist I certainly see them as essential for the production and maintenance of warranted Christian belief.

Bibliography

Annis, D. "Knowledge and Defeasibility." *Philosophical Studies* 24, no. 3 (1973) 199–203.

Freud, Sigmund. *The Future of an Illusion*. Translated and edited by James Strachey. New York: Norton, 1961.

Gettier, Edmund. "Is Justified True Belief Knowledge?" *Analysis* 23, no. 6 (1963) 121–23.

Gregg, Steve. *All You Want to Know about Hell: Three Christian Views of God's Final Solution to the Problem of Sin*. Nashville: Nelson, 2013.

Koehl, Andrew. "On Blanket Statements about the Epistemic Effects of Religious Diversity." Religious Studies 41, no. 4. (2005) 395–414.

———. "Reformed Epistemology and Diversity." *Faith and Philosophy* 18, no. 2 (2001) 168–91.

Lewis, C. S. *The Problem of Pain*. New York: Macmillan, 1944.

Plantinga, Alvin. *Warrant: The Current Debate*. New York: Oxford University Press, 1993.

Roberts, Benjamin T. "In Deep Affliction." *The Earnest Christian* (February 1875) 63.

———. *Pungent Truths: Being Extracts from the Writings of The Rev. Benjamin Titus Roberts, A.M.* 1912. Repr., Salem, OH: Schmul, 1973.

9

Amazing Grace in the Life of the Earnest Christian

—Rodney L. Bassett

When on a journey, it is good to have a map. This chapter is a map for considering the psychology of grace within the life of an earnest Christian. Looking through the lens of psychology, this chapter considers what might happen to a "brain on grace."

B. T. Roberts was clearly convinced of the centrality of God's grace in redemptive human history. That which was (and is) fallen and totally depraved was (and is) redeemed. Wounded souls are being restored, all by God's grace.

> Thus, though we are saved by *grace through faith,* yet the faith that saves is not fruitless. Every step taken towards God in faith, leaves behind it a plain track discernible by all.[1]

Roberts did not spend a lot of time in his writings reflecting directly on the construct of grace. Instead, he seems to have aligned himself with the theological framework of John Wesley.[2] In particular, Wesley emphasized prevenient, justifying, and sanctifying grace. All of these types of grace are captured within three stanzas of Charles Wesley's 1939 hymn, *And Can It Be that I Should Gain.*

---

1. Roberts, *Pungent Truths,* 116.
2. Snyder, email to the author.

And can it be that I should gain
An interest in the Savior's blood!
Died he for me? Who caused his pain!
For me? Who him to death pursued?
Amazing love! How can it be
That thou, my God, shouldst die for me?
Amazing love! How can it be
That thou, my God, shouldst die for me?

. . .

Long my imprisoned spirit lay,
Fact bound in sin and nature's night;
Thine eye diffused a quickening ray;
I woke, the dungeon flamed with light;
My chains fell off, my heart was free,
I rose, went forth, and followed thee.
My chains fell off, my heart was free,
I rose, went forth, and followed thee.

. . .

No condemnation now I dread;
Jesus, and all in him, is mine;
Alive in him, my living Head,
And clothed in righteousness divine,
Bold I approach th' eternal throne,
And claim the crown, through Christ my own.
Bold I approach th' eternal throne,
And claim the crown, through Christ my own.[3]

Wesley's concept of prevenient grace bears some resemblance to the Calvinists' common grace.[4] It is the manifestation of God's grace that restrains evil in the world, allows people to have some intimation of God's moral code, and quickens one's conscience.[5] Wesley saw all of these manifestations of God's grace as indications that "God so loved the world." (John 3:16) What separated Wesley's view of prevenient grace from a Calvinist's

---

3. Wesley, "And Should It Be That I Should Gain," stanzas 1, 3, 5.
4. See Coppedge, *Shaping the Wesleyan Message*.
5. See Collins, *The Theology of John Wesley*.

common grace was the restoration of some measure of free will. Wesley believed that in our fallenness, human beings are enslaved to sin. However, prevenient grace frees individuals, but typically does not require of them, to choose salvation by exercising faith in the atoning work of Jesus Christ.

Justifying grace flows out of the priestly role of Jesus Christ. Because of human fallenness a relationship with God can only be reestablished through the work of a Mediator. As the perfect High Priest, Christ atoned for our sins and made it possible for us to reestablish relationship with a loving and holy God through his sacrifice. On Calvary, God's justice and love were reconciled. Wesley was clear that he believed the atoning work of Christ could be accessed by anyone, although everyone might not choose to take advantage of this amazing grace.[6]

Sanctifying grace involves the gradual process of moving toward Christian perfection (Phil 3:12–15). Wesley believed that Christian perfection occurred after justification since justified persons are to go on to perfection (Heb 6:1).[7] It also could occur before death since St. Paul wrote of living persons that were perfect (Phil 3:15). It is not absolute but rather improvable. Sanctifying grace is perfect love (1 John 4:18), and the fruits of Christian perfection include rejoicing evermore, praying without ceasing, and in everything giving thanks (1 Thess 5:16). It does not make a person infallible, and it is something that can be lost.

B. T. Roberts seemed to implicitly agree with all of these views regarding grace.[8] Roberts certainly taught explicitly that the experience of God's grace was, is, and will be transformative in the lives of believers.

> No one should be satisfied with his present attainments. Christ is the portion of his people, but he will continue to satisfy their hearts only as they continue to grow in grace and in the knowledge of the truth. Life and growth are essential to fruit bearing. Dead trees do not have foliage or fruit. The fruitless fig-tree was cursed. Let us see to it that we bear much fruit; so shall we be his disciples.[9]

Thus, a grace-filled life will be fruitful as an indication of the work of grace within that believer's life. And, Roberts was convinced that one essential fruit of a grace-imbued life was holiness. For Roberts holiness meant a life of purity, following the Golden Rule of treating others as you would want to be treated, and regularly living out charity. Apparently, living out charity

6. See Cullum, *Grace Unfolding*.
7. Ibid.
8. Snyder, email to the author.
9. Roberts, *Pungent Truths*, 118.

roughly corresponded to manifesting the fruit of the Spirit: "But the fruit of the Spirit is love, joy, peace, forbearance, kindness, goodness, faithfulness, gentleness and self-control." (Gal 5:22–3)

Grace in Psychological Literature

The fruit of the Spirit seems to be largely addressed within the field of virtue psychology, which is an off-spring of positive psychology.[10] Without necessarily realizing it, psychologists have recently given a fair amount of thought to what an earnest Christian would call the fruit of the Spirit. What psychologists have paid little attention to is grace. In fact, Bassett has noted that one of the amazing things about grace is that psychologists interested in spirituality and religious experience have paid so little attention to a construct that is so central to the Christian faith. Thus, the purpose of this chapter will be to map out possible mechanisms by which grace transforms the human mind and further map out the possible physiological, cognitive, emotional, and behavioral manifestations of this transformation within the context of B. T. Roberts's understanding of the earnest Christian. An implicit assumption of this work will be that a creative God can and will work through God's creation. God can use the human brain/mind to accomplish God's purposes (including moving people toward holiness).

The little work that has been done on grace has focused on prevenient and justifying grace. Researchers have attempted to operationalize the extent to which persons are grace-oriented as well as some of the psychological and spiritual implications of this orientation. Perhaps the earliest efforts to operationalize grace were reported by Watson et al..[11] More recently, there have been essentially five efforts to spell-out and study the construct of grace. Payton et al. and Spradlin et al. have developed multiple versions of a grace-orientation scale.[12] Bassett notes: "Casual observation of the items suggests some of the following themes: (a) God manifesting unconditional love, (b) family history related to patterns of forgiveness and feelings of love, shame and anger, (c) relating to others in a 'golden rule' manner or an 'eye for-an-eye' manner, (d) inclinations to ruminate over past wrongs, and (e) the distinction between living well because of love or living well

---

10. See Plante, *Religion, Spirituality, and Positive Psychology*.
11. Watson et al., "Grace and Christian Psychology."
12. See Payton et al., "A Measure of Grace"; and Spradlin et al., "Shame, Grace, and Spiritual Well-Being."

to be loved."[13] Spradlin et al. also reported that grace-orientation predicts enhanced spiritual well-being and reduced levels of dispositional shame.

Sisemore et al. developed the Richmont Grace Scale. The original version contained thirty-four items and, in one study, was found to be positively correlated with an intrinsic religious orientation and a healthy and realistic view of sin. In a second study, the Richmont Grace Scale was used to consider the relationship between grace and mental health. In this study, the scale correlated negatively with all three measures of mental distress, and higher levels of grace were associated with greater mental health.

Watson et al.[14] presented a shorter version of the Richmont Grace Scale that contained twenty-seven items and was designed to tap four main constructs: forgiveness through grace, grace and responsibility, avoiding personal legalism, and avoiding interpersonal legalism. This version of the scale was found to relate inversely to extrinsic personal motivation, depression and anxiety. And, scores on this scale were directly related to intrinsic orientation (largely internalized faith), self-compassion, and a realistic view of sin. The authors reported that items in the current version of the scale seemed to share a common theme and items seemed to split into about nine different aspects of grace.

Bronte and Wade examined the experience of grace through thematic analysis of in-depth interviews. Interviewers asked open-ended questions about the experience of grace and the change brought about because of the experience. This analysis identified four common components of grace: mode of transmission, subjective impulse to change, emotional experience, and external effects. The mode of transmission reflected several options including: intuition, auditory experience, vision, feeling a presence, dreams, and experiencing grace through other people. In experiencing grace, many participants reported effortless subjective impulses to change, as well as spontaneous surrender. Participants reported feeling enlivened, surprised, loved, comforted, calmed, humbled, and sometimes pained by the experience of grace. The experience of grace was more likely to cause change when it was supported by environmental factors and often change-experiences were found to have a positive impact on others.

Bassett developed The Amazing Grace Scale to assess internalization of faith, an understanding of grace, resulting gratitude, and a transformed life. Exploratory factor analyses, a statistical strategy for highlighting the basic elements of a scale, revealed the items of the scale largely comprised two factors: grace identified (e.g., internalization) and grace awareness (e.g.,

13. Bassett, "An Empirical Consideration," 44.
14. Watson et al., "Grace and Christian Psychology."

understanding). Higher overall scores on this measure of grace were associated with higher scores on Christian identity, comfort-providing faith, intrinsic faith, gratitude, and identified faith. This measure of grace was also found to be independent of social-benefits faith, quest faith, and internalized but not personalized faith. In a second study, the scale also demonstrated direct relationships with empathic concern, other-forgiveness, and situational forgiveness. There was also a direct relationship between The Amazing Grace Scale and the measure of grace-orientation developed by Payton et al. and Spradlin et al.[15]

Finally, Bassett et al. did a study with Christian undergraduate students to see if they would differentiate within John Wesley's grace typology (prevenient grace, justifying grace, and sanctifying grace).[16] The students were given descriptions of each type of grace and then they were asked to rank them along fourteen evaluative dimensions. Generally, less spiritually mature students perceived more differences between the three types of grace than more spiritually mature students. That finding was unexpected. One possible explanation proposed by the researchers was that as one grows in relationship with God, that person may grow to recognize common patterns and themes in the handiwork of God. This may be akin to becoming familiar with an author and being able to recognize common themes across that author's many books. After all, it is the same author, or, in this case, the same God.

Considering what has been done empirically with grace, the dominant methodology has involved the questionnaire. Grace has also largely been construed in dispositional terms (people have been thought of as grace-oriented rather than simply having a grace moment). And, grace-orientation has predicted spiritual maturity and psychological well-being. However, sometimes dispositional constructs (a way of being) can be manipulated in a state (in the moment) fashion. Examples of that strategy can be found within the attachment literature.[17] These efforts have involved a prompt designed to boost a particular attachment state temporarily. Some of these prompts have been subliminal (e.g., brief exposure to the names of individuals previously identified as security-enhancing attachment figures) and some of these prompts have been supraliminal (e.g., recalling a past interaction with security-providing attachment figures). Findings from this body of research suggest that dispositional constructs (like

---

15. Payton et al., "A Measure of Grace"; and Spradlin et al., "Shame, Grace, and Spiritual Well-Being."

16. Bassett et al., "Is All Grace the Same?"

17. See Campbell and Mitchell, "Anxious Attachment"; and Mikulincer, "Attachment, Care-Giving, and Altruism."

attachment) can, in fact, be boosted in a state fashion producing results consistent with those constructs.

As a preliminary effort in that direction, Bassett et al. attempted to manipulate the construct of saving grace in a state fashion (to make God's grace cognitively salient).[18] Specifically, supraliminal prompts were used to make justifying grace cognitively salient for individuals who had already experienced God's grace. This initial effort seemed to indicate that focusing upon God's unmerited favor impacted unforgiveness, the personal reflection upon God's grace seemed to make people more inclined to forgive those who had transgressed against them.

In a more recent effort, Bassett et al. gave Christian undergraduate students twenty dollars and asked them to decide to keep all, or part, of the money or give all, or part, of the money to homeless individuals who were needy (and blameless) or who were needy (because they had made a lot of bad choices).[19] Some of the students had already experienced a grace-salience manipulation and the other students had spent their time, before the money allocation task, coloring geometric and neuroanatomical figures. The grace-salience students gave away more, and thus kept less, of the money. Also, there seemed to be a tendency for students who had thought about God's unmerited favor to make less of an issue of how meritorious the homeless individuals were when giving them money.

The Physiological Manifestations of Grace

So, what might be the physiological underpinnings of making God's grace salient? At a neurotransmitter and hormonal level, several possibilities come to mind. For example, there are the neuropeptide hormones oxytocin and vasopressin produced by the posterior pituitary gland. Research suggests that oxytocin and vasopressin systems play a role in the establishment of social bonds, mother-infant attachment, and becoming calm and less anxious.[20] If the key to establishing a relationship with God is accepting God's grace, then experiencing God's grace may co-vary with the release of oxytocin and vasopressin in our brains as the bond between us and God is forged. And then there are the neurotransmitters serotonin and glutamate.[21] Both have been associated with learning and memory, and the activity of both neurotransmitters has been identified as playing a role in mood disorders.

18. Bassett et al., "Grace Salience."
19. Bassett et al., "Considering the Impact of Grace Salience."
20. Kalat, *Biological Psychology*.
21. Ibid.

High levels of glutamate activity may predict mania and low levels of serotonin activity predict depression. As people experience justifying grace they often report feeling centered and right—not too high and not too low. After all, everything has been set right through the atonement of Jesus Christ. And, as people experience sanctifying grace they learn to live in ways that are consistent with God's character. They begin to develop holy habits. Relative levels of serotonin and glutamate may play a role in both these types of grace. Finally, there is the neurotransmitter dopamine. Dopaminergic systems are found throughout the brain and serve a variety of functions.[22] One role of dopamine involves human sexuality. A moderate release of dopamine can stimulate sexual receptivity. During orgasm, there is a sudden release of dopamine in several areas of the brain. Dopamine also plays a key role in the reward centers of the brain. God's people have been referred to as the bride of Christ (Rev 21:2–4). In Matthew 22:30, Jesus suggested that in the life to come, ". . . we're beyond marriage. As with the angels, all our ecstasies and intimacies then will be with God."[23] People who know God have reported euphoric and ecstatic moments as they contemplate the wonder of God and God's actions.[24] A neuroscientist might well say that these moments were undergirded by dopaminergic systems within the brain.

Religion, Spirituality, and the Fruits of Faith

Just as interesting as the bio-chemical underpinnings of grace are the psychological implications of being impacted by grace. As God's grace impacts the human brain, what happens "downstream" in terms of behavior, emotions, and cognition? When considering where to look for such implications a good place to begin would seem to be the fruit of the Spirit (Gal 5:22; Col 3:12–15). Although not much has been done empirically regarding grace, there are growing literatures that have considered the relationships between religion/spirituality and the fruits of faith.[25]

In this literature, religion and spirituality are typically not seen as synonymous. Sadly, there is not a clear consensus among psychologists as to the nature and definition of religion and spirituality.[26] Both seem to refer to our relationship with the transcendent. That which is transcendent can range from the Divine to that which is ideal and praiseworthy within

22. Ibid.
23. Translation, *The Message*.
24. Seybold, *Explorations in Neuroscience*.
25. Plante, *Religion, Spirituality, and Positive Psychology*.
26. Zinnbauer and Pargament, "Religiousness and Spirituality."

human experience. Most people refer to themselves as religious *and* spiritual. However, there are a growing number of people who identify themselves as spiritual and not religious. Religion is perceived as more institutional, organized, and social. In contrast, spirituality is usually conceptualized as more personal and individualistic. In empirically considering the fruits of faith it must be kept in mind that there are no universal definitions for "religious" or "spiritual."

Gratitude and Grace

Colossians 3:12–15 identifies being thankful as a fruit of the Spirit. B. T. Roberts had the following to say about thanksgiving:

> Paul tells us to make our requests known to God *with* thanksgiving. The sails of the ship cost little, compared with the rest of the ship. But they are of great importance to a sailing vessel. A ship may be steered toward Liverpool, but is not likely to reach there unless its sails are spread. So, thanksgiving adds wings to our prayers, and impels them on to the throne of God. A devout spirit is a thankful spirit. Notice how full the Psalms are of expressions of praises to God. In the worst calamities, there is still something to be thankful for. The father of John and Charles Wesley, seeing the parsonage and all their earthy substance burning up, was full of thankfulness that his wife and all the children were saved. Let us cultivate a thankful spirit.[27]

From a psychological perspective, thanksgiving sounds a lot like experiencing gratitude. Gratitude involves recognizing that one has received a valuable benefit.[28] That benefit can be received from another person or that benefit can be received from God. If grace involves receiving God's unmerited favor, then grace-salience should certainly make a believer feel grateful. Gratitude can also be conceptualized as a state or a trait. So, gratitude can be a transient emotional response to a "good gift" (a state). However, it is also true that some people are simply more inclined than others to respond to "good gifts" with gratitude (a trait). Both state and trait gratitude have been found to predict psychological, social, and physical well-being.[29]

What connections can we make between gratitude and grace? Emmons and Kneezel suggest that because of the centrality of gratitude in Christian

---

27. Roberts, *Pungent Truths*, 334.
28. Emmons and Mishra, "Gratitude."
29. Ibid.

theology (see Col 3:15–17), gratitude is at the heart of the gospel.[30] In addition, Karl Barth suggested, "Grace evokes gratitude like the voice an echo. Gratitude follows grace like thunder lightning."[31] Interestingly, Watkins et al. reported that those who were intrinsically religious (those for whom their faith and their relationship with God was an end in itself) were dispositionally inclined to be grateful.[32] Those who were extrinsically religious (for whom religion tended to be a means to an end) were dispositionally inclined to be less grateful. Presumably, individuals who had experienced God's grace and/or for whom grace was salient would more likely be intrinsically inclined toward their faith and be more likely to experience gratitude.

Emmons and Kneezel reported a study with a largely Christian and interesting sample: adults with congenital and later-onset neuromuscular diseases.[33] Within this population, the researchers found that measures of striving for sanctification and a measure of desiring closeness with God both predicted higher levels of daily and dispositional gratitude. However, when the sample was divided into those who identified as Christian (the clear majority of the sample) and those who identified as non-Christian (a small fraction of the sample), Christians scored higher on dispositional gratitude but not on daily gratitude.

A study by Rosmarin et al. considered what factor might mediate the connection between religiousness and gratitude.[34] It also addressed the issue of whether religious gratitude (e.g., gratitude toward God) contributed to well-being independently of general gratitude. Using a relatively diverse sample of adult individuals, the researchers were able to demonstrate that the connection between religiousness and gratitude was mediated by gratitude toward God. This gratitude toward God (for religious individuals) also contributed to well-being (happiness, increased positive emotions, decreased negative emotions, and mental health) above and beyond general dispositional gratitude.

Humility and Grace

Another fruit of the Spirit is humility or meekness (Col 3:12–15). B. T. Roberts seemed to see a clear connection between humility and being able to experience God's grace.

30. Emmons and Kneezel, "Giving Thanks."
31. Cited in Boulton, "We Pray by His Mouth," 70.
32. Watkins et al., "Gratitude and Happiness."
33. Emmons and Kneezel, "Giving Thanks."
34. Rosmarin et al., "Grateful to God."

> The presence of Christ in a congregation met for worship does not depend upon the place in which they are assembled. The character of the edifice has nothing to do with it. The place may be an upper room; it may be a loghouse—it may be a cathedral. This has not the slightest influence in securing the presence of Christ. The sunshine in a house depends, not upon its construction, but upon the opportunity the sunshine has to get in. So, the manifested presence of Christ in a meeting depends upon the humble, consecrated souls who are willing to receive him. He comes as a King to rule, if he comes to stay. As such he must be received. From the proud and the self-willed he turns sadly away. With formalists and hypocrites he has no more sympathy than he had when he denounced in such burning words the scribes and the Pharisees—the men of the greatest literary and the men of the greatest religious pretensions. He makes his abode with the poor in spirit, and the pure in heart.[35]

It is true that psychologists have not done a lot of empirical investigating of humility.[36] However, there has been a growing interest in that virtue. One of the challenges has been the use of self-report to assess humility. It is probably a given that as soon as someone publicly identifies himself/herself as humble, that person is not in a state of humility. Yet, there has been some consensus in regards to how psychologists define humility. These definitions have not involved having a lowly opinion of oneself; thus, perhaps they are inconsistent with Roberts's notion of being "poor in spirit." Instead, psychologists have tended to define humility as including the parameters of: (a) having a realistic view of self (perhaps this would be consistent with being "poor in spirit" when the realistic comparison is between the individual and an infinite and supreme God), and (b) not having an egocentric preoccupation with self. Tangney has pointed out that both arrogance and self-deprecation share a common focus upon self (either because one is so praiseworthy or so not), which is inconsistent with humility.[37]

A reasonable definition of humility, as a multifaceted construct, has been provided by Tangney.

- accurate assessment of one's abilities and achievements (*not* low self-esteem, self-deprecation).
- ability to acknowledge one's mistakes, imperfections, gaps in knowledge, and limitations (often vis-à-vis a "higher power").

35. Roberts, *Pungent Truths*, 136.
36. Tangney, "Humility."
37. Ibid.

- openness to new ideas, contradictory information, and advice.
- keeping of one's abilities and accomplishments—one's place in the world—in perspective (e.g., seeing oneself as just one person in the larger scheme of things).
- relatively low self-focus, a "forgetting of the self," while recognizing that one is but one part of the larger universe.
- appreciation of the value of all things, as well as the many ways that people and things can contribute to our world.[38]

Such a conceptualization has been divided into state-humility and trait-humility (humility in the moment versus dispositional humility). However, as noted by Halling et al., doing research in humility has been humbling.[39] The main challenge, as mentioned above, has been developing self-report measures of humility.[40] However, given that limitation, some early conclusions do seem reasonable. First, humility seems to predict greater physical health among the elderly.[41] Second, among the elderly, feeling closer to God predicts greater humility.[42] Third, humility predicts greater integrity in decision-making and more of an equality-approach to others.[43] And fourth, Worthington reported that humility tends to be indicative of a pro-social personality; the humble person is someone people like to be around.[44]

What might be a connection between grace-salience and humility? For example, justifying grace seems to involve the triple-pronged awareness among human beings that one is needy, one is profoundly loved by God, and that God has provided a solution (through the death and resurrection of Jesus Christ) for human neediness. The awareness of God's unconditional love should free individuals to honestly acknowledge their shortcomings and their strengths. After all, one does not have to fake being good to get God's love; it simply is. The degree of self-focus may depend upon which prong of salvation-grace is cognitively salient. If one is focused upon one's neediness, then there may be a large amount of self-focus. As David proclaimed, "For I know my transgressions, and my sin is ever before me." (Ps 51:3) But if one is focused on the amazing love of God and God's redemptive plan, then one may be much less self-focused.

38. Ibid., 73–74.
39. Halling et al., "The Contributions of Dialogal Psychology."
40. Tangney, "Humility."
41. Krause, "Religious Involvement."
42. Ibid.
43. Ashton and Lee, "Empirical, Theoretical, and Practical Advantages."
44. Worthington, "Helping Clinicians and Researchers."

Forgiveness and Grace

Another fruit of the Spirit is forgiveness (Col 3:12–15). Regarding forgiveness, B. T. Roberts said the following:

> A Christian cannot hold a grudge. We must be of a forgiving spirit. In dealing harshly with those who have gone astray we may say that we give them no more than they deserve. That may be true, and it may not be true. There may be animosity nestled in the heart, the presence of which we have not discovered. But if there is not, still we should leave them, as far as is consistent with our duty, in the hands of God. He is the judge.[45]

Clearly, in this passage Roberts was concerned about granting forgiveness, forgiving those who have offended us. However, psychologists see two sides of the forgiveness equation. Seeking forgiveness is one side of that equation,[46] and involves seeking forgiveness or simply apologizing.[47] Also, seeking forgiveness or apologizing can be aimed at the person harmed and/or at God.[48] The *granting* side of the forgiveness equation can involve emotional or decisional forgiveness.[49] And, forgiveness can be granted to self,[50] the transgressor,[51] or even a situation that was beyond anyone's control.[52] Self-forgiveness can assume the forms of self-forgiving, condoning, and self-punishing.[53] Finally, forgiveness can be granted by people or God.[54]

Psychologists have been so interested in forgiveness because of the general connection between forgiveness and well-being.[55] Generally, unforgiveness is conceptualized as triggering negatively valenced emotional states such as guilt and anger, while forgiveness is conceptualized as triggering positively valenced emotional states, such as peace and harmony. Thus, unforgiveness becomes a stressor that can predict negative effects on physical health, mental health, and relationships.

45. Roberts, *Pungent Truths*, 97.
46. Sandage et al., "Seeking Forgiveness."
47. Exline et al., "Is Apology Worth the Risk?"
48. Sandage et al., "Seeking Forgiveness."
49. Worthington and Scherer, "Forgiveness Is an Emotion."
50. See Fisher and Exline, "Self-Forgiveness versus Excusing"; and Tangney et al., "Forgiving the Self."
51. Sandage et al., "Seeking Forgiveness."
52. Thompson et al., "Dispositional Forgiveness of Self."
53. Fisher and Exline, "Self-Forgiveness versus Excusing."
54. Toussaint and Williams, "National Survey Results."
55. Worthington, *Handbook of Forgiveness*.

So, what happens when someone experiences grace-salience? The story of justifying grace is the story of forgiveness. God, through Jesus Christ, has paid the penalty for our sins. We can thus accept God's forgiveness for our sins, since the debt has been paid, and our relationship with God can now be restored. Since human beings tend to treat others as they have been treated, making God's forgiveness of us salient should make us forgiving of others. In fact, an initial effort to manipulate grace-salience tended to reduce unforgiveness and bitterness toward past offenders.[56] This connection between being forgiven and in turn forgiving is so clear that in the Lord's Prayer the forgiveness we receive from God appears to be contingent upon the forgiveness we extend to others. "And forgive us our debts, *as* we also have forgiven our debtors." (Matt 6:12)

Hope and Grace

Although hope is not specifically listed in the Galatians and Colossians listings of the fruit of the Spirit, it seems to be implied by other fruit-like virtues, such as patience, peace, and faithfulness. In addition, I Corinthians 13 indicates that three things that have abiding value are faith, hope, and love (1 Cor 13: 13). In regards to hope, B. T. Roberts had the following to say:

> Good Christians sometimes forget that "we are saved by hope" (Romans 8:24). They deprive themselves of much comfort by always looking at the dark side. They anticipate the worst, and their fears sometimes bring upon the calamities which they dread . . . In the thickest darkness we must exhort ourselves as did the Psalmist: "Why art thou cast down, O my soul? And why art thou disquieted within me? Hope thou in God: for I shall yet praise him, who is the help of my countenance, and my God" (Ps 42:11).[57]

Within psychology there has been an effort to distinguish between several related constructs: optimism, self-efficacy, and hope. According to Magaletta and Oliver, the three constructs are similar in that they are all determinants of behavior and focus on expectancies and individual goals or outcomes.[58] Optimism is the general expectancy that one will experience positive outcomes in life. Self-efficacy more specifically relates to an individual's belief that he/she can effectively accomplish tasks or behaviors that

---

56. Bassett et al., "Grace Salience."
57. Roberts, *Pungent Truths*, 178–79.
58. Magaletta and Oliver, "The Hope Construct."

result in desirable outcomes. Hope involves both the belief in one's ability to successfully meet goals (agency) and belief in one's capacity to generate routes for meeting these goals (pathways).

Thus, Carver and Scheier argued that optimism relates mostly to general outcome expectancies whereas hope relates to both outcome expectancies and personal agency.[59] Likewise, Peterson stated that an optimist might believe that positive outcomes will occur but might fail to reflect upon the pathways necessary to pursue these outcomes. A person with hope, on the other hand, might demonstrate the belief in positive outcomes and do the reflection necessary in generating routes to obtain these outcomes.[60]

Bryant and Cvengros examined whether optimism and hope were two separate constructs or reflections of the same general construct.[61] The researchers used the twelve-item Life Orientation Test to assess dispositional optimism and both the Adult Hope Scale and Herth Hope Scale to assess hope. The researchers also considered the relationship between the two aspects of hope: *agency* and *pathways*. The results of the study showed agency and pathways to be related but separate aspects of goal-orientation. Agency was shown to have a stronger correlation with general self-efficacy than pathways. The researchers found that optimism was more closely related to positive reappraisal coping than hope, whereas hope was more closely related to general self-efficacy than optimism. Therefore, optimism may have more to do with cognitive evaluations of goals and outcome while hope may have more to do with beliefs about personal abilities. In summary, this study suggested that optimism and hope are similar but separate constructs.

What might this psychological work on hope have to do with grace-salience? Certainly, grace as unmerited favor says much more about God than about us. However, once someone is set free to have a relationship with God through justifying grace, then that person, with God's help, can experience sanctifying grace and begin to act and think more like a child of God. Thus, one way to frame justifying and sanctifying grace is that people are now empowered through the Holy Spirit (agency) and given a plan through God's revealed word (pathway) for living life in full-colored holiness. Thus, grace-orientation may well contribute to hope on the part of the believer.

---

59. Carver and Scheier, "The Hopeful Optimist."
60. Peterson, "The Future of Optimism."
61. Bryant and Cyengros, "Distinguishing Hope and Optimism."

Conclusion

This chapter began by acknowledging the importance of grace in the thinking and work of B. T. Roberts. How Roberts thought about grace was then elaborated by considering the views of John Wesley on different types of grace. Thinking about grace from a psychological perspective, we considered the possible biochemical underpinnings of the experience of grace. We considered the possibility that a Christian may be grace-oriented but we also considered the state quality of grace-salience. We proposed that the work of grace in someone's life may connect to the roles of oxytocin, vasopressin, glutamate, serotonin, and dopamine within the human brain. We also proposed that grace-salience may make the fruit of the Spirit more abundant in the life of a believer (Galatians 5:22, Colossians 3:12–15). More specifically we considered the possibility that grace-salience may enhance one's gratitude, humility, forgiveness, and hope. The next step would seem to be empirically clarifying those connections between grace-salience, the workings of the human brain, and the fruit of the Spirit. There is much work to be done!

Bibliography

Ashton, Michael C., and Kibeom Lee. "Empirical, Theoretical, and Practical Advantages of the HEXACO Model of Personality Structure." *Personality and Social Psychology Review* 11, no. 2 (2007) 150–66.

Bassett, Rodney L. "An Empirical Consideration of Grace and Legalism within Christian Experience." *Journal of Psychology and Christianity* 32, no. 1 (2013) 43–70.

Bassett, Rodney L., et al. "Considering the Impact of Grace Salience in the Dictator Game." Presentation at the Christian Association for Psychological Studies International Conference. Pasadena, CA. March 10, 2016.

———. "Grace Salience: Possible Methodologies for Making Unmerited Favor Cognitively Salient." Presentation at the Christian Association for Psychological Studies East Regional Conference. Bethesda, MD. November 14, 2014.

———. "Is All Grace the Same?" Presentation at the Christian Association for Psychological Studies International Conference. Pasadena, CA. March 10, 2016.

Boulton, Matthew. "'We Pray by His Mouth': Karl Barth, Erving Goffman, and a Theology of Invocation." *Modern Theology* 17, no. 1 (2001) 67–83.

Bronte, Jacelyn C., and Jenny Wade. "The Experience of Grace: Divine Assistance in Making a Change." *The Journal of Transpersonal Psychology* 44, no. 2 (2012) 182–200.

Bryant, Fred B., and Jamie A. Cvengros. "Distinguishing Hope and Optimism: Two Sides of a Coin, or Two Separate Coins?" *Journal of Social and Clinical Psychology* 23, no. 2 (2004) 273–302.

Campbell, Lorne, and Tara Marshall. "Anxious Attachment and Relationship Processes: An Interactionist Perspective." *Journal of Personality* 79, no. 6 (2011) 1220–49.

Carver, Charles S., and Michael F. Scheier. "The Hopeful Optimist." *Psychological Inquiry* 13, no. 4 (2002) 288–90.

Collins, Kenneth J. *The Theology of John Wesley: Holy Love and the Shape of Grace.* Nashville: Abingdon, 2007.

Coppedge, Allan. *Shaping the Wesleyan Message: John Wesley in Theological Debate.* Nappanee, IN: Evangel, 2003.

Cullum, Douglas. *Grace Unfolding: The Journey of Faith from a Wesleyan Perspective.* Presentation at Pearce Memorial Church Lecture Series. North Chili, NY. 2014.

Dudley, Roger L. "Grace, Relevancy, and Confidence in the Future: Why Adventist Young Adults Commit to the Church." *Journal of Psychology and Christianity* 14, no. 3 (1995) 215–27.

Emmons, Robert A., and Anjali Mishra. "Gratitude." *Religion, Spirituality, and Positive Psychology: Understanding the Psychological Fruits of Faith*, edited by Thomas G. Plante, 9–29. Santa Barbara, CA: Praeger, 2012.

Emmons, Robert A., and Teresa T. Kneezel. "Giving Thanks: Spiritual and Religious Correlates of Gratitude." *Journal of Psychology and Christianity* 24, no. 2 (2005) 140–48.

Exline, Julie, et al. "Is Apology Worth the Risk? Predictors, Outcomes, and Ways to Avoid Regret." *Journal of Social and Clinical Psychology* 26, no. 4 (2007) 479–504.

Fisher, Helen E., et al. "Defining the Brain Systems of Lust, Romantic Attraction, and Attachment." *Archives of Sexual Behavior* 31, no. 5 (2002) 413–19.

Fisher, Mickie L., and Julie J. Exline. "Self-Forgiveness versus Excusing: The Roles of Remorse, Effort, and Acceptance of Responsibility." *Self and Identity* 5, no. 2 (2006) 127–46.

Halling, Steen, et al. "The Contributions of Dialogal Psychology to Phenomenological Research." *Journal of Humanistic Psychology* 34, no. 1 (1994) 109–31.

Kalat, James W. *Biological Psychology.* 10th ed. Belmont, CA: Wadsworth, 2009.

Krause, Neal. "Religious Involvement, Humility, and Change in Self-Rated Health over Time." *Journal of Psychology and Theology* 40, no. 3 (2012) 199–210.

Magaletta, Philip R., and J. M. Oliver. "The Hope Construct, Will, and Ways: Their Relations with Self-Efficacy, Optimism, and General Well-Being." *Journal of Clinical Psychology* 55, no. 5 (1999) 539–51.

Mikulincer, Mario, et al. "Attachment, Caregiving, and Altruism: Boosting Attachment Security Increases Compassion and Helping." *Journal of Personality and Social Psychology* 89, no. 5 (2005) 817–39.

Payton, J. T., et al. "A Measure of Grace: Preliminary Development of a Grace Scale." Presentation at the Christian Association for Psychological Studies International Conference. Tulsa, OK. March, 2000.

Peterson, Christopher. "The Future of Optimism." *American Psychologist* 55, no. 1 (2000) 44–55.

Plante, Thomas G., ed. *Religion, Spirituality, and Positive Psychology: Understanding the Psychological Fruits of Faith.* Santa Barbara, CA: Praeger, 2012.

Roberts, Benjamin T. *Pungent Truths: Being Extracts from the Writings of the Rev. Benjamin Titus Roberts Compiled and Edited by W. B. Rose.* Chicago: Free Methodist, 1912.

Rosmarin, David H., et al. "Grateful to God or Just Plain Grateful? A Comparison of Religious and General Gratitude." *The Journal of Positive Psychology* 6, no. 5 (2011) 389–96.

Sandage, Steven J., et al. "Seeking Forgiveness: Theoretical Context and an Initial Empirical Study." *Journal of Psychology and Theology* 28, no. 1 (2000) 21–35.

Seybold, Kevin S. *Explorations in Neuroscience, Psychology and Religion*. London: Ashgate, 2007.

Shorey, Hal S., et al. "Author's Response: Somewhere over the Rainbow: Hope Theory Weathers its First Decade." *Psychological Inquiry* 13, no. 4 (2002) 322–32.

Sisemore, Timothy A., et al. "Grace and Christian Psychology—Part I: Preliminary Measurement Relationships, and Implications for Practice." *Edification: The Transdisciplinary Journal of Christian Psychology* 4, no. 2 (2011) 57–63.

Snyder, Howard. Email to the author. August 1, 2014.

Spradlin, Jill D., et al. "Shame, Grace, and Spiritual Well-Being: Preliminary Findings." Graduate School of Clinical Psychology, George Fox University, 2011.

Tangney, June P. "Humility: Theoretical Perspectives, Empirical Findings and Directions for Future Research." *Journal of Social and Clinical Psychology* 19, no. 1 (2000) 70–82.

Tangney, June P., et al. "Forgiving the Self: Conceptual Issues and Empirical Findings." *Handbook of Forgiveness*, edited by Everett L. Worthington Jr., 143–58. Abingdon: Routledge, 2005.

Thompson, Laura Y., et al. "Dispositional Forgiveness of Self, Others, and Situations." *Journal of Personality* 73, no. 2 (2005) 313–59.

Toussaint, Loren L., and David R. Williams. "National Survey Results for Protestant, Catholic, and Nonreligious Experiences of Seeking Forgiveness and of Forgiveness of Self, of Others, and by God." *Journal of Psychology and Christianity* 27, no. 2 (2008) 120–30.

Watkins, Philip C., et al. "Gratitude and Happiness: Development of a Measure of Gratitude, and Relationships with Subjective Well-Being." *Social Behavior and Personality* 31, no. 5 (2003) 431–51.

Watson, Paul J., et al. "Grace and Christian Psychology—Part II: Psychometric Refinements and Relationships with Self-Compassion, Depression, Beliefs About Sin, and Religious Orientation." *Edification: The Transdisciplinary Journal of Christian Psychology* 4, no. 2 (2011) 64–72.

———. "Sin and Self-Functioning: I. Grace, Guilt, and Self-Consciousness." *Journal of Psychology and Theology* 16, no. 3 (1988) 254–69.

———. "Sin and Self-Functioning: II. Grace, Guilt, and Psychological Adjustment." *Journal of Psychology and Theology* 16, no. 3 (1988) 270–81.

Worthington, Everett L., Jr. *Handbook of Forgiveness*. Abingdon: Routledge, 2005.

———. "Helping Clinicians and Researchers Understand, Deepen, and Promote Humility." Presentation at the Christian Association for Psychological Studies International Conference. Pasadena, CA. March 10, 2016.

Wesley, John. "And Should It Be That I Should Gain." 1879. http://www.umcmission.org/Find-Resources/Global-Praise-/Charles-Wesley-Hymns/And-Can-It-Be-That-I-Should-Gain. Accessed March 23, 2017.

Worthington, Everett L., and Michael Scherer. "Forgiveness is an Emotion—Focused Coping Strategy that Can Reduce Health Risks and Promote Health Resilience: Theory, Review, and Hypotheses." *Psychology & Health* 19, no. 3 (2004) 385–405.

Zinnbauer, Brian J., and Kenneth I. Pargament. "Religiousness and Spirituality." *Handbook of the Psychology of Religion and Spirituality*, edited by Raymond F. Paloutzian and Crystal L. Park, 21–42. New York: Guilford, 2005.

10

Piety, Virtue, Industry, and Economy

The Habits of B. T. Roberts and Christian Nursing Education

—Susanne M. Mohnkern and Cheryl B. Crotser

In the mid-1860s, B. T. Roberts wrote that "a number of persons . . . desirous of doing all the good in their power, [undertook] to establish a school, in which all shall be done that can be done, to train up youth to habits of *piety, virtue, industry* and *economy*, while they are acquiring the elements of a sound education.[*italics added*]"[1] 150 years later, the school Roberts established has grown into two institutions, Roberts Wesleyan College and Northeastern Seminary, which together serve over 1,700 students and offer over sixty undergraduate, thirteen graduate (including one doctoral), and four degree-completion programs. The College mission declares a "commitment to historic Christianity and a desire to prepare thoughtful, spiritually mature, service-oriented people who will help transform society."[2] The nursing program, added in the 1950s, is deeply committed to this mission.

The chapter that follows is a systematic study of the relevance of B. T. Roberts's ideas of piety, virtue, industry, and economy to Christian nursing today, and more specifically to Christian nursing education at the school that Roberts founded. We start by defining these four concepts, and then proceed to a brief review of the nursing literature in which we find that the habits that Roberts calls "piety, virtue, industry, and economy" are essential

1. Roberts, "A School Project," 161.
2. Roberts Wesleyan College Mission Statement.

to the discipline of nursing today. We then present the methodology and design of our study discussing the results. For each of the four habits, we reflect on themes from our interviews with participants with regards to three questions: how they understand these habits in nursing practice, how they see them employed and inculcated through the nursing program at Roberts, and suggestions they have for how to further imbed these values in the nursing program going forward. We believe that this study provides significant insights into the nature of nursing today, deepens our understanding of the core habits of piety, virtue, industry, and economy, and stimulates thinking on how to strengthen Christian education for character not only in nursing, but across the disciplines.

Definitions of B. T. Roberts's "Habits"

First we will clarify the meaning of the four habits as used by B. T. Roberts, in the context of common usage in the 1860s.

- *Piety*—Stemming back to John Wesley's phrase, "all inward and outward holiness," piety refers to grounding one's life in God, using spiritual disciplines and pursuing ongoing sanctification. This grounding results in a godly life that seeks the best for all people and contributes to the general welfare.[3]

- *Virtue*—Virtue is "a particular moral excellence; a special manifestation of the influence of moral principles in life or conduct."[4] It is similar to today's usage of the word, "values," and is directly related to one's character.[5]

- *Industry*—Industry is a virtue including both study and diligence,[6] the opposite of idleness, as well as careful stewardship of time and other resources.[7]

- *Economy*—Economy is the careful management of resources to make them go as far as possible, orderly conduct and productiveness. It is closely related to industry,[8] involves not wasting resources or energy and means living simply but well.[9]

3. Snyder, email message to author.
4. *Oxford English Dictionary,* "Virtue."
5. Snyder, email message to author.
6. *Oxford English Dictionary,* "Industry."
7. Snyder, email message to author.
8. *Oxford English Dictionary,* "Economy."
9. Snyder, email message to author.

Piety, Virtue, Industry, and Economy in Nursing Literature

Christianity has been influential on the history of nursing. There are at least forty-one distinct healing works of Jesus in the New Testament,[10] with perhaps the most pointed of Jesus' teachings in this area being the story of the Good Samaritan (Luke 10:30–6). Nursing grew out of this Christian worldview that inspires loving service to others.[11] Phoebe, a deaconess in the early Christian church, started a tradition continued by followers of Jesus in monastic and religious orders of providing loving ministrations to the sick and injured.[12] Florence Nightingale, considered the founder of modern nursing, believed that as nurses care for the sick, they work with the temple of the Holy Spirit.

> "Nursing is an art: and if it is to be made an art, it requires an exclusive devotion as hard a preparation as any painter's or sculptor's work; for what is the having to do with dead canvas or dead marble, compared with having to do with the living body, the temple of God's spirit? It is one of the Fine Arts: I had almost said, the finest of Fine Arts."[13]

Sr. Mary Elizabeth O'Brien suggests that nurses meet God in the needs of patients—their whimpers, moans, nervous questions, and anger—and we should "[take] off our shoes" (stripping away whatever prevents us from experiencing the holy) because we are standing on holy ground.[14] Sometimes that ground becomes hot, dry, and rough as life's difficulties bear down on us, and it is at such times that the Christian nurse will seek *shalom* through Christ.[15] *Shalom*, a Hebrew word meaning "peace," in a Christian context means "a God-centered community that shares the hope of Jesus Christ, bringing health, welfare, friendship, and security."[16] These two tenets of Christian nursing, standing on holy ground when ministering to patients and living in *shalom*, are a modern instantiation of Roberts's concern with "piety."

---

10. Swartley, *Health*, 67–68.
11. Shelly and Miller, *Called*, 17–18.
12. O'Brien, *Spirituality*, 7–8.
13. Nightingale, *Una and the Lion*, 6.
14. O'Brien, *Spirituality*, 7.
15. Shelly, "Walking," 3.
16. Ibid.

Christian nurses see the Holy Spirit as a source of strength, peace, grace, renewal, and inspiration when providing spiritual care.[17] O'Brien shares how, after hurricane Katrina, nurses who felt hopeless and abandoned as they cared for hospitalized patients waiting for evacuation relied on their faith and Scriptures for sustenance.[18] In their major work, *Called to Care: A Christian Worldview for Nursing*, Shelly and Miller define Christian nursing as "a ministry of compassionate care for the whole person, in response to God's grace toward a sinful world, which aims to foster optimum health (shalom) and bring comfort in suffering and death for anyone in need."[19] Nurses provide spiritual care as a result of their understanding of God's grace, an understanding that comes from knowledge of and devotion, reverence and obedience to God.

Patient-centered care, an essential focus on the modern discipline of nursing, requires customization of care according to the patient's needs, values, and preferences.[20] True patient-centeredness demands whole-person care, and this includes spiritual care.[21] Murphy and Walker propose that being in tune with God through the indwelling of the Holy Spirit provides guidance for Christian nurses as they go beyond the diagnosis and treatment of physical illness to whole-person care.

A common theme in spiritual care is the emotional cost[22] to the nurse of being authentically present to the patient,[23] building a relationship, and "diving down deep."[24] The secular nursing literature echoes these thoughts in the work of Patricia Benner, one of the most well-known contemporary nurse scholars. Benner and colleagues write that nursing judgment is heavily contextualized and requires skills of involvement and "emotional labor."[25] These authors point out characteristics of nursing that relate to piety and virtue—providing contextualized care (which necessarily includes spiritual care) in difficult situations, and seeking the best for all people.

B. T. Roberts's next recommended habit, *virtue*, is a "particular moral excellence or character; a special manifestation of the influence of moral

---

17. Deal and Grassley, "Spiritual Care," 475; Murphy and Walker, "Spirit-Guided," 147; Shelly and Miller, *Called*, 259.

18. Ibid., 382.

19. Shelly and Miller, *Called*, 344

20. IOM, *Quality Chasm*, 6.

21. Deal and Grassley, "Spiritual Care," 472.

22. Ibid., 476.

23. O'Brien, *Standing*, 129.

24. Deal and Grassley, "Spiritual Care," 476.

25. Benner, *Expertise in Nursing*, 197.

principles in life or conduct."[26] Contemporary nursing is usually seen as a virtuous profession whose practitioners are noble, altruistic and caring.[27] In a 2013 Gallup poll, the American public rated nurses as having the highest standards of honesty and ethics of any profession for the fifteenth consecutive year.[28]

There is some concern, however, with the idea of nursing as a virtuous profession. Some hold that this "one-dimensional" understanding of nursing could prove unattractive to generations of professionals who have many career options.[29] This position seems to wrongly assume that if a profession is seen as virtuous, it cannot also be grounded in scientific knowledge and skill. The practice of virtue by nurses cannot be separated from the science of caring,[30] as such care involves contextualized, skillful use of knowledge.[31] Patricia Benner and colleagues have outlined three "apprenticeships" of nursing education: acquiring and using knowledge and science, using clinical reasoning and skilled know-how, and ethical comportment and formation.[32] Ethical comportment includes spiritual care and the virtues of compassion, honesty, courage, justice and altruism, as well as "demonstrating appropriate use of knowledge, skills of care and relations, and communication with patients and colleagues" [33]

The third and fourth habits mentioned by B. T. Roberts are *industry* and *economy*. The desire to make health care affordable and accessible in the twenty-first century has led to a special emphasis on these habits in nursing. Bogossian et al. describe the demanding workload and severe working conditions faced by nurses as "nursing at the 'coal-face.'"[34] A nurse who thrives in this trying environment must exhibit economy, wisely organizing the work and carefully using resources of time and materials. Articles about the economic and quality benefits of increased levels of nursing care,[35] cost control in nursing homes by means of economy of scale,[36] and doing the right

26. *Oxford English Dictionary*, "Virtue."
27. Price, "Choosing Nursing," 306.
28. Gallup, Inc. "Honesty/Ethics in Professions."
29. Price, "Choosing Nursing," 305.
30. Murphy and Walker, "Spirit-Guided," 146.
31. Benner, *Expertise in Nursing*, 316.
32. Benner, *Educating Nurses*, 26–28.
33. Ibid., 26.
34. Bogossain, "The Pure Hard Slog," 377.
35. Twigg, "The Economin Benefit," 2253–61; Aiken, "Hospital Nurse Staffing," 1987–93; and Aiken, "Educational Levels," 1617–23.
36. Hoess, "Cost Control," 45–63.

thing for less,[37] demonstrate that modern nurses must be acutely aware of their use of time, energy and physical resources.

Our Study and Its Methods

B. T. Roberts's ideas of piety, virtue, economy, and industry are not only addressed in the nursing literature, but they are foundational to the Christian approach to nursing that is the focus of the curriculum, the faculty, and many of the students in the School of Nursing at Roberts Wesleyan College. How precisely *do* current faculty, staff, and alumni understand the habits B. T. Roberts wanted to instill in young people? Does the current curriculum foster these habits? What could be done to improve the nursing curriculum and co-curriculum in these areas? To answer these questions, nursing alumni, faculty, and staff from the School of Nursing at Roberts Wesleyan College were interviewed as part of a descriptive, qualitative study. This study was designed to determine the current influence on nursing education of Roberts's ideas and strategies for strengthening piety, virtue, industry, and economy in our nursing programs going forward.[38]

Qualitative, descriptive methodology[39] was used to produce a "comprehensive summary of events in the everyday terms of those events."[40] Using a semi-structured interview process, respondents were asked to reflect on the importance to nursing of the habits of piety, virtue, industry and economy. Participants were identified via purposive and snowball sampling, with interviews taking place at a time and place convenient to the respondents, usually in the researcher's private office in an academic setting. As part of the recruitment efforts, prospective participants were given definitions of the four habits being examined. After obtaining informed consent, interviews were audio-recorded to promote accurate analysis of data. The interview schedule shaped the conversation and the researcher followed up with probing and clarifying questions. Participants were given ample time to form their thoughts and to deeply explore their own understanding of the four habits and how they relate to their experiences.

Emergent design, which allows methods to develop and "[emerge] during the course of the data collection" and analysis,[41] was employed

37. Tonges, "Quality with Economy," 205–11.

38. The concrete, practicable suggestions for curricular changes have been included in this chapter, while some more general responses have not been.

39. Brown, *Evidence-Based Nursing*, 43; Sandelowski, "Qualitative Description," 335.

40 Ibid., 334.

41. Polit and Beck, *Nursing Research*, 59.

within descriptive qualitative methodology. Interviews were transcribed by the researcher, then analyzed within the context and structure of the interview schedule. A second researcher with experience in qualitative methodology analyzed the interviews and provided additional perspectives and confirmation of emerging themes. An iterative process was used as data were reduced, and themes were identified as they emerged. In all, seven interviews took place. Three faculty, one staff person, and three recent nursing alumni participated. As part of the data-reduction process, member checks were completed with all respondents confirming the identified themes.

Findings

All those interviewed agreed that habits of piety, virtue, industry and economy remain as pertinent, essential, and integral components in Christian nursing and nursing education. It was immediately evident in each interview that the respondents identified with the defined habits as part of their current experience. The findings related to each of the four habits are described and explicated in the following sections.

Piety

> "I always have a sense of a higher calling . . . you see past the difficulties that our patients present . . . you need to realize these people are in a lot of pain."
>
> —*respondent*

Participants talked with ease about the characteristics and behaviors of the Christian nurse exemplifying piety. The concept of caring and all of its components are at the core of piety in nursing for these respondents. These components include compassion, authentic presence, altruism, kindness, empathy, developing helping-trusting relationships, teaching and learning that address individual needs, love, sharing, stress alleviation, and surveillance.[42] Respondents see themselves as providing whole-person care as a result of their calling to serve others as a nurse. When reflecting on what piety in nursing meant, participants described it as being a "servant of the most high God," as having a "higher calling," and as practicing "servant leadership." Whole-person care for these respondents involves assisting with physical, emotional, social, and spiritual needs of the care recipient in the context of family or significant others.

---

42. Leininger, "Overview of Leininger's Theory"; Watson Caring Science Institute, "Core Concepts."

Whole-person care emphasizes identifying, not ignoring, spiritual distress and intervening appropriately by building a trusting relationship with even the most difficult patients. Nurses, relying on their spiritual grounding, share their experiences and make themselves available to struggling patients. One participant stated, "You have no idea . . . what you are going to face, like the patient who is trying to bite everybody. Those are my specialty. We go in and we talk and we cry together and I ask, 'Are you hurting?', and they say 'Yes!'" This nurse's way of intervening is grounded in an empathy and humility that issue from her Christian piety. As one respondent said, "There's something in their spirit that makes them treat you the way they do, and it brings up the whole different type of perspective and it also teaches you how to love people in a different way."

The Christian nurse sees beyond the hectic inpatient environment and the current crisis to empathize with a fearful patient in spiritual, physical, and emotional pain. During limited encounters, using an altruistic approach, the nurse identifies what is best for the patient and provides a calming, Christ-like presence. Physical care delivered with a positive, uplifting spirit and compassionate sharing of needed information soothes fears and helps the patient and family face their future—whether it be surgery, difficult days of recovery, and/or care transitions such as a discharge to home.

Motivated by a desire to be like Christ, Christian nurses exhibit piety by investing in others' lives, establishing caring relationships with those who start out as strangers. One respondent believes that finding something in common with the patient and using an empathetic approach is a sure way to discover opportunities to "pour Christ's love" into the patient. Another respondent characterizes her approach as being "God's hands and feet here on earth."

The piety of Christian nurses leads them to treat others—patients, families, and co-workers—with kindness. Seeing beyond the negativity, aggression, or difficult behaviors in others puts Christian nurses on a different trajectory, which is sometimes misunderstood by those around them. One respondent was told by a co-worker, "You're so nice to everyone. You say 'please' and 'thank you' and you always ask people, 'Are you too busy to help me?'" Being set apart and behaving differently are explored more in the section on virtue below.

Piety and the Roberts Wesleyan College Nursing Program

Respondents from the nursing faculty found that they were able to "do and say what God wants" at the college. This freedom allows them to integrate their faith into their professional role and connects them more deeply to colleagues and students. Faculty members emphasize that that their goal is not to indoctrinate, but to develop students as whole persons by intentionally showing the relevance of faith to the subject matter of their classes. Sharing their worldview and applying their Christianity in all they do (e.g., class preparation, grading, and communicating with students) enables faculty to plant seeds of Christian faith so that "God can grow them."

Nursing faculty who live their faith inside and outside of the classroom are role models for students. One alumna respondent stated, "Teachers are examples of who Jesus wants us to be." There is a distinctive connection between students and faculty members that draws students into conversations about what it means to care, love, and display the fruits of the Spirit. In and out of the classroom, in co-curricular events like service projects and ministry opportunities, and in informal gatherings, faculty invest in students' lives by coming alongside them in love. One alumna put it this way: "RWC presents Christ to students in so many ways . . . It's there for you to see all the way through." The alumni respondents found that the sincere prayers offered by faculty for students drew them into spiritual disciplines and Bible study. Faculty use encouragement forums in the course management system, reflective journaling, simulation, and roleplays to address the wholistic needs of the students. Alumni interviewed particularly cited simulation and roleplay as effective in helping them to practice communication and build their confidence in addressing some of the more difficult spiritual issues with patients.

When respondents were asked what more could be done in the Roberts Wesleyan College nursing curriculum to help develop habits of piety, they suggested:

- increased use of simulation, with a focus on a debriefing process in which the learner can reflect and think critically about actions taken
- making sure there is room for rest and balance in the program
- having an intentional, program-wide structure for faith-integration
- adding junior-level interprofessional education (IPE) simulation to prepare students for the major IPE simulation in the senior year
- providing a course on Christian spiritual care that biblically explores themes such as how to deal with unanswered prayers for healing
- giving students the chance to do physical hygiene care in clinical to "open a place to talk"
- having seasoned graduates return to the classroom to address the difficult realities of in-patient care
- focusing clinical experiences more on the development of communication skills with difficult patients

Virtue

> "I came out of college with a philosophy, with an idea of what I wanted to make nursing to be and every day I go to work, I try to maintain that."
>
> —*respondent*

Virtue is seen by the respondents to include integrity, honesty, respect and right treatment of others, dependability, courage, authenticity, and being open and transparent. These qualities are deemed essential and non-negotiable. Nursing faculty mentioned academic integrity as a precursor to having integrity in nursing practice. One respondent views virtuous behavior to include "no short cuts, not half-hearted . . . no option for cheating." Seen as part of professional behavior, virtue prepares students to practice independently as professionals. Although it is not unique to Christian nursing, virtue is "inherent in our ways."

Respondents clearly articulated the importance of having courage to go against the prevailing culture of the patient-care arena by taking time to be authentically present for vulnerable patients and their family members, who are seen as integral to the patient care milieu created by the nurse. What our respondents saw as "being there" for patients sometimes engendered criticism from co-workers, who saw them as spending *too much* time with patients. Respondents are willing to disregard such criticism when they perceive that they need to spend extra time (e.g., thirty minutes) talking with, listening to and/or teaching patients and family members. One commented, "We're just going to agree to disagree on that," because the patient is the priority. Participants also communicate the importance of vigilance and advocacy, which require "keeping an eye on what is important" and speaking up if something is not right.

Alumni consistently discussed being set apart, behaving differently from colleagues. One alumna stated,

> Maybe I'm just an anomaly . . . but there are days that I feel very different and removed in the way I approach situations, different from how some of my nurse colleagues approach it. Sometimes their remarks kind of rub me the wrong way because that's not how I would address it or sometimes they ignore things that a patient has said . . . I would want to sit down and say, "Hey, . . . what's your concern?" . . . I don't know how to say this because it's something I struggle with . . . I feel like I care a bit differently . . . more compassionate not just toward my patients but [also] the people I work with.

This new nurse realizes that sometimes the patient is not getting the best of care from co-workers, has found the courage to remain true to her own standards, but struggles with what she sometimes observes.

Participants communicated the related need to avoid the incivility and bitterness that unfortunately arise in the difficult situations common in health care workplaces. Respondents see nursing as "hard," and mention that it is emotionally risky to "put yourself out there." At times, authentic caring must be maintained in the face of patient indifference. Respondents have an intrinsic drive to develop civility, kindness, and perseverance in the face of such challenges.

Respondents felt that integrity involved keeping themselves educated as new or unfamiliar treatments or problems arose, and having the honesty and courage to admit mistakes. Recognizing that nurses are human and the fast pace of acute care can create possibilities for error, immediately reporting, for example, a medication error, is essential to virtuous nursing practice. In the same vein, these respondents highlighted trustworthiness and dependability ("doing what you say you're going to do") as key habits of a Christian nurse.

The final virtue discussed by respondents involves ensuring that meaningful human interaction is the focus of care, that technology doesn't become an unnecessary barrier between the nurse and the patient. Computers-on-wheels, for instance, can form a physical barrier between nurse and patient and can, along with other monitor screens in the room, attract the eye contact of the nurse over eye contact with the patient. Giving the verbal and non-verbal message that they are "there for the patient," listening carefully, and responding to the assessed needs are important ways of responding to this problem.

Virtue and the Roberts Wesleyan College Nursing Program

Alumni respondents were quick to identify nursing faculty as examples of ethical practice marked by virtue. Stories told by teachers create a place for students to develop their moral imaginations, and as faculty share mistakes they have made in the past, students can see that their professors "survived" and went on to be good nurses and nurse-educators. Such faculty stories give the students a way to deal with their anxiety about possibly committing an error in the future, and a model of how to proceed should an error occur. In addition, nursing faculty are seen as modeling excellence in grading and providing feedback, interacting with students, keeping abreast of developments in nursing, and being energetic about their teaching roles.

Respondents noted that integrity is addressed in every syllabus and taught as essential to certain nursing skills—such as the six to ten rights associated with medication-administration. Clinical experiences are particularly good opportunities for student nurses to practice performing each task with integrity. Integrity is connected to honesty, and as such the support of faculty when students make mistakes encourages them to disclose any errors they might make and to grow through the process.

Debates used as a teaching strategy helped students clarify their own values, examine their prejudices, and learn how to respond in a non-judgmental manner. Participants believed that student diversity helped them understand different perspectives. Also, since faculty encourage inquisitiveness, the school is seen as a good and safe place to ask hard questions. Alumni respondents remember examining case studies about caring for vulnerable populations, hearing from consumers of mental health care, and writing guided reflections in their clinical journals. Each of these experiences helped respondents develop the virtue of empathy.

Suggested curricular changes to increase the development of virtue in the Roberts Wesleyan College student nurse included:

- sharing of more nursing faculty stories that make it clear that faculty are fellow-journeyers
- assuring that faculty members are currently practicing
- forming an alumni mentoring group
- using simulation of extremely difficult situations (with experienced alumni present) and discussing errors made by students as part of the "safe" debriefing conversation
- creating a separate ongoing reflective journal that is maintained across all clinical settings in which students reflect on difficult or emotional situations in clinical practice

Industry and Economy

" . . . someone is paying for all this!"

—*respondent*

The habits of *industry* and *economy* recalled the concept of *stewardship* for respondents, and they saw stewardship as using God-given gifts and resources (including nursing skills) fully and wisely. One faculty respondent emphasized that professors should exercise excellence in advising so that students could satisfy nursing degree requirements as efficiently as possible. Most students have limited resources, so faculty must carefully plan the sequencing of courses. A faculty advisor should also facilitate student transfer into Roberts from a community college, since that is a cost-saving choice for a significant portion of students. A staff respondent highlighted the innately economical non-traditional program delivery method that supplements one night a week with web-supported activities, helping working adults to get a degree in a "fiscally responsible way." It can be noted that fully online education is also economical in this way.

As alumni moved into their practice roles, they learned to be careful with supplies provided to the patient at discharge. There is a delicate balance between providing what patients need for a successful transfer to home and not being wasteful of resources. As in-patient health care providers, these nurses clearly understood that a failed discharge would result in a readmission costing their facilities tens of thousands of dollars in lost reimbursement from third-party payers. It is much more economical to orchestrate a good discharge by providing all necessary supplies than to shortchange this opportunity and perhaps sabotage the transition in care.

Alumni respondents said that careful time management and a strong work ethic helped them prioritize their work, organize themselves, and accomplish tasks early whenever possible. They believe that being resourceful and organized at work creates time for them to get to know their patients. In this way, industry and economy relate to piety and virtue in nursing practice. Respondents talked about being energetic, not sitting too much, and helping out even if the one in need is not their patient. Again, this approach brought notice from co-workers who suggested that they should not be so industrious and should let someone else—perhaps the unlicensed assistive person or technician—do the work. In this way lessons learned at school about how to approach work open doors for discussions with coworkers during which alumni can share their perspectives on nursing practice.

Alumni respondents often mentioned the importance of seeing the big picture and keeping the "end in view." One respondent reflected on changing her major after sensing a call to be a nurse, how that call set her "on fire" to "see it happen" even though she knew that the pre-nursing science requirements would be a struggle. Another participant reflected on perspective by recounting how she shared an intravenous pump (an important resource) with the emergency room, which was having a much busier day than her unit. She was chastised by a co-worker, who instructed her to never share equipment. Her response, "We are in the same hospital!", illustrates the larger perspective that she holds regarding her work.

In-patient care calls for awareness of the environmental and budgetary impact of health care decisions. Student clinical practice involved charging supplies to a budget as they were used. With faculty guidance, students learned to avoid being wasteful, carefully thinking through the supplies needed to complete a procedure so as not to be wasteful. One respondent related how a recycling program on four in-patient units in her hospital saved $12,000 in one year, in addition to decreasing the demand for natural resources.

Industry and Economy and the Roberts Wesleyan College Nursing Program

Faculty believed that the rigor of the nursing program curriculum requires diligence in study and good stewardship of time (including making time for sleep). Alumni respondents added that they had to defer gratification (i.e., parties, fun) to get their course work completed. Students learned that being idle was not an option as they found their way through the multiple assignments, exams, laboratory and clinical experiences required. Alumni also found that challenging projects with strict deadlines led to industrious habits and that faculty members were available to step in and help should the student be struggling. They also mentioned that classmates "watched out for each other" and encouraged a good balance between work and rest.

Students at Roberts also report acquiring the teamwork skills that are essential for industry and economy in the workplace. Alumni respondents felt that diversity in the student body helped them learn to work well with people different from themselves, and faculty found that service projects with marginalized or vulnerable populations helped students understand the richness of their available resources. Students came to understand wastefulness in a different way as these experiences broadened their perspectives.

Suggested curricular changes to increase the habits of industry and economy in the Roberts graduate included:
- using simulation to train students to integrate care as opposed to focusing on one task at a time
- using clinical-setting learning activities such as:
    - pre-brief opportunities to increase understanding of workflow on a particular unit
    - having students create their own clinical worksheet to learn how to organize their time more efficiently
    - unfolding case studies to help students envision themselves dealing with complex situations
- creating more test questions that involve "all that apply" versus "choose the best answer," as these are more realistic

Discussion

Nurses can encounter moral distress when they find themselves "participating in perceived moral wrongdoing" due to the high-stakes pressures of the job.[43] The ability to cope with moral distress is captured in the virtue of resilience. Resilience is defined as "the ability to adapt coping strategies to minimize distress"[44] or "to bounce back [and] cope successfully despite adverse circumstances."[45] External resilience involves problem-solving skills and engaging in a variety of activities outside of work. Internal resilience includes meeting spiritual needs such as hope, meaning and purpose in life and the sense of the value of life even under difficult circumstances.[46] There is an obvious connection between internal resilience and spiritual health or maturity,[47] making an even stronger case for increased intentionality in spiritual development of students in Christian nursing programs.

Another risk of nursing practice is compassion fatigue, "the physical, emotional, and spiritual result of chronic self-sacrifice and/or prolonged exposure to difficult situations that renders a person unable to love, nurture, care for, or empathize with another's suffering."[48] Wende recognized that "[nurses] perform a number of concrete functions, but the essential product they deliver is themselves."[49] The virtue of "caring for self" is essential to a long and productive nursing career, as are interventions such as "time outs," journaling, and collective grief-sharing.

Conclusion

B.T. Roberts's vision for Christian education was that "all shall be done that can be done to train up youth to habits of piety, virtue, industry, and economy."[50] We sought to understand the degree to which that vision guides the nursing program at the school Roberts founded, some 150 years later. We discovered that our respondents had insightful reflections on the nature of these habits, could relate them to their experiences in the program and in professional practice, and had useful suggestions on how to further ingrain

---

43. Rushton, "Burnout and Resilience," 413.
44. Ibid, 413.
45. Hart, "Resilience in Nurses," 7–20.
46. Rushton, "Burnout and Resilience," 413.
47. Shelly and Miller, *Called*, 96.
48. Harris and Griffin, "Nursing on Empty," 82.
49. Joinson, "Coping," 116–17.
50. Roberts, "A School Project," 161.

these habits in our students going forward. The experiences and stories shared by the participants in this research clearly chronicle the embodiment of the habits in question as the nurse educators, administrative staff, and practicing nurses associated with today's Roberts Wesleyan College fulfill their vocation.

Christianity has a long history of and deep resources for effective patient-centered, whole-person care. Christian piety means "taking off our shoes," standing on holy ground as we minister to patients, and providing spiritual care that issues from our own experience of God's grace. Our participants articulated many habits crucial to nursing practice and education, including wise self-care, counter-cultural courage, civility and relationship-building, excellent mentoring and advising, perspective and perseverance, budget- and environmental-consciousness, and integrity—which to them means continuing education, admitting errors, and being honest, trustworthy, and dependable.

Respondents see Christian nursing education at Roberts as exemplifying core values related to piety, virtue, industry, and economy such as wisdom, respect, spiritual discipline, prayer, vulnerability, humility, honesty, courage, tolerance, inquisitiveness, empathy, community, mutual accountability, and teamwork. They have recommended eighteen initiatives for improving the nursing curriculum and co-curriculum. These include creative and advanced use of simulation and case studies, ongoing journaling focused difficult situations in clinical practice, more involvement of experienced alumni in contextual education, an intentional program-wide structure for faith-integration, more intentional sharing of faculty experiences, making sure that faculty are currently practicing, a course in the biblical foundations of spiritual care, and more clinical experiences focused on developing communication skills with patients and families.

Preparing nurses who have well-developed habits of piety, virtue, industry, and economy should continue to be a priority in Christian nursing education. Since health care, patient needs and characteristics, and the nurses entering practice are constantly changing, the challenge for Christian nurse educators is to remain relevant and to provide pertinent learning opportunities and coaching situations for students at all levels, so that we can continue being, in one participant's words, "God's hands and feet here on earth."

Bibliography

Aiken, Linda H., et al. "Educational Levels of Hospital Nurses and Surgical Patient Mortality." *Journal of the American Medical Association* 290, no. 12 (2003) 1617–23.

———. "Hospital Nurse Staffing and Patient Mortality, Nurse Burnout and Job Dissatisfaction." *Journal of the American Medical Association* 288, no. 16 (2002) 1987–93.

American Nurses Association. *Code of Ethics for Nurses with Interpretive Statements.* 2015 ed. http://www.nursingworld.org/MainMenuCategories/EthicsStandards/CodeofEthicsforNurses/Code-of-Ethics-For-Nurses.html. Accessed March 23, 2017.

Begley, Ann M. "A Virtue-Based Exploration of a Dilemma in Practice." *International Journal of Nursing Practice* 14 (2008) 336–41.

Benner, Patricia, et al. *Educating Nurses: A Call for Radical Transformation.* San Francisco, CA: Jossey Bass, 2010.

Benner Patricia, et al. *Expertise in Nursing Practice: Caring, Clinical Judgment, and Ethics.* New York: Springer, 2009.

Bogassian, Fiona, et al. "'The Pure Hard Slog that Nursing is . . .': A Qualitative Analysis of Nursing Work." *Journal of Nursing Scholarship* 46, no. 5 (2014) 377–88.

Brown, Sarah J. *Evidence-Based Nursing: The Research-Practice Connection.* Burlington, MA: Jones & Bartlett, 2014.

Bureau of Labor Statistics, U.S. Department of Labor. "The Economics Daily: Largest Industries by State, 1990–2013." Bureau of Labor Statistics. July 28, 2014. http://www.bls.gov/opub/ted/2014/ted_20140728.htm. Accessed March 23, 2017.

Deal, Belinda, and Jane S. Grassley. "The Lived Experience of Giving Spiritual Care: A Phenomenological Study of Nephrology Nurses Working in Acute and Chronic Hemodialysis Settings." *Nephrology Nursing Journal* 39, no. 6 (2012) 471–81.

Gallup, Inc. "Honesty/Ethics in Professions." Last modified December 26, 2015. http://www.gallup.com/poll/1654/honesty-ethics-professions.aspx. Accessed March 23, 2017.

Harris, Chelsia, and Mary T. Griffin. "Nursing on Empty: Compassion Fatigue Signs, Symptoms, and System Interventions." *Journal of Christian Nursing* 32, no. 2 (2015) 807.

Hart, Patricia L., et al. "Resilience in Nurses: An Integrative Review." *Journal of Nursing Management* 22, no. 6 (2014) 720–34.

Hoess, Victoria, et al. "Cost Control in Nursing Homes by Means of Economies of Scale and Care Profile Optimization." *Nursing Economics* 27, no. 1 (2009) 45–63.

Institute of Medicine. *Crossing the Quality Chasm.* Washington, DC: National Academy, 2001.

Joinson, Carla. "Coping with Compassion Fatigue." *Nursing 92*, no. 4 (1992) 116–21.

Kangasniemi, Mari, et al. "Professional Ethics in Nursing: An Integrative Review." *Journal of Advanced Nursing* 71, no. 8 (2015) 1744–57.

Kavey, Rae-Ellen. "Health Care Professionals." In *Leadership Commitments to Improve Value in Healthcare: Finding Common Ground: Workshop Summary.* Washington, DC: National Academies, 2009. http://www.ncbi.nlm.nih.gov/books/NBK52843/. Accessed March 23, 2017.

Leininger, Madeleine. "Overview of Leininger's Theory of Culture Care Diversity and Universality." Last modified 2008. http://www.madeleine-leininger.com/cc/overview.pdf. Accessed March 23, 2017.

Murphy, Lyn S., and Mark S. Walker. "Spirit-Guided Care: Christian Nursing for the Whole Person". *Journal of Christian Nursing* 30, no. 3 (2014) 1441–52.

Nightingale, Florence. *Una and the lion*. Cambridge: Riverside, 1871. https://archive.org/stream/unaandlionoonighgoog#page/n9/mode/2up. Accessed March 23, 2017.

O'Brien, Mary E. *Spirituality in Nursing: Standing on Holy Ground*. Sudbury, MA: Jones & Bartlett, 2011.

Polit, Denise F., and Cheryl T. Beck. *Essentials of Nursing Research*. New York: Lippincott Williams & Wilkins, 2006.

Price, Sherry. L., et al. "Choosing Nursing as a Career: A Narrative Analysis of Millennial Nurses' Career Choice of Virtue". *Nursing Inquiry* 20, no.4 (2013) 305–16.

Roberts, B. T. "A School Project." *The Earnest Christian* (May 1866) 160–61.

Roberts Wesleyan College Mission Statement. https://www.roberts.edu/about/what-we-believe.aspx. March 23, 2017.

Rushton, Cynda H., et al. "Burnout and Resilience Among Nurses Practicing in High-Intensity Settings." *American Journal of Critical Care* 24, no. 5 (2015) 412–20.

Sandelowski, Margarete. "Whatever Happened to Qualitative Description?" *Research in Nursing & Health* 23 (2000) 334–40.

Shelly, Judith A. "Walking on Holy Ground". *Journal of Christian Nursing* 20, no. 3 (2003) 3.

Shelly, Judith A. and Arlene B. Miller. *Called to Care: A Christian Worldview for Nursing*. 2nd ed. Downers Grove, IL: Intervarsity, 2006.

Snyder, Howard A. Email message to the author. September 14, 2014.

Snyder, Howard A. *Populist Saints: B. T. and Ellen Roberts and the First Free Methodists*. Grand Rapids: Eerdmanns, 2006.

Swartely, William M. *Health, Healing and the Church's Mission: Biblical Perspectives and Moral Priorities*. Downers Grove, IL: Intervarsity, 2012.

Tourangeau, Ann E., et al. "Impact of Hospital Nursing Care on 30-day Mortality for Acute Medical Patients." *Journal of Advanced Nursing* 57, no. 1 (2007) 32–44.

Tonges, Mary Crabtree. "Quality with Economy: Doing the Right Things for Less." *Nursing Economics* 3 (1985) 205–11.

Twigg, Diane E., et al. "The Economic Benefits of Increased Levels of Nursing Care in the Hospital Setting." *Journal of Advanced Nursing* 69, no. 10 (2013) 2253–61.

Watson Caring Science Institute. "Core Concepts of Jean Watson's Theory of Human Caring/Caring Science." Compiled by A.L. Wagner. 2010. https://www.watsoncaringscience.org/files/Cohort%206/watsons-theory-of-human-caring-core-concepts-and-evolution-to-caritas-processes-handout.pdf. Accessed March 23, 2017.

11

Faithful Engagement

The Role of Spirituality and Religion in Social Policy Practice

—Lori M. Sousa

Introduction

In the social work profession, there is a renewed emphasis on the importance of integrating knowledge about religion and spirituality (RS) into practice, research, and education.[1] Most of the literature about religious and spiritual integration in social work, however, centers on some aspect of direct practice. The role of RS in policy practice has received little attention.[2] With regards to the neglect of RS in policy practice, scholars have argued that there needs to be a stronger infusion of social science theory to examine this phenomenon.[3] The lack of literature on the role of RS in social policy practice is surprising, given that social policies reflect societal values, and religious and spiritual beliefs often inform these values. Yet, with the increasing secularization of academic disciplines, the professionalization of social work, and a desire to keep church and state separate (in the United States), it is apparent that the role of RS has been overlooked in social policy analysis.

1. See Canda, "The Future," 97–180; Canda and Furman, *Spiritual Diversity*, 9–10; Derozotes, *Spiritually Orientated*, 1; Hodge and Bushfield, "Developing Spiritual Competency in Practice," 101–27.

2. See Canda, "The Future," 97–180; Evans, "Influencing," 26–37; Holt-Oliver, "Integrating Faith," 130–44; Hutchison, "Spirituality, Religion," 105–27; Sheridan, "Introduction," 1–8; Staral, "Observational," 4–14; Thomas, "Living Critically," 240–62; Wald et al., "Making Sense," 121–43.

3. Wald et al., "Making Sense," 121–43.

There are two major impasses faced by policy practitioners who desire to integrate knowledge about spirituality into practice. First, in social work academic settings where evidence-based practice is standard, integrating practices and *ways of knowing* that are unique to spirituality can pose a significant challenge to traditional academic paradigms. Vokey posits that spiritual knowledge, if it is to be fully appreciated, must have room to be explored in western academic cultures traditionally dominated by *mechanistic* or scientific ways of knowing.[4]

Second, because the literature and empirical research on the integration of RS in policy practice has been scant, practitioners often have difficulty conceptualizing and operationalizing a useful model of integration. Despite these challenges, Crowley and Derezortes encourage the persistent inquiry into this realm:

> Seeking elusive data about spiritual dimensions and non-ordinary states of consciousness will undoubtedly require non-ordinary research measures. Social work educators and researchers need to be resolute in remembering that rationality is not more scientific than intuition; it is simply more accurate when measurable information is available. Those who do research on higher states of consciousness must resist intimidation by those who would denigrate intuition, naturalistic data, or qualitative phenomenological research as ways of knowing.[5]

Despite the dominance of mechanistic ways of knowing in academic settings and the difficulty of conceptualizing spiritual phenomenology, the renewed emphasis on the importance of integrating knowledge about RS into practice warrants a critical inquiry into this area.

Central Question and Purpose of Study

The purpose of this study is to examine the process of integrating RS in social policy practice. For this study, *religious and spiritual integration* is defined as the process by which individual policy practitioners utilize religious and/or spiritual experiences, beliefs, practices, and values to inform their engagement in social policy practice. *Social policy practice* is defined as, "efforts to change policies in legislative, agency, and community settings, whether by establishing new policies, improving existing ones, or defeating

---

4. Vokey, "Spirituality," 97–120.
5. Crowley and Derezotes, "Transpersonal," 38.

the policy initiatives of other people."[6] Therefore, this study explores the religious and spiritual experiences, beliefs, practices and values of policy practitioners (those who engage in social policy practice) and the process by which RS informs their social policy practice. This study is designed to answer the following central question: *What is the process by which policy practitioners utilize religious and spiritual experiences, beliefs, practices and values to inform policy practice activities?*

Literature Review

With regards to religious and spiritual integration in social work, Furman et al. found a positive correlation between social workers who received training on religious and spiritual integration and their utilization of RS in practice.[7] When examining social workers' attitudes toward RS, these authors found that Christian social workers held positive attitudes about integrating RS in practice and education. However, half of those surveyed in the Furman study believed that social workers did not have the necessary skills to work with clients on spiritual or religious issues.[8] In addition, seventy-three percent of social workers surveyed believed that social workers should become more knowledgeable about spiritual matters.[9] When comparing social workers who had received training on spiritual integration with social workers who had not, those who had not received training were not as comfortable raising the topic of RS with clients. Furman and his colleagues also found that social workers who had not received spiritual integration training were not as likely to utilize RS in practice as social workers who had received training.[10]

The study conducted by Furman et al. focused on spiritual integration by social workers in direct practice; however, their findings underscore the significance of education on RS in practice for all social workers. Given the lack of literature on the role of RS in social policy practice, one must question what resources and models are being used to instruct future social workers. This writer argues that serious attention must be given to the process of spiritual integration in social policy practice. This is critical, considering the Council on Social Work Education's (CSWE) insistence that social

---

6. Jansson, *Effective Policy*, 14.
7. Furman et al., "Christian Social Workers," 175–97.
8. Ibid., 196
9. Ibid.
10. Ibid.

workers "understand religion and spirituality to develop a wholistic view of the person in environment."¹¹

The Origins of the Issue

The absence of RS in academic disciplines is not peculiar to social work. When one considers the role of RS in social policy practice, it becomes clear that there has been a historic neglect of this topic in other disciplines as well. Wald et al. note that, until recently, even though religion has been a constant in human society, there has been scant attention given to this area by political scientists.[12] In fact, these scholars point out that until about fifty years ago, religion was considered to be epiphenomenal and in opposition to modernization and effective development. These views of religion began to change as historical events such as the Islamic Revolution in the late 1970s and the rise of the New Christian Right began to garner scholarly attention. As powerful, religiously-motivated activism emerged, scholars were ill-prepared to make sense of these movements. Political science and related disciplines lacked appropriate paradigms and theories for understanding religiously-motivated social movements. They tended to portray such activity as "irrational, dangerous, and socially marginal."[13] The emergence of religiously-motivated mass movements in the 1970s and 1980s coincided with an alternative approach to mass politics that was emerging based on European traditions of social theory. This approach known as *Social Movement Theory (SMT)*, examined mass movements by legitimizing political participants and attempting to assess the reasons for their motives. SMT examined social movements by trying to understand the motives, means, and opportunities of the participants.[14] As SMT began to gain popularity, the central questions posed by SMT began to open the door to understand, rather than pathologize, the influence of religion in social policy.[15]

Similar to other academic disciplines, the role of RS has had a complex and nuanced history in social work. Canda suggests that the relationship of social work with RS in the United States has moved through three broad and overlapping phases and that we are now in the midst of the fourth phase, characterized by *transcending boundaries*.[16] According to Canda, the

11. Council on Social Work Education, *Religion and Spirituality Clearinghouse*.
12. Wald et al., "Making Sense," 121–43.
13. Ibid., 123.
14. Ibid., 121–43
15. Ibid.
16. Canda, "The Future," 97–180.

following are some of the trends of this fourth phase: an increase in the rate of research and publication on the relationship between social work, spirituality, and religion; the formulation of frameworks for spiritually sensitive practice; and curriculum guidelines, courses, and textbooks about spirituality being widely established.[17] Canda marks the beginning of the fourth phase in the mid-1990s, when a change in the CSWE guidelines returned attention to belief systems, religion, and spirituality. The amended CSWE guidelines state the following:

> Given the pervasiveness of religion and spirituality throughout people's lives and cultures, social workers need to understand religion and spirituality to develop a wholistic view of the person in environment and to support the professional mission of promoting satisfaction of basic needs, well-being, and justice for all individuals and communities around the world.[18]

Despite the recognition of the importance of faith integration in all areas of social work, research on spiritual integration with policy practice has been neglected.[19]

Sheridan conducted a search of social work abstracts and found that there were 2,137 publications that focused on spirituality, religion, or faith. Of these publications, the vast majority focused on some aspect of direct practice.[20] There were sixty-one articles that focused on practice related to larger client systems, and only five articles that addressed some aspect of spirituality or religion and policy development or legislative advocacy.[21] Since that date, four additional articles that examine spirituality and religion in policy practice have been published in social work journals.[22] Six of the articles are theoretical, two are commentaries, and only one is a research article. These nine articles serve as a basis for understanding how religion, spirituality, and policy practice are portrayed in social work literature.

17. Ibid., 100.

18. Council on Social Work Education, *Religion and Spirituality Clearinghouse*.

19. See Canda, "The Future," 97–180; Evans, "Influencing," 26–37; Holt-Oliver, "Integrating Faith," 130–44; Hutchison, "Spirituality, Religion," 105–27; Sheridan, "Introduction," 1–8; Staral, "Observational," 4–14; Thomas, "Living Critically," 240–62; Wald et al., "Making Sense," 121–43.

20. Sheridan, "Introduction," 1–8.

21. See Evans, "Influencing," 26–37; Holt-Oliver, "Integrating Faith," 130–44; Marx and Hooper, "Faith-Based," 280–82; Straal, "Observational," 4–14; Thomas, "Living Critically," 240–62;

22. See Campbell, "Explosion," 34–43; Hutchison, "Spirituality, Religion," 105–27; Sheridan, "Introduction," 1–8; Sheridan, "Spiritual Activism," 193–208.

Methodology, Approach, and Philosophical Assumptions

The methodology used for this study is based on the philosophical assumptions of *critical theory* and the methodological approach of *grounded theory*. To understand the process of religious and spiritual integration in social policy practice, the researcher utilized dialogic methods to foster conversation and reflection while interviewing social policy practitioners who self-identified that RS plays a significant role in their practice. The focus of the interviews was on understanding the central question—*What is the process by which policy practitioners utilize religious and spiritual experiences, beliefs, practices and values to inform policy practice activities?*

Use of Critical Theory

It is generally accepted that values inform social policies; however, in a culture that seeks to keep religion and policy separate, secularly influenced values are esteemed in the policy arena while religiously and spiritually inspired values are disparaged. One could argue that the cultural paradigm of separation of church and state has contributed to the marginalization of the role of RS in policy practice in the United States. Additionally, spirituality and spiritual ways of knowing have been marginalized in western academic settings dominated by a mechanistic worldview.[23] This culturally sanctioned dominance of mechanistic knowledge serves to esteem secular intellectual paradigms at the expense of alternative ways of knowing. The emancipatory characteristic of critical theory begs a discriminating examination of the neglected role of spirituality in policy analysis. Critical theory can, therefore, provide the necessary theoretical perspective for considering the role of RS in social policy practice.

Critical theory's exploration of what knowledge is, how it is constructed, and for whom it is constructed is of central importance when examining this arena. Perhaps spirituality has been underutilized, in part because scholars and educators have failed to conceptualize and tap into its unique contribution potential. One of critical theory's defining features is its rejection of naturalism—the assumption that methods of scientific inquiry can be applied to the study of human beings in social action.[24] Lincoln et al. also note the need for liberation from the domination of scientific ways of knowing. They state:

---

23. Vokey, "Spirituality and Professional," 79–120.
24. Thomas, "Living," 505–24.

> Arguably axiology has been "defined out" of scientific inquiry for no larger a reason than that it also concerns religion. But defining religion broadly to encompass spirituality would move constructivists closer to participative inquirers and would move critical theorists closer to both (owing to their concern with liberation from the oppression and freeing of the human, spirit both profoundly spiritual concerns).[25]

Vokey points out that in social work academic settings, integrating practices and ways of knowing that are unique to spirituality can pose a significant challenge to traditional academic paradigms. Yet, Vokey argues that an exploration of *transpersonal knowledge* as an alternative way of knowing may offer some hope.[26] Transpersonal knowledge can be defined as knowledge that transcends the limits of body, ego, and linear space and time.[27] A distinguishing feature of RS is the ability of adherents to gain transpersonal knowledge. Though methods and practices differ, knowledge gained through sacred texts, prayer, meditation, and oral traditions are a defining and foundational feature of most religious and spiritual traditions. Vokey argues that for spiritual integration to be fully appreciated, the knowledge that is central to spirituality must not only be welcomed, but also valued in academic settings.[28]

In an era where RS appears to be exercising increasing influence in the policy area, a critical assessment of the influence of RS on social policy is crucial. Thomas argues that religion will be a major force in shaping policy in the twenty-first century; therefore, critical theory (holding true to its claims of emancipation) must develop a more complex understanding of religion.[29] Instead of viewing religion as part of the problem, critical theorists can take into account spiritual and theological interpretive views of the world that promote emancipation and social justice. According to Thomas:

> It is often thought that in critical theory, religion is a part of the problem rather than the solution, in so far as it is indebted to Marxism—from Marx, Engels and Feuerbach, to Gramsci and Nietzsche, and the Frankfort School. Religion is a little more than false consciousness, an ideological subterfuge; it is one of the main ideological pathologies, forms of capitalist hegemony, that seeks to legitimate the status quo, to mask the potential for

25. Lincoln et al., "Paradigmatic," 116.
26. Vokey, "Spirituality and Professional," 97–120.
27. Coholic, "A Review," 167–85.
28. Vokey, "Spirituality and Professional," 97–120.
29. Thomas, "Living Critically."

social justice and emancipation, and to reinforce the fear and coercion that maintain the prevailing domestic and international order . . . When critical theorists have recognized religion's potential for promoting social justice and emancipation, it has been on the basis of mainly finding cognate ideas, concepts and thinkers acceptable to critical theory and its emancipatory project.[30]

As Thomas articulates, efforts to bring religion back into critical theory must be part of a more complex understanding of modern-day RS. According to Thomas, RS are "tradition-dependent, and cannot be detached from the traditions and communities through which most people in the world live out their moral and social lives."[31]

The perspective offered by Thomas resonates with the dialectic approach articulated by Theodor Adorno in *Negative Dialectics*. In this work, Adorno insists that the dialectic approach is not a midpoint between absolutism and reality. In fact, he argues against the idea that critical theory should merely criticize one point of view in favor of another.[32] Yet in some regards, critical theory's negative treatment of religion has done this by marginalizing voices who view spirituality as a significant contributor to social policy practice. Given the neglect of spirituality in policy practice analysis, and its central importance in the twenty-first century, spirituality in social policy practice warrants further examination.

In accordance with the objectives of critical theory, this study deconstructs the experiences, beliefs, practices, and values of social policy practitioners to examine the role of RS in social policy practice. The use of critical theory in this manner can be transformative by allowing conceptual space to consider how RS influences social policy practice.

Use of Grounded Theory

Since there is little scholarship on the process of integrating RS into policy practice, studies are needed to discover a unified theoretical explanation of the process by which policy practitioners utilize religious and spiritual experiences, beliefs, practices, and values to inform policy practice activities. According to Creswell, "The intent of a grounded theory study is to move beyond description and to generate or discover a theory, a unified

---

30. Ibid., 509–10.
31. Ibid., 512.
32. Stanford Encyclopedia of Philosophy, "Theodor W. Adorno."

theoretical explanation for a process or action."[33] In keeping with Creswell's description, this study uses grounded theory methodology to examine the process by which policy practitioners utilize RS to inform policy practice activities.

Purposive Sample and Data Collection Procedures

Based on the assumptions of critical theory, the researcher conducted interviews with policy practitioners in a manner that fostered conversation and reflection. As a critical theorist, the researcher recognized the inherent problems with the subject-object label. Rather than merely describing and reflecting the thoughts of the *subject,* the researcher viewed the interview as transformative. For this study, the researcher began with the following assumptions:

1. RS influences personal values.
2. Personal values influence social policy.
3. Due to predominant cultural paradigms, the inquiry into religious and spiritual integration in social policy practice has been marginalized.
4. For the phenomena of religious and spiritual integration in policy practice to be explored, the researcher and subject must be purposeful in their inquiry of RS.

The researcher engaged the subjects in conversations about various aspects of RS in a process of mutual discovery. Through this dialogic process, the critical researcher challenged and deconstructed the dominant paradigm that does not take into account the role of RS in social policy practice, and utilized the interview process to reconstruct a paradigm that is open to the influence of RS on social policy practice. This study used the grounded theory *systematic procedural approach* of Strauss and Corbin.[34] The process of data collection and data analysis were an ongoing and overlapping process in this grounded theory study.

Purposive Sample

The study utilized criterion-based snowball sampling to select a sample of seventeen individuals who met the following criteria: They were individuals

---

33. Creswell, *Qualitative,* 84.
34. Strauss and Corbin, *Basics of Qualitative,* 195.

who utilized social work skills to propose, change or influence policies in order to achieve the goal of social or economic justice in all practice settings;[35] individuals who were engaged in promoting social change, empowerment, and/or liberation of people to enhance well-being; and individuals who identified religion or spirituality as a factor that influenced their policy practice activities.

Initially, two social workers who met the sample-selection criteria were selected. The initial sample was comprised of individuals who were identified by gatekeepers. In accordance with theoretical sampling guidelines, not all participants were selected prior to data collection, but once data emerged, subject selection was guided by the emerging data.[36] Additional subjects were selected based on referrals and the proposed sample emerged in the process of data collection. In accordance with theoretical sampling guidelines, data collection and data analysis involved an iterative process.[37] After an initial round of interviews, interviews were transcribed and analyzed for salient themes, further data collection occurred with additional participants as needed. The additional interviews were compared to the initial categories. This process continued until the theoretical categories being developed reached saturation.

Data Collection and Analysis

Data was collected by conducting semi-structured, open-ended interviews. The questions that were asked during the interview were designed to explore the religious and spiritual experiences, beliefs, practices and values of policy practitioners, as well as the process by which RS informs their social policy practice. The interview utilized a semi-structured, inductive process, comprised of the following three main sections: questions about RS; questions about religious and or spiritual integration in policy practice; and questions about core beliefs and values that influence policy practice. In addition to these main questions, participants were asked to answer demographic questions prior to the interview. These included questions about age, gender, academic degrees acquired, years of policy practice, and religious affiliation.

Seventeen subjects were interviewed. All interviews were audiotaped, transcribed, and coded in ATLAS.ti. The selective coding method of data analysis was used. Selective coding is the process of: selecting the core category that emerges from the data; systematically relating the core category

35. Director and Clark, *Defining*, 2.
36. Drauker et al., "Theoretical," 1137–48.
37. Creswell, *Qualitative*, 86.

to other categories that emerge; validating those relationships; and filling in the categories that need further refining (through theoretical sampling). This writer used open coding to examine the data and label the emerging categories. During the initial phase of data collection, the interview transcripts and the reflective journal were analyzed for salient categories. Similar concepts were grouped together under main categories and these emerging categories were labeled. Using the constant comparative approach, this researcher continued to code and collect data as necessary until the categories were saturated. Once the categories were saturated with the full range of properties, the categories were dimensionalized and presented on a continuum. Once axial coding was complete, selective coding was utilized to generate a hypothesis. Next, this researcher engaged in discriminate sampling to maximize the relationship between categories. Data was then analyzed to determine where the data was the strongest and where it was weakest. Once the data was full, this researcher used the data to articulate a theory of the interrelationship of the categories and the core phenomenon.

Results

There were seventeen subjects who were interviewed. Participants ranged from age thirty-eight to seventy-seven with a mean age of fifty-four and a half years. Nine of the participants were men and eight were women. Ten participants received formal training in policy practice and seven received no formal training. The participants identified their religious or spiritual affiliation as follows: three were Jewish (two identified themselves as agnostic and one as reformed); one Muslim; five Catholics (three identified with Roman Catholicism); three Christians (no denomination specified); four Baptists (one American Baptist; one evangelical Southern Baptist; two Southern Baptist) and one Protestant.

Six of the participants held a social work degree, three held a law degree, four held a ministry degree, and five held another non-specified degree. Some participants held more than one degree.

Religious and Spiritual Integration in Social Policy Practice (RSSPP)

Interviews with policy practitioners who identified RS as a significant factor influencing their social policy practice provided substantial data to construct a preliminary model that elucidates the role of RS in social policy practice. The *Religion and Spirituality in Social Policy Practice* model

(RSSPP) (see figure 1) presents a framework for conceptualizing the process by which policy practitioners integrate RS in social policy practice.

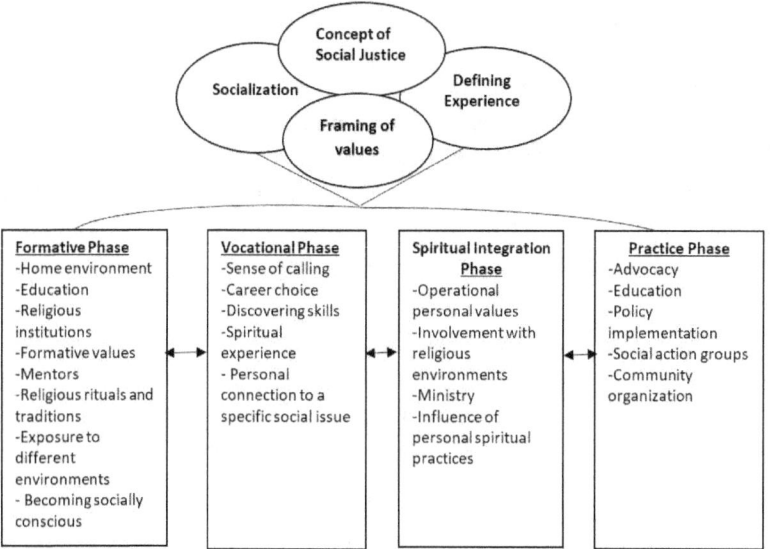

Figure 1. RSSPP Model illustrates the four phases of religious and spiritual integration impacting social policy practice.

The RSSPP model is based on the most salient beliefs, core values, and defining experiences that shape the integration of RS in social policy practice. First, the model identifies the following four developmental phases by which RS integration occurs:

1. Formative Phase;
2. Vocational Phase;
3. Spiritual Integration Phase; and
4. Practice Phase.

These phases are not necessarily progressive and practitioners can move back and forth between the phases several times throughout their life. Next the model identifies: Socialization; concepts of social justice; defining experiences; and framing of values as the four primary factors that shape each of the developmental phases. The four developmental phases are discussed in detail below.

1. Formative Phase

The formative phase is characterized by experiences that powerfully impact the shaping of core values and beliefs. This phase often occurs early in life, where culture and family serve as a primary force of socialization. This phase, however, is not limited to early experiences or chronological age. Policy practitioners can experience formative experiences throughout life. The primary defining feature of this phase is its distinct role in impacting practitioners as they forge fundamental values and beliefs that guide their decisions and approach to social policy practice. One participant (Jack) discussed his formative years and how his childhood environment seemed to draw his interest in social justice:

> Very early, in this very tough town I was growing up in, I had the sense that I should resolve to live my life in a different way than I saw in my neighborhood, and so forth. There was a very early sense that I ought to try and convince other people that this is actually what the founders said, that only a virtuous people could remain free—that if America was going to succeed, we had to avoid unbridled freedom and instead get that ordered liberty under God that the founders thought about. So, for me, it wasn't just about the way I lived, it was about how I make a living—if I'm not going to be a preacher, which I didn't really feel called to, how can I convince others these things are really important if America is going to survive?

For Jack, a commitment to America, as envisioned by our founding fathers, would become a defining feature of his life's work.

Other subjects talked about being advocates for social justice as something that was just part of who they are. Policy practice was not something that they learned about in a formal way; instead, it was something that emanated from a core sense of justice that was often instilled by their parents and primary caregivers. Tony expressed his involvement in social justice as almost an instinctive part of his core identity:

> Well, this is how it came for me; it was very organic. There was not a situation where we took social policy lessons or classes, so I learned about segregation and desegregation in my living room, in my mom's sewing room . . . I learned these things just growing up between being in church and hearing messages, hearing the Scripture, going to Sunday school, and my mom talking with pride about the African American community. That's just how I came up. So, it wasn't a stated social-gospel type of thing for me; it was just this sense of right and wrong, a good

work ethic, a sense of pride in community, doing things to help your community, being respectful, recognizing that you—when you're out in the community, you're representing yourself, your family, your church, and yourself as a Christian.

Often the exposure to, and discussion of, social issues of the day had a potent impact on value development during the formative phase. Frequently, the formative phase led to, or overlapped with, the vocational phase.

2. Vocational Phase

The vocational phase is characterized by a discovery or decision to enter the field of social policy practice. During this phase, all individuals interviewed reported sensing a call to justice or discovering skills or talents that aided them in social policy practice. Four participants reported that their decision to become involved in social policy led to a vocation in ministry, and three others reported that a sense of justice inspired them to seek a career in law. All participants interviewed reported being involved with policy practice long before it became their profession. Samuel articulated his start in social policy practice using the example of notable social justice leaders who were inspired by faith. He underscored the idea that social justice in the life of these prominent leaders was not something they learned. Rather, it was inspired by their spiritual life and was part of who they were as people:

> So to them, speaking out against injustice was just part of who they were. It wasn't something they went to school for; like today you can go to school and study social justice, which is good and bad. The good part, obviously—it teaches you to be aware, and the sad part is that social justice isn't an academic exercise. It is actually something that is born out of your spiritual life. This is how it happened for me . . . I remember, years ago, I guess in my twenties or thirties, I remember some op-ed was written about the Black church that was really racist. So, I sat down and wrote a letter to the editor. My parents never taught me to write letters. They didn't tell me when you get mad, write a letter to your senator. But I started doing stuff like that.

Eventually, Samuel would become a pastor, a community organizer, and an international leader of a social justice organization. Like many participants, he did not take an academic course on social policy practice; instead, his advocacy efforts were an outgrowth of his faith and his desire to stand against injustice.

One notable trend that emerged during this study was the diversity of academic degrees earned by participants. Even though a snowball sampling strategy was used to identify two social workers who met the sample-selection criteria, and the initial sample was comprised of individuals identified by gatekeepers, many of the subsequent participants held academic degrees outside of social work. Only six of the seventeen subjects held MSW, BSW or PhDs in social work. In selecting participants, it also became apparent that, for those outside of the social work profession, there were misconceptions about what constitutes social work and social policy practice. For example, some potential participants that seemed to be engaging in social policy practice did not identify their work as such. Yet when they were given the definition of social policy practice, they agreed that it was, in fact, an accurate description of their work. Because of this, the sampling selection criteria were amended so that the definitions of social work and social policy practice were used in the selection criteria instead of the unfamiliar terms. In doing this, the researcher was able to engage policy practitioners from various disciplines.

3. Spiritual Integration Phase

The spiritual integration phase is characterized by the recognition and use of religious and spiritual beliefs and values to impact policy practice. This phase describes the period when practitioners actively utilize religious and spiritual integration skills to understand or frame policy practice. During this phase, policy practitioners use RS and apply critical thinking to understand social issues. This phase also involves the use of skills necessary for engaging other religiously or spiritually affiliated groups in social policy practice. The following are three of the main practices or trends noted during this phase: the framing of values; the nuanced nature of RS; and the use of spiritual ways of knowing.

Framing Values

Joseph, who identified himself as agnostic, explained his use of framing to engage the Christian faith community:

> So when I wrote in Israel, and I thought about issues in Israel, it was different. In Israel, religion can be expressed, discussed, and acknowledged. When you work in the current-day United States, unless your audience is amenable to it, you don't bring in

> any religious context. So, when I talk about ex-prisoners here, I talk about second chances; I talk about the cost to society; I talk about lost working days; I talk about the future of children. I purposely and intentionally don't bring anything that can be constructed as religious or spiritual.

Here Joseph underscores the role of culture in the successful framing of social issues. It is significant because he contrasts the role of religion and policy in the Unites States with that of Israel, a country where religious framing is acceptable. This finding may suggest that the culture of separation of church and state in the United States has had conceptual and linguistic ramifications that make it difficult for subjects to clearly identify or articulate how their religiously or spiritually-inspired values influence their policy practice. Fifteen of the participants, when asked about core values that inform their policy practice, focused on connecting their policy activities to what they considered to be basic inherent human values. Even though all participants stated that RS impacts their policy practice, these fifteen participants needed to be engaged with probing questions in order to articulate the way that RS influenced their practice. Often the religious or spiritual connection to concepts of social justice and human rights was not initially evident.

The nuanced nature of RS

Another eminent trend involved the nuanced role of RS. Participants appeared to be considerably influenced by the specific values and beliefs of their religious or spiritual tradition. For example, Maria, who was affiliated with a conservative evangelical tradition, focused almost exclusively on the inerrancy of the Bible. Whereas other participants, influenced by the social-gospel lens or Catholic social teaching, gained their perspective of social justice through the examples observed in the gospel and lived experiences. They emphasized the example of Jesus and its modern application over the infallibility of Scripture. Paul, who identified himself as an evangelical Southern Baptist, explained his position:

> I think the more likely a denomination is to reject that inerrancy of Scripture, the more likely they are to embrace the latest wind that comes through the culture. It is a big difference. The other thing . . . I go back to history. The early church, being closer to the living Christ, is going to reflect more accurately the message of the Scriptures. The early church took root in the Roman world where infanticide and sexual immorality was rampant. And the early church stood, at great cost, against these practices.

On the other hand, Alex, who identifies himself as an American Baptist, explained his position on social justice as emanating from the Bible, but denied the inerrancy of Scripture:

> Well, you know, I would say it's more of my sense of what is right, and that part comes from my faith. So, I don't see the Bible as infallible or the literal word of God, but I think its principles are very inspirational and that there's direction there. But you can't take everything from a first-century context and prior to that, and translate it automatically into today. So, part of it has to do with looking at some of the guiding principles of who Christ was, his example, what he thought was important and what I then gain from that, and then to see the thread that runs throughout the Bible. My dialog with persons of other faiths is a part of it, in terms of seeing things from how other people see things. So, I would say it really is a whole, you know, all together. But I mean, when I hear something's going on, and I recognize that it doesn't seem right, doesn't seem fair, doesn't seem just, that evaluation comes from my faith.

The nuanced dynamic of religion is significant because it accentuates the variegated nature of religiously inspired values. Individuals who state that their religious beliefs and values influence their social justice positions, who affiliate with the same religion (e.g., Christian, Jewish, Muslim), can arrive at divergent positions on social justice issues based on varying factors that influence their core values, and inspire their personal spiritual identity. It appears that different religious practices, sources of guidance, interpretational paradigms, and spiritual experiences greatly inform individual social policy practice.

Spiritual ways of knowing

One of the most interesting findings involved transpersonal experiences. When subjects were asked about religious and spiritual experiences, by far most participants, regardless of denominational or religious affiliation, identified having spiritual experiences that could be considered transpersonal in nature. Transpersonal experiences can be described as mystical and intuitive occurrences or expansive states of consciousness that appear to go beyond limited biological and psychological selves.[38] Some participants described these experiences as *thin spaces* or *God moments,* times that stand out as defining moments and hold significant meaning for

---

38. Braud and Anderson, *Transpersonal,* xxi–ii.

individuals. Often these experiences were said to be spiritual experiences that provided guidance or direction involving current social policy work. Jacob, a subject involved in social policy work on poverty, described such an experience as a *thin space*, a unique time in his life in which he was keenly aware of spiritual direction:

> There's just certain times or certain places where . . . there's this idea of thin spaces, where the gap between God and man, or God and people really seems thin. And these experiences are very powerful. I mean, you think about going to a mountain, standing on the mountain, it just seems like there is something majestic about it, or you're sitting out looking over the ocean. Or sometimes being in a beautiful chapel . . . Sometimes it can be by yourself in your room, a place where you go daily to pray . . . and I think it can also be a time period. For me, the time around when I encountered the St. Francis story began a time period of probably three or four years where I was experiencing kind of a thin place. It just seemed like everything was very profound and real, almost like the colors of life were richer.

Jacob described this period in his life as one of keen spiritual awareness. During this time, his spiritual experience evoked greater connectivity with human suffering that compelled him to utilize his skills to change policy and alleviate these conditions. Jacob explained:

> I think it's those kinds of experiences, those thin places where I encountered a lot of this economic suffering that causes suffering in other ways . . . I mean you know a prostitute gets beat up incredibly badly. I mean on any given night they can be beat to death or beat within an inch of their life. So, if I have the skill set, and can develop the skill set or knowledge base to be able to do something about that, and I don't, it's hard for me to think that I'm loving my neighbor as myself. If I'm just choosing to be present with them or friends with them because that makes me feel good, or because I have that direct contact with them, but I have the ability to engage the power structure to change things, and I don't, that to me seems selfish. And so for me, that's why we get into policy. Because by and large they don't need me to be friends with them. They have friends. So, I think that's part of what drove me in this particular direction.

Many participants who identified transpersonal experiences as being a significant impetus in their lives, actively engaged in practices to become more sensitive to spiritual direction. Robert, for example, described some methods that helped him become more open to spiritual experiences. Robert talked about the importance of giving attention to spiritual ways of knowing. He explained:

> The doorway to spiritual experiences is paying attention and focus. So, meditation and techniques that increase our focus tend to encourage spiritual experiences. Things like opening our human heart, or creativity can foster greater spiritual sensitivity. Like poets, for example—they may be going through the very same process, but they've got to give attention to their subject in order to create. They've got to open themselves to this thing, this process, this awareness, this knowing. I think that traditions such as mindfulness and contemplation can open us to these experiences, but so can service, so can yoga. Like, literally, physically moving our body in certain ways, I think, can also do that.

Six participants talked about utilizing the Ignatius contemplative approach or incorporating meditative practices into their daily routine.

While six of the seventeen participants talked about having spiritual experiences that provided direction for future policy work, others identified having these experiences in relation to other areas of their life. Six participants reported having an overwhelming sense of knowing related to the need of a loved one or involving formative years. Almost all participants identified one or more experiences that they considered to be transpersonal in nature. Interestingly, two participants who identified themselves as agnostic did not recall having this type of spiritual experience and seemed to imply that some of their lack of identification with such an experience may, in part, have to do with framing and interpretation of such events. For example, Joseph, who identified himself as agnostic, explained:

> Now there is some type of spirituality where people tell me they look at the tree and say, "My heart is pounding, and my head is whatever . . . and I feel like connecting with nature." Fine. That is an emotion that I can't describe . . . I can't explain. Sometimes I go to a museum and I stand in front of a picture and I have this sense of connectedness with the universe. But I don't call it spirituality. I call it excitement or whatever . . .

This example underscores the significance of cognitive interpretations of spiritual experiences. Additional research on spiritual experiences may provide greater insights into how these unique events are perceived and interpreted.

4. Practice Phase

This phase is characterized by efforts to change policies in legislative, agency, and community settings, by establishing new policies, improving existing ones, or by defeating policy initiatives of other people.[39] Although the spiritual integration and practice phases often occur simultaneously, some participants identified times when their involvement in policy practice did not necessarily involve the assimilation of religion or spirituality. Markus, for example, described his initial involvement in social policy practice and shared how his early years in social work led to his career in social policy practice:

> Like many people, I thought that I was going to do clinical work, that I would be a practitioner in an office and have clients, and I would be the next Sigmund Freud ... But very soon I realized that that's not my abilities. My skills, my advantages are elsewhere. So, I moved into administration and policy, mostly as a reaction to my limited clinical skills. So, one of my professors came to me and said, "You know you will struggle to be a mediocre practitioner or a clinical practitioner, but you will be an amazing person in (what we now call) macro practice." And I said, "Really?" and he said, "Yes." So, I gave it a chance. And so, I went to work for the government, and I became engaged in national policy ... So, everything came together. It all evolved naturally.

Markus did not identify religion or spirituality as a motivating factor in his decision to engage in policy practice. His decision to engage in macro practice occurred after he took stock of his skills and decided to employ them to help others in the most effective way. Even though this practitioner did identify with a belief in the dignity and worth of the individual, he viewed these values in more of a humanistic manner. He explained:

> I was fortunate to be at the right place with the right people and most of them shared my values, or even they influenced my values in the sense that they were committed—some from a humanistic perspective, some from a religious perspective. They were all committed to human dignity, to communal responsibility through policy.

In this example, Markus underscores the significance of shared values for effective policy practice, even if the values originate from varying sources. The idea that individuals can have similar core values, regardless of religious

---

39. Jansson, *Effective Policy*, 14.

identity or spiritual beliefs, has significant implications for social policy practice. Becoming sensitive to the spiritually and secularly influenced values in the communities where policy practice is occurring can serve to empower communities. With this perspective, communities with diverse RS traditions can work together effectively for change, by unifying around shared functional values regardless of their origin. Even though this participant identifies himself as an agnostic, as his career progressed, he began to work effectively with Christian communities by utilizing his understanding of Christianity to garner support for innovative faith-based projects that were consistent with shared community values.

Discussion

The data provided by policy practitioners were used to develop the model for understanding the Integration of Religion and Spirituality in Social Policy Practice (RSSPP). This framework can be used to conceptualize the salient features that impact religious and spiritual integration in social policy practice. This is a useful model for visualizing the process by which RS impacts social policy practice. In addition to yielding this model, the data also indicated some notable trends that have implications for policy practitioners. These trends are noted below.

Early Socialization

Primary forces of socialization early in life appear to play a significant role in making participants mindful of issues related to social justice, regardless of the origin of their faith tradition. The data suggest that primary caregivers who engaged children in conversations about current events, involved them in social policy, and modeled activism seemed to be a factor in forging conceptions of social justice. While the influence of primary caregivers was remarkable, additional impressions garnered from the childhood environment of policy practitioners also appear to have made a significant contribution to a practitioner's involvement in social policy. This may shed some light on recent research that has suggested that formative values seem to powerfully influence an individual's selection of their specific religion or spiritual path.[40] In other words, contrary to the popular belief that involvement in a particular religion influences political ideology, Campbell and Putnam suggest that core values may be more likely to determine reli-

---

40. Campbell and Putnam, "God and Caesar," 34–43.

gious and spiritual affiliation and expression. That is to say that core values, seem to influence religious affiliation and political leanings. When giving consideration to how primary values impact social policy practice, this data provides compelling evidence to support additional focus on primary socialization.

Spiritual Ways of Knowing

This study provided convincing evidence for a greater appreciation for alternative ways of knowing. The data suggests that transpersonal experiences may offer a powerful source of guidance and direction when it comes to social policy practice. There are, however, serious challenges in attempting to garner additional insight in this area.[41] Unless the unique contributions that spirituality offers are valued in academic settings, attempts to integrate spirituality in educational curricula will not be sustainable. Vokey notes the significance of recognizing spiritual ways of knowing as a primary and unique feature of spirituality. Specifically, he posits that spiritual knowledge, if it is to be fully appreciated, must have room to be explored in academic settings that have traditionally been dominated by mechanistic or scientific ways of knowing (particularly in the West). A distinguishing feature of religion and spirituality is the ability of adherents to gain transpersonal knowledge. Though methods and practices differ, knowledge gained from sacred texts, prayer, meditation, and oral traditions are a defining and foundational feature of most religious and spiritual traditions. Vokey argues that in order for spiritual integration to be fully appreciated, the transpersonal knowledge that is central to spirituality must not only be welcomed, but also valued in academic settings.[42] Thomas further argues that spiritual practices such as prayer, meditation, and contemplation are of the utmost importance for the promotion of social change and political transformation.[43] If these spiritual practices are a core feature of the integration of faith in practice, as the data, Vokey, and Thomas suggest, then additional research is warranted in this area.

---

41. Vokey, "Spirituality and Professional," 97–120.
42. Ibid.
43. Thomas, "The Variations," 230–62.

The Role of Social Policy in Social Work

One of the most surprising outcomes of the data involved the role of the social work profession in social policy practice. Since this research was designed to examine the integration of religion and spirituality in social policy practice, the sampling frame was not limited to individuals with social work degrees. Instead, the researcher utilized criterion-based snowball sampling to get the most salient sample. Even though the criteria did not limit participants by academic degree, by using criteria that were familiar to social workers, the assumption was that most individuals referred by gatekeepers (who had their degrees in social work) would also hold degrees in social work. Surprisingly, only six of out of the seventeen participants included in the sample held social work degrees. What was most remarkable was the realization that participants from other disciplines, who were actively engaged in what would be considered *social policy practice*, were not familiar with this term. However, once these practitioners were given the definition of social policy practice, they confirmed that they were, in fact, involved in what social work refers to as *social policy practice*.

Because of these challenges with semantics, the definition of social work and social policy practice were added as part of the sample criterion. The modified criterion was changed as follows: The sample will be comprised of individuals who: are involved in efforts to change policies in legislative, agency, and community settings, whether by establishing new policies, improving existing ones, or defeating the policy initiatives of other people;[44] individuals who engage in promoting social change, empowerment, or the liberation of people to enhance well-being; and individuals who identified religion or spirituality, as a factor that influenced their policy practice activities. This amendment was made to allow the inclusion of individuals who were engaging is social policy practice from other disciplines. Next to social work, degrees in law and theology or ministry were the most prevalent in the research sample.

Aside from the challenges with discipline-specific language, the preliminary results seem to indicate that there is some need to give more intentional focus to this area of social work practice. If the data is, indeed, indicative of the low representation of social workers engaging in social policy practice, additional research may be justified to determine the factors contributing to this trend, and to explore the implications for social work as a profession.

---

44. Jansson, *Effective Policy*, 14.

Framing Values

Another unexpected finding involved the framing of core values. All participants were given information about the study in advance of the interview (i.e., the central question, the interview guide, and information about the nature of the study). In addition, to meet the criteria necessary to be included in the study, participants self-identified that religion or spirituality was an influencing factor in their policy practice. Despite this, many of the practitioners who participated in the study did not initially frame their core values in a religious or spiritual manner, nor did they identify their core values as having a spiritual foundation. Often they used language devoid of religious or spiritual indications. When this researcher utilized probing questions to explore the origin of their values, some subjects voluntarily spoke about the religious or spiritual foundation of their core values, yet others did not. Of all the preliminary findings, this was perhaps the most daunting because it presents a challenge when attempting to assess how RS influences social policy practice. It also seems to indicate that the religious and spiritual impetus for social policy practice many not initially be apparent.

Even though these data were somewhat surprising, it was not completely unanticipated. In fact, the use of critical theory in the research design was based on the primary assumption that RS is marginalized in the social policy arena. The initial data collected during the preliminary interviews seems to confirm the use of the philosophical assumptions of critical theory for this study. With these initial findings, this researcher formulated probing questions that elicited information about the religious, spiritual or secular influence of core values. In reflecting on this outcome, this writer suggests the following implications: First, language itself is a powerful tool used by skilled policy practitioners who are gifted in framing ideas and values in a manner that garners public support. One could argue that in the United States, values framed as religious or justified on the basis of religious beliefs do not resonate with policy makers and do not make effective political arguments. Perhaps spiritually motivated policy practitioners are no less motivated by their faith, but they have become accustomed to discussing these values in a manner that resonates with policymakers. Jacob, a policy practitioner who received his social work training in Israel before coming to the United States, relays the following story that illustrates this point:

> I'll tell you an anecdote, so you understand where I'm going. When I came to do my doctoral work here (in the U.S.), during the first semester I had to write a paper on policy and I wanted to use a quote from the Bible, from the book of Amos. So, I went

> to the library and the only Bible I read before was in Hebrew, so I took the Bible from the library and went to the right passage, and to my chagrin it didn't say what I wanted to say. So, I went back to my fellow students and I told them what happened. So, they looked at me with disbelief and said, "How does a smart person like yourself not know anything?" And they said to me, "If you don't like it take another Bible." And I said, "What do you mean?" And they said, "There are many translations; find a translation that says what you think it should say." But then they said, "Look, you're not in Israel. Here when you write an academic paper, don't use biblical quotes or your professor will think that you don't have intellectual rigor if you resort to writing just biblical stuff—we don't do it." So, I asked my mentor and she said, "Oh no! Don't do it!" So, in most academic settings here you have this division of what you bring into public sphere and what you don't bring into the public sphere. So, when I wrote in Israel and I thought about issues in Israel, religion can be expressed, discussed, and acknowledged. But when you do work in the United States today, unless your audience is amenable to it, you don't bring in any religious content.

This story, relayed by Jacob, seems to capture the essence of a cultural dynamic indicative of current American political spheres. Perhaps religious and spiritual language has successfully been divorced from political discourse, making it difficult to gain a full appreciation of the role of RS in policy practice.

This dynamic also prompted this writer to think about values in general. The two agnostics who participated in this study did so because of their recognition of the impact that religion has on social policy practice. While they may not be personally inspired by religion in their work, they both recognize the functional role of RS in the policy arena. Much of their work involved working with the religious community to harness the shared values for the betterment of society. Jack, an agnostic practitioner, shared the following when discussing his work with congregants of a church:

> Most of them shared my values or even influenced my values in the sense that they were committed—some from a humanistic perspective, some from a religious perspective. They were all committed to human dignity and to communal responsibility through policy.

What seemed to matter most to Jack was shared functional values that were empowering. The origin of these values was of little concern. This realization has significant implications. In this example, Jack was savvy in his ability to harness the functional values of religion and unite the community around shared values, even though he identified himself as agnostic. This may seem like an obvious intervention, yet in today's increasingly polarized political arena where activists utilize faith to justify their political stances, uniting people around shared values can pose significant challenges. Those committed to social justice find themselves dealing with increasingly complex and divisive social issues. By recognizing the empowering and functional contributions that can be harvested from RS, policy practitioners may find significant value in unifying religiously diverse communities around shared functional values. Perhaps, in the same way that this writer encountered cultural and linguistic challenges when using the term *social policy* with people outside of the social work profession, similar cultural and linguistic challenges exist when people of various religious and spiritual traditions endeavor to engage in the political realm. If this is the case, it may be feasible for astute policy practitioners, who see the unique value contribution that religion and spirituality offer, to assist individuals and communities in bridging this cultural and linguistic gap.

Despite the immense challenges, there are significant implications for understanding how values are framed. As social policy practitioners endeavor to engage in spiritually sensitive practice, the issue of framing can be explored so that all values, including religiously inspired ones, are assessed and utilized for community empowerment. The preliminary findings of the role of culture in the successful framing of social issues suggest that the culture of separation of church and state in the United States has had conceptual and linguistic ramifications. This framing may hinder subjects from their ability to clearly conceptualize or articulate how religious or spiritual values influence their policy practice. In order to empower individuals and communities to utilize the unique contributions of religion and spirituality, an assessment instrument was created to make room for religiously inspired values. This instrument is designed to aid policy practitioners with the means to critically assess their own spiritual beliefs and values.

Below, Figure 2 presents a model for a Spiritually Sensitive Community Assessment Instrument (SSCAI). It is designed by this researcher to be a conceptual map where religious and non-religiously inspired values are assessed, legitimized, and operationalized to forge a unified community-policy assessment instrument.

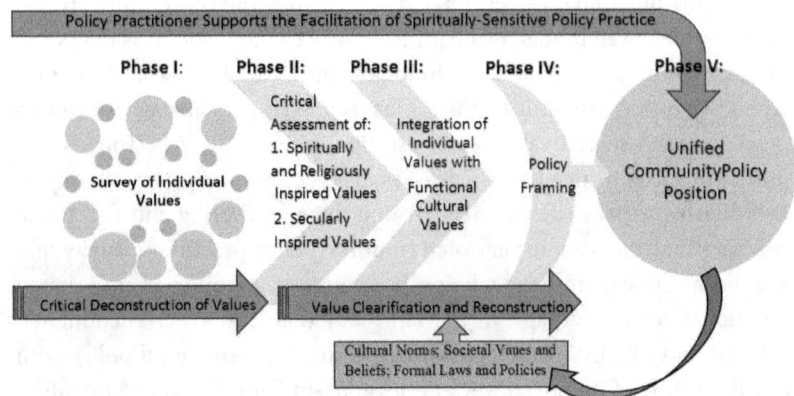

Figure 2. Spiritually Sensitive Community Assessment Instrument (SSCAI)

The SSCAI is designed to enable practitioners to be more sensitive to the primary values that inform their policy paradigm. In addition, this instrument is constructed to equip practitioners with the means to frame values in language that resonates with functional cultural values. Specifically, the SSCAI would increase policy practitioners' awareness of how values impact their practice; enable practitioners to assess their values in light of functional cultural values; empower practitioners with the skills necessary to effectively integrate RS in practice while engaging in spiritually sensitive practice; and equip practitioners with an instrument to empower individuals and communities to voice their primary values. The SSCAI would aid practitioners as they work with communities so that all values (secularly and religiously inspired) are recognized, legitimized, and have room to operate in the policy arena. In addition to equipping policy practitioners, individual communities would be empowered with a model that evokes greater awareness and understanding of core community values, while eliciting participation from marginalized voices.

Limitations

One of the limitations of this study is the lack of dimensionalization in the category of religious diversity. Due to the vast diversity of religious traditions and spiritual expression in the United States, it was not feasible to select a sample that included a full range of religious expression. Thirteen of the participants were affiliated with Christian denominations. Instead of selecting a theoretical sample that contained greater religious diversity, this researcher focused on building a purposive sample that focused on the primary categories that emerged during open coding. Because religious diversity was not part of the sampling strategy, the findings may disproportionately reflect the manner in which the religious traditions included in the sample integrate RS in social policy practice.

Conclusion

The data from seventeen policy practitioners who identified spirituality and religion as a significant factor influencing their social policy practice provided substantial information to construct a preliminary model that elucidate the role of religion and spirituality in social policy practice (RSSPP). The RSSPP model presents a framework for conceptualizing the formative experiences, beliefs, core values, and defining experiences that shape the integration of spirituality and religion in social policy practice. The model indicates that the four salient themes of socialization, concepts of social justice, defining experiences and framing of values, influence and shape the four developmental phases.

In the RSSPP model, similar concepts were grouped together under main categories and these emerging categories were labeled. Using the constant comparative approach, this researcher coded and collected data, until the primary categories were saturated. Research analysis continued until a theoretical model (RSSPP) emerged that illustrated the process by which policy practitioners utilize RS to inform social policy practice. The RSSPP model illustrates the interrelationship of the four primary phases' categories and their relationship to the core phenomenon of spiritual integration in policy practice.

The RSSPP model has significant implications for spiritually sensitive social policy practice. As this model emerged, data provided by this study also produced the conceptual framework for the creation of the Spiritually Sensitive Community Assessment Instrument (SSCAI). This assessment emerged from the core findings of this study. These findings indicate that the framing of values and the secularization of the policy arena in the United States has significant implications for spiritually sensitive policy practice. The formulation of this assessment instrument is intended to critically deconstruct and assess societal values to make room for the full range of values (spiritually and secularly inspired) that exist in a particular community. Additional research will be needed to develop, test and implement this assessment instrument.

Bibliography

Braud, William, and Rosemary Anderson. *Transpersonal Research Methods for the Social Sciences: Honoring Human Experience.* Thousand Oaks, CA: Sage, 1998.

Bohman, James. "Critical Theory." *The Stanford Encyclopedia of Philosophy.* Fall 2016 ed., edited by Edward N. Zalta. http://plato.stanford.edu/archives/fall2016/entries/critical-theory. Accessed March 23, 2017.

Campbell, David E., and Robert D. Putnam. "God and Caesar in America: Why Mixing Religion and Politics is Bad for Both." *Foreign Affairs* 91 (2012) 34–43.

Campbell, Simone. "Explosion of the Spirit: A Spiritual Journal into the Health Care Reform Legislation." *Journal of Religion and Spirituality in Social Work: Social Thought* 31 (2012) 85–104.

Canda, Edward. R. "The Future of Spirituality in Social Work: The Farther Reaches of Human Nature." *Advances in Social Work* 6 (2005) 97–108.

Canda, Edward R., and Leola D. Furman. *Spiritual Diversity in Social Work Practice.* 2nd ed. New York: Oxford, 2010.

Coholic, Diana. "A Review of Spiritually Sensitive and Wholistic Social Work Methods: Current Emphases and Future Directions for Research and Practice." In *Spirituality in Social Work and Education: Theory, Practice, and Pedagogies,* edited by Janet Groen et al., 167–185. Waterloo, OT: Laurier, 2012.

Corradetti, Claudio. "The Frankfurt School and Critical Theory." In *The Internet Encyclopedia of Philosophy,* ISSN 2161–0002. http://www.iep.utm.edu/frankfur/. Accessed March 23, 2017.

Corbin, Juliet M., and Anselm Strauss. "Grounded Theory Research: Procedures, Canons, and Evaluative Criteria." *Qualitative Sociology* 13, no. 1 (1990) 3–21.

Council on Social Work Education. *Religion and Spirituality Clearinghouse.* http://www.cswe.org/centersinitiatives/curriculumresources/50777.aspx. Accessed March 23, 2017.

Cowley, Au-Deane S., and David Derezotes. "Transpersonal Psychology and Social Work Education." *Journal of Social Work Education* 30, no. 1 (1994) 32–41.

Creswell, John W. *Qualitative Inquiry and Research Design: Choosing among Five Approaches.* Thousand Oaks, CA: Sage, 2013.

Derezotes, David S. *Spiritually Oriented Social Work Practice.* Boston: Pearson, 2006.

Director, N. E., and Elizabeth J. Clark. "Defining Policy Practice in Social Work." In *Policy Practice for Social Workers: New Strategies for a New Era,* 1–25. Boston, MA: Allyn & Bacon, 2011.

Draucker, Claire B., et al. "Theoretical Sampling and Category Development in Grounded Theory." *Qualitative Health Research* 17, no. 8 (2007) 1137–48.

Evans, E. N. "Influencing Decision-Making in Public Policy: Religious Organizations and Political Process." *Journal of Religion & Spirituality in Social Work: Social Thought* 31, nos. 1–2 (2012) 26–37.

Furman, Leola D., et al. "Christian Social Workers' Attitudes on the Role of Religion and Spirituality in U.S. Social Work Practice and Education: 1997–2008." *Social Work and Christianity* 38, no. 2 (2011) 175–97.

Hodge, David R., and Suzanne Bushfield. "Developing Spiritual Competence in Practice." *Journal of Ethnic and Cultural Diversity in Social Work* 15, nos. 3–4 (2007) 101–27.

Horkheimer, Max. *Critical Theory.* New York: Seabury, 1982.

Hoyt-Oliver, Jane. "Integrating Faith and the Study of Social Policy: Translating God's Will into Earthen Vessels." *Social Work & Christianity* 25, no. 2 (1998) 130–44.

Hutchison, Elizabeth D. "Spirituality, Religion, and Progressive Social Movements: Resources and Motivation for Social Change." *Journal of Religion & Spirituality in Social Work: Social Thought* 31, nos. 1–2 (2012) 105–27.

Jansson, Bruce. *Becoming an Effective Policy Advocate: From Policy Practice to Social Justice*. 5th ed. Belmont, CA: Cengage, 2007.

Kellner, Douglas. "Critical Theory and the Crisis of Social Theory." *Sociological Perspectives* 33, no. 1 (1990) 11–33.

Lincoln, Yvonna S., et al. "Paradigmatic Controversies, Contradictions, and Emerging Confluences, Revisited." *The Sage Handbook of Qualitative Research* 4 (2011) 97–128.

Marx, Jerry D., and Fleur Hopper. "Faith-Based versus Fact-Based Social Policy: The Case of Teenage Pregnancy Prevention." *Social Work* 50, no. 3 (2005) 280–82.

Sheridan, Michael J. "Introduction: Connecting Spirituality and Social Justice within Macropractice." *Journal of Religion & Spirituality in Social Work: Social Thought* 31, nos. 1–2 (2012) 1–8.

———. "Spiritual Activism: Grounding Ourselves in the Spirit." *Journal of Religion & Spirituality in Social Work: Social Thought* 31, nos. 1–2 (2012) 193–208.

Staral, Janice M. "Observations from the Field of Faith-Based Organizing: Revitalizing Social Work Skills in Policy and Social Action." *Professional Development-Philadelphia* 5, no. 2 (2002) 4–14.

Strauss, Anselm, and Juliet Corbin. *Basics of Qualitative Research: Techniques and Procedures for Developing Grounded Theory*. Newbury Park, CA: Sage, 1998.

Thomas, M. Lori. "The Variations and Strategies of Faith-Based Advocacy Organizations in Virginia." *Journal of Policy Practice* 9, nos. 3–4 (2010) 240–62.

Thomas, Scott M. "Living Critically and 'Living Faithfully' in a Global Age: Justice, Emancipation and the Political Theology of International Relations." *Millennium-Journal of International Studies* 39, no. 2 (2010) 505–24.

Wald, Kenneth D., et al. "Making Sense of Religion in Political Life." *Annual Review of Political Science* 8 (2005) 121–43.

Vokey, Daniel. "Spirituality and Professional Education: Contributions Toward a Shared Curriculum Framework." In *Spirituality in Social Work and Education: Theory, Practice, and Pedagogies*, edited by Janet Groen et al., 79–120. Waterloo, OT: Laurier, 2012.

Zuidervaart, Lambert. "Theodor W. Adorno." *The Stanford Encyclopedia of Philosophy*. Winter 2015 ed., edited by Edward N. Zalta. http://plato.stanford.edu/archives/win2015/entries/adorno/. Accessed March 23, 2017.

Index

Abel, 154, 168
Abell, Asa, 17, 78, 105
ăbôdâ (work), 151
abolition. *See* justice (social)
Abraham, 47, 165
action-orientation, 59–60, 68
Adam, 45, 50, 147–48, 155, 160, 166–71
ădāmâ (earth), 145, 147, 151–52, 156, 165–66
Adorno, Theodor, 233
Allen, William, 86
Allis, Asa, 78
Alston, William, 173
Anderson, Galusha, 104
Anderson, Martin, 80, 90
Andover Academy and Theological Seminary, 110
Annis, D., 195, 207
Anthony, Susan B., 27, 45, 50, 138
anxiety, 8–9, 175, 194–96
    faculty sharing failures reduces, for students, 218
    Fall led to, 158
    grace mollifies, 194
apostles, 16, 37, 42, 45–48, 50, 51, 53, 108, 170
apostolos (apostle), 42
Aristotle, 37–38, 40, 47
Arthur, William, 136–138
Asbury, Francis, 102, 104
Augustine, 144, 168

Baptist, 104, 122, 236, 241–42
Barr, James, 151, 170
Barth, Karl, 199
Bassett, Rodney, xv, 190
Bates, Mary Lou, 76
Bear Ridge, NY, 6
Beck, Cheryl T., 223, 225
Beers, Adelaide, 96
Benner, Patricia, 211–12, 224
Bergen camp ground, 65, 69, 78, 103–9, 116–17
Bergen Camp Meeting. *See* camp meetings
Berry, Elvera B., xii, 30
Berry, Wendell, 112–14, 117
Black Creek Camp Meeting, 5–6, 8, 91
Black Friday, 89
Blatchly, Sister, 20
Bogassian, Fiona, 212, 214
Bornstein, David, 57–61, 63, 70, 72
Boulton, Matthew, 199, 205
Brackett, L. P. 39
Bronte, Jacelyn C., 194, 205
Brooks, Arthur C., 14, 57, 59, 60, 72
Brown, Sarah J., 213, 224
Brown, William P., 152, 170, 213, 224
Brummett, Barry, 44, 54
Bryant, Fred B., 204–205
Buffalo, NY, ix–x, 5–6, 19, 31, 66, 69, 78–79, 96–97, 110, 121
Buffalo Road, 81, 84–85, 88
Burke, Kenneth, 28, 32, 4–44, 54

burned-over district, 3, 27, 86, 120, 138
Bushfield, Suzanne, 226, 254

Cain, 154, 166, 168
calling (vocation), ix–x, 3, 6, 31–33, 70
    to care for others, 211, 214, 220
    to dissent, 33, 47
    equality of men and women in
        pursuing, 34
    to evangelism, 8, 11, 135
    of humanity in general, 54, 108, 112,
        147–55, 165
    to justice, 239
    to piety, 33
    to social policy practice, 237–240
    of women to domestic life, 22–23
    of women to preach, xii, 4–7, 8–11,
        15–16, 22, 24–25, 34–35, 37, 44,
        48, 50, 53
Calvin, John, 148, 170, 191
camp meetings, 3, 5–8, 12, 14, 18, 19,
    35, 56, 65, 78, 96, 107–108, 175
    Bergen Camp Meeting, 7, 17, 65,
        104–6, 118
    Coldwater Camp Meeting, 12
    Gasport Camp Meeting, 5
    Lyndon Camp Meeting, 14, 19
    Pekin Camp Meeting, 17, 121
    West Falls Camp Meeting, 9–11
Campbell, David E., 246, 254
Campbell, Levi, 86
Campbell, Lorne, 195, 205
Campbell, Simone, 230, 254
Canal Street Mission, ix, 66–67, 110
Canda, Edward R., 226, 229–30, 254
Canon, Charlie, 76
Carver, Charles S., 204, 206
Caryville, NY, 6
Catarack Milling Company, 94–95
Catholicism, 44, 144, 236, 241
Cattaraugus Trail, 81
Chautaqua, 31
Chesbrough, A. M., x, 69, 92–95
Chili Seminary, ix–xii, 12, 22, 73, 77,
        79, 102
    150th anniversary of, xi, 71
    behavioral rules of, 114
    Carpenter Hall, 98

Chesbrough Seminary, name
        changed to, 94
    Cox Hall, 96–98
    fire at, 95–96
    first classes of, held in B. T. Roberts's
        home, 85
    founding of, x, xvi, 31, 67, 69–70,
        82–84, 109
    legacies supporting, 91–97
        Chesbrough, A. M., 92–95
        Cox, Edward P., 96–97
    manual labor school and farm,
        conducted as, 68, 89–90, 109–
        12, 114
    populist ethos of, 114
    real estate transactions regarding,
        69, 81–99
    Roberts Junior College, name
        changed to, 94
    Roberts Wesleyan College, name
        changed to, 94
    seminary building of, constructed
        and dedicated, 87, 90
    students of, from moderate and low
        income families, 89
    survival of, when similar institutions
        were failing, 98
    tuition and board of, 89
Chopin, Kate, 34
Christianizing the Social Order
    (Rauschenbusch), 129
Clarke, Adam, 25, 47, 50
Clothilde, 50
Clovis, King of the Franks, 50
Coates, Gregory R., 102, 114, 117
Coldwater Camp Meeting. *See* camp
    meetings
College Greene, 85
Collins, Patricia, 38
compassion, 130, 182, 184, 187, 243
Connell, Jack, xiii, 55
Corbin, Juliet M., 234
Cox, Edward P., 80, 96
Creswell, John W., 233–35, 254
Crothers, William, 75
Crotser, Cheryl B., xvi, 208
Cullum, Douglas R., xii, 3, 32, 37, 192
Curley, Christine, 163–65
Cvengros, Jamie A., 204

Dakota Conference, 7
Davis, Susan, 57, 59, 61, 72
deacon, office of, 27, 32–33, 37, 42, 48–49, 53, 144
deaconess, office of, 27, 37, 42, 48–49, 210
death,
    of animals, 166
    disobedience the cause of, 158
    Fall the cause of, 162–68
    judgment after, 183–84
    meaning of, in *Genesis 2*, 158–59
Deborah, 64
DeCastilley, Cristoval, 52
Declaration of Sentiments, 30
Dees, Gregory J., 57
Derezotes, David, 226–27
diakonos (deacon), 42
Dibble, Joseph, 91
Dick, Mendal, 112
Douglass, Frederick, 32, 79, 120
Downing, Moses, 7
Draucker, Claire, 235
Dunbar, E. W., 19
Dunning, Jane, 69

Earnest Christian, 12, 66–67, 69–70, 87–88, 112, 126, 131
    building purchased for, 79
    circulation of, 79
    founding of, x, 66, 70, 121, 138
    fundraising, vehicle for, 91, 96, 109,
    Golden Rule merged with, 111n52
    inaugural issue of, 130
    production moved to North Chili, NY, 138
Eastern Orthodoxy, 144, 160, 166
Eden, 108, 148–51
elder, office of, 27, 32–33, 42, 60, 144
Eldridge, Cynthia, 5
Ely, Richard, 129
Emmons, Robert A., 198–99
Engels, Friedrich, 232
entrepreneurism, social, xiii, xvii, 55–61, 64, 68, 70, 72
    attributes of, 58–60, 68
        action-orientation, 58, 68
        collaboration, 59, 69
        determination, 60, 70
        innovation, xii, 58, 108–9, 150, 168, 170, 223
        resource acquisition, 60, 69, 87
    curricula, recommended for, 71
environmentalism. *See* justice (environmental)
Erie Canal, 55, 78, 81
evangelicalism, xiv, 101, 110, 120, 133, 138
evangelism, xiv, 8–9, 11, 37, 49, 65, 103, 175
    and abolitionism, 123–24
    and holiness, 131–32
    social reform dependent on, 131–132, 138
    social reform a form of, 134–135
evangelist, office of, 23–25, 32–33, 37, 55, 134–35, 144
Evans, Christopher H., 125–126, 129, 139
Evans, E. N., 226, 230
Exline, Julie, 202

faith, 5, 63, 68, 99, 111, 129, 230
    choices and motivations influence on, 173–75
    fear overcome by, 8–9
    fruits of, 136, 174, 176, 190, 192, 197–204, 216
    gifts of, 10, 17
    grace required for, 192
    in guidance, 20
    healing as a result of, 13
    integration of, with the nursing profession, 215–16
    integration of, with the social work profession, 226–53
    internalization of, 194–95
    intrinsic, related to gratitude, 199
    religious experience essential to maintaining, 173
    social action the result of, 128, 242
    social justice leaders inspired by, 239
    social justice influence on, 188–89
    strength increased through, 211
    transformation required for, 173–74

Fall (of humanity), 45, 157–69, 190
    arguments from the, concerning
        women's ordination, 45–46, 53
    consequences of, 162–69
        banishment from the garden,
            166–67
        death, 162–63
        diminished life for the man,
            164–66
        diminished life for the woman,
            163–64
        judgment, 162–63
        mediator needed, 192
        sin, growing domination of, 168,
            192
    creation often conflated with, 144
    God's grace in response to, 166
    restoration through Christ from,
        169–70, 190, 203
    upwards, 159n48–160n48
fanaticism 5, 13–19
    abolition rejected as, 38–39
    and divine gifts, 13, 16, 17, 19
    extravagances of, distinguished from
        genuine power of God, 19
    and healing, 13, 16
    Nazarites practitioners of, 13n38,
        16–19, 104–5
    and physical manifestations, 19
    and women preaching, 13–14, 17
Finney, Charles G., 3, 30, 32, 110, 120
First Lessons on Money (Roberts), xiv,
    98, 129, 132
flourishing. *See* human nature
forgiveness, xvi, 174, 176, 205
    being forgiven leads to, 203
    flourishing promoted by, 202–3
    forgiving others a requirement for
        God's, 203
    grace-orientation leads to, 194–95,
        202–3
    self-, 202
Francis of Assisi, 71, 243
Frankfurt School, 232
Fredonia, NY, 115
Freeland, Mariet H., xii, 4–7, 11–12,
    14–15
    call to exhort of, 4–5
    preaching of, 6–7, 14–15

Free Methodist Church, ix, xii, 33, 144
    Eastern Convention of, 15, 16,
        19–20, 23
    founding of, x, 31, 62, 78, 121
        Chesbrough family pivotal to, 69
        Cox family pivotal to, 80
    headquarters of, in Buffalo,
        purchased, 79
    theology of,
        fanaticism, 13–15; miraculous
            gifts, resolution against,
            16–17
        revivalism, 120
        salvation, 120, 123
        social reform, 123–24
    women, non-ordained ministry of,
        xii, 15, 16, 18–27, 32–35, 46,
        48–51, 53, 144n4
        deacons, licensing as, 32–33
        evangelists, licensing as, 24,
            32–33
        "labors" versus preaching, 20–21,
            23
        lay delegates to the General
            Conference, 144n4
        licensure versus ordination, 24
        preaching, 6–7, 10–15, 20–23, 32
        resolution against, of the Eastern
            Convention, 21
        social, 23
        women, of, to other, 23
    women, ordained ministry of, xiv,
        13, 46, 48 32–35, 37–41, 44, 45,
        50, 51, 53, 77, 100
        and abolition, 25, 37–40, 51
        and baptizing, 49–50
        as deacons: full ordination,
            144n4; without access to
            senior pastor position, 144n4
        as elders, 27; approval of, 32–33
        and governing, involvement in 24
        as ministers: approval of, 27;
            consideration of, 24–25;
            rejected, by only four votes,
            144n4; resistance to, 15;
            symbol of God's call, 44
        See also Ordaining Women
Fretheim, Terence, 168

Freud, Sigmund, xv, 160, 161, 167, 177–78, 227
Furman, Leola D., 226, 228

Gainesville Female Seminary, 5–6
Garden of Eden, 143–44, 146–52, 158–162, 166–67
Gasport Camp Meeting. *See* camp meetings
gender equality. *See* justice (social)
Genesee Campground Association, 105
Genesee Wesleyan Seminary, 4, 13, 111, 121
George, Henry, 129
Gihon, 149
Gilman, Charlotte P., 34
Gowanda, NY, 31
grace, 10, 63, 114, 176, 190–99, 201–205, 211, 223
  in Christian nursing, 211
  courage essential for experiencing, 176
  humility essential for experiencing, 200
  physiological manifestations of, 196–97
    neuropeptide hormones: oxytocin and vasopressin, 196
    neurotransmitters: serotonin, glutamate, and dopamine, 196–97
  prejudice overcome by, 40
  in psychological literature, 193–96
  and social reform, 130–32
  varieties of,
    justifying, xv, 10, 63, 190, 192–93, 195–97, 201, 203–4
    prevenient, xv, 190–92, 193, 195
    sanctifying, iv, xiv, xv, 65, 102, 131, 190–92, 195, 197, 199, 204, 209
grace-orientation, 193–95, 204–5
  anxiety improved by, 194
  character, created by, 197
  depression improved by, 194
  forgiveness of others increased by, 195, 202–3
  gratitude increased by, 198–99
  humility correlated with, 199–201
  realistic view of sin correlated with, 194
  scales of,
    Amazing Grace Scale, 194–95
    Richmont Grace Scale, 194
  self-compassion correlated with, 194
  shame reduced by, 194
grace-salience xvi, 196, 198, 199, 201, 203–5
  forgiveness of others increased by, 196, 203
  generosity increased by, 197
  judgmentalism decreased by, 197
Gramento, Jean, 12
Gramsci, Antonio, 232
Grassley, Jane S., 211
gratitude, xvi, 193, 194–95, 198–99, 205–6
  flourishing promoted by, 198–99
  grace-orientation increased by, 198–99
  religious people more likely to have the habit of, 199
Gregg, Steve, 184
Griffin, Mary T., 222
Griffith, G. W., 24, 28
Gütersloh, 121

ḥai (living), 164
Hall, Stuart, 38
Hannah, Thomas, 85
Harding, Sandra, 38
Harford, Charles, 86
Harris, Chelsia, 222
Hart, E. P., 12
Hart, Patricia L., 222
Haudenosaunee Confederacy, 82
Haudenosaunee Road, 81
Hauerwas, Stanley, 132–34
Havilah, 149
ḥavvâ (Eve), 164
ha'ādām (the human), 147, 148, 155, 165–67
heaven, 108, 130n35, 131, 144n2, 146, 149, 156n39, 170, 175

hell, xv, 104, 172, 173, 175–77, 179–88
    annihilationism, 184
    eternal abandonment view of, 172, 181–84
        epistemic impacts of, 183–84
    fear of, 172–77, 180–84, 186–89
        rationality of, 180–81
    restorationism, 184
Hell's Kitchen, 124, 127
Hempton, David, 103, 114
Henry, Matthew, 45
hērôn (childbearing), 163
Hodge, David R., 226
Hoess, Victoria, 212
Hogue, Wilson T., 7, 21
holiness, xi, xvi, 3, 4, 7, 33, 62, 121, 145, 170, 204
    camp meetings a place to promote, 65
    care for others, essential to, ix, 137, 209, 214–16
    care for others an outgrowth of, 70, 123, 131–32, 189
    evangelism an outgrowth of, 131–32
    grace leads to, 192, 197
    humility an aspect of, 215
    levity a threat to, 114
    nature can provide a sense of, 107–8
    prohibition an issue of, 128
    purity part of, 192
    revival leads to, 131
    servant leadership an aspect of, 214
    social, xv, 145, 170, 192
    theology of,
        heaven, a place for the disembodied saints, 108, 114
        personal conversion emphasized over social transformation, 120n2, 137
Holy Spirit,
    fear a hindrance to receiving guidance from, 8–9
    filled with, being, 10
    gifts of, 13, 15–16
        healing, 13, 210
        prophecy, 10, 17
    humility required to experience the presence of, 200
    manifestations of, 19, 103
    movement of, 4, 9, 10, 12, 14, 19
    promptings of, 4–5, 8–9, 10, 14, 44, 133, 174–75
    resisting the, 174
hope, xvi, 108, 185, 203–5, 222
    Herth Hope Scale, 204
    optimism, distinguished from, 204
Hopkins, John H., 25, 38
Hudson, Winthrop S., 124, 133–35, 137
Huldah, 46
human nature, 53
    complete corruption of, not indicated in *Genesis*, 167–69
    and creativity, 150
    and decision-making, 153–54
    epistemic blindness part of, 173–75
    flourishing of, xv, 112, 158–59
        and the Fall, 162–69
        and forgiveness, 202–3
        God's original intent for, 145–57; mutuality of men and women, 152–57; primal harmony, 146, 152, 156, 161, 164–65; work and sustenance, 145–55, 165
    and grace, 194
    and gratitude, 198–99
    "life" in *Genesis* 2 refers to, 158
    and relationship between human and earth, 145
    shalom central to, 212
    this-worldly, 132–34, 137
    and freedom, 123
    gender differences in, 47, 53
    and labor, xv, 26, 90, 110, 112, 122–24, 165
        agrarian, value of, 124–25, 147–52
        and community health, 113
        manual, inferiority of, according to Aristotle, 38
        psychological value of, 110, 114
        requirement of, at Chili Seminary, 90
        spiritual value of, 110
        workaholism, 165
    mortality part of first people's, 148n14

and mutuality of man and woman, 145
original "sin nature" not part of, 129–30, 143–44, 168
slavery and, according to Aristotle, 38
humility, xvi, 96, 135, 169, 174, 182, 187–88, 215, 223
Hutchison, Elizabeth D., 226, 230

Ignatius, 244
Imago Dei, 123, 150, 171
In Darkest Africa (Livingstone), 39
intrapreneurs, 63–64, 72
îš (man), 145, 153, 155–56, 164
iṣābôn (pangs), 163, 165
Israel, 124, 152, 158, 162, 240–41, 249–50
iššâ (woman), 145, 153, 155–56, 164

Jacobsen, Thorkild, 150
Jansson, Bruce, 228, 245, 248
Jeffries, Delia, 70
Jerusalem, 149, 151, 170
Joan of Arc, 48
Johnson, Samuel, 41
Joinson, Carla, 222
Jones, George, 78
justice (economic), ix–x, 31, 63, 66, 71, 114–16, 124–26, 129–32, 235
  and abolition, 130
  and Jubilee, ix, 125, 130
  New York State Farmers' Alliance, 68, 101–2, 114, 116
  and prohibition, 126–27
  and sabbath years, 125
justice (environmental), xiii, 58, 100–117, 151, 223
  manual labor movement, affinities with, 110–13
  stewardship, 101, 145, 209, 220–21
justice (social), xiii, xvi, 4, 30–33, 63, 71, 120–24, 129, 131–32, 154, 235, 242, 253
  abolition, 53, 79, 86, 110, 120, 122–23, 125–28, 232–33
    and holiness and revivalism, 123
    and manual labor movement, 110

  and prohibition, 130
  and women's ordination, 37–40
  evangelism a kind of, 134–35
  gender equality, 4, 30, 34, 37
    authority shared in society, 51
    biblical teaching of, 143–45, 152–57, 169–70
    differences between church and society regarding, 36, 45–46
    suffrage, women's, 25, 30, 34, 120
    wives and husbands, between: biblical support for, 45–46, 53; ownership of wife by husband, 39–40
    women in ministry. See Free Methodist Church
  humanistic, spiritual, and religious motivations for promoting, 250–52
  knowledge, impact on, 188–89
  personal conversion necessary for, xiv, 70, 136
  personal conversion not sufficient for, 137
  prohibition, 126
    and abolition, 130
    business helped by, 127
    and colleges, 128
    and holiness, 128
  religious diversity not prohibitive in the pursuit of, 245–46, 251
  religious worldviews that promote, 232–33
  and revivalism, 123, 130–31
  social entrepreneurs needed to promote, 71
  social gospel, xiv, 119–20, 129–38
    impact of, on social policy practitioners, 238, 241
    and religious experience, 133
  socialization creates concern for, 238–39, 246
  and spiritual practices, 241–42, 247
justification. *See* grace: varieties of
Kalat, James W., 196
Kendall, Martha, 8, 11
Kendall, William, 69, 81
kĕnegdô (as his partner), 152
kerux (preacher), 42

264　　　　　　　　　　　　　　　　INDEX

kingdom of God, 35, 101, 108, 112, 114, 120, 132, 134, 135
knowing (atheistic), xv, 173, 177, 184–86
　challenges to, from fears and inducements, 184–86
knowing (Christian), 172–82, 184, 186, 188–89
　challenges to,
　　from fear of hell, 175–77, 179–86, 188–89
　　from inducements, 176–77, 182
　　from religious diversity, 183
　　from wish-fulfillment, 178–79
　choices and motivations influence on, 173–74
　cognitive design plan determinant of, 173, 178–83
knowing (general religious), x, xvii, 10
　critical theory approach to, 231
　religious experiences a means of, awareness heightened in, 243
　doctrines produced through, 120, 188
　dopaminergic systems influence on, 197
　epistemic challenges, a possible defeater of, 183
　fear an influence on, 176
　focus a tool for heightening, 244
　framing and interpretation of, 244
　God's grace encountered in, 194, 197
　guidance provided by, 243, 247
　humility a prerequisite for, 200
　Ignatian contemplation, 244
　ineffability of, 42
　knowledge of God produced by, 133–34, 173
　meditation, 244
　nature a feature in, 243–44
　needs of others often the focus of, 244
　serving the needy a source of, 210
　social gospel rooted in, 133
　"thin spaces" a description of, 242
　transpersonal experiences, 232, 242–44; values influenced by, 246–47
　western academic settings, ignored in, xvii, 227
Koehl, Andrew C., xv, 172, 173, 183, 188
Kramarae, Cheris, 38
Krause, Neil, 201
Krober, Al, 76

labor. *See* human nature
Leininger, Madeleine, 214
lĕ'ādām (to/for the human), 147–48
Lewis, C. S., 166, 169–70, 184
Lily Dale, NY, 30–31
Lincoln, Yvonna, 231–32
Livingstone, David, 39
Lockport, NY, 6
Lodi, NY, 104
Lyndon Camp Meeting. *See* camp meetings

Magaletta, Philip R., 203
Mahnke, Dale, 112
Mahnke, Leo, 112
Marsden, George, 103
Marston, Leslie, 13, 16, 25, 27
Martin, Roger L., 59
Martindale farmstead, 91
Marx, Jerry D., 230
Matthews, J., 70
McCreery, Joseph, 6
McDowell, Catherine L., 150
McPherson, Jeffrey L., xiv, 119
Merritt, Abram, 92–93
Methodist Episcopal Church, 3, 6, 62–65, 69–70, 78, 100, 104–5, 121–22
　abolitionism, opposition to x, 25, 38
　Bergen Camp Meeting a source of controversy in, 65, 105
　camp meetings used as a means to reform, 104
　Freeland, Mariet H., ministry overseen by, 6
　Genesee Campground Association placed under the jurisdiction of, 105
　pew rental in, 32, 122

Meyer, Lucy R., 27
Middleton, Richard J., xiv–xv, 108, 109, 112, 143, 149–51, 158–59, 161, 163, 167, 170
Mikulincer, Mario, 195
Mill, John Stuart, 39
Miller, Arlene B., 210–11, 222
Miller, Patrick D., Jr., 152
Miriam, 46
Mishra, Anjali, 198
Mohnkern, Susanne, xvi, 208
Moore, Carl C., v, 73–76
    book of, preserved by William Crothers, 75
Moore, Matthew Dwight, 73, 84
Muir, John, xii, 100, 106–7
Müller, Max, 43–44
Murphy, Lyn S., 211–12

naming, 153–56
    arguments, 44
    animals, 153–54
    deaconesses while withholding the essence of the office, 49
    Eve by Adam, after the Fall, a form of domination, 164
    partnership precluded by, 154
    vocation transformed by, 154
National Grange, 115
nature, xiii, 100, 102–5, 116–17, 147, 149, 191, 244
    Fall did not corrupt, 167
    holiness in, 106–7
    and human purpose, 146–52
    and religious experience, 243, 244
    restoration of, promised in Scripture, 170
Nazarites. *See* fanaticism
nepeš ḥayyāh (living being), 148
New Evangelism (Rauschenbusch), 134–35
New School Methodism (Roberts), x, 64, 121
New York State Farmer's Alliance, 68, 101–2, 114, 116
New York, western, hotbed of religious and social activism, 3, 30, 120

Niagara Street Church, 121
Nietzsche, Friedrich, 232
Nightingale, Florence, 61, 210
Noadiah, 46
Noll, Mark, 102–3
North Chili, NY, x, xiv, 22, 27, 56, 74–75, 80–82, 84–87, 90, 96, 100, 110, 117, 121, 138
North Chili Tavern, x, 67, 75, 84–88, 90, 91
Northeastern Seminary, ix–xi, 88, 208
Nubia, 149
nursing, 50, 210–15
    Christianity influence on, 210–11
    compassion fatigue, 222
    emotional labor, 211
    patient-centered care, 211
    technology, a threat to, 218
    and vulnerability, 215
    spiritual care,
        and patient-centered care, 211
        understanding God's grace a motivation for, 211
nursing (Christian), 50, 208, 210–11, 217–18, 222–23
    empathy in, 214–15
    industry and economy in, 219–21
    and perspective, 220
    and living in *shalom*, 210
    piety in, 214–16
    and standing on holy ground, 210
    virtue in, 212–13, 217–19
        courage, 217–18, 223
        empathy, 214, 215, 219
        friendliness, 215, 218
        honesty, 217
        humility, 205, 215
        integrity, 218
        perseverance, 218, 222
        trustworthiness, 218
        vulnerability, 215, 218
        wisdom, 223
nursing education, 208, 223
    diversity important to 219
    online an economical mode of, 220
    School of Nursing at Roberts Wesleyan College, of 208

nursing education *(continued)*
   piety exemplified in, and suggestions to improve, 215–16
   industry and economy exemplified in, and suggestions to improve, 220–21
   virtue exemplified in, and suggestions to improve, 218–19
   social entrepreneurship recommended for, 71
   spiritual care course recommended for, 216

Oberlin College, 22, 30, 112
O'Brien, Mary E., 210–11
Ogden, Edna, 76
Old Pearl Street Theater, x, 78–80
Olin, Stephen, 31, 174
Oliver, J. M., 203
Oneida Institute, 110–12
Oneida Society, 120
Ordaining Women (Roberts) xii, 26, 27, 30–54, 144
   rhetoric of, xii, 25, 30–33, 41, 51–52
   appeals to authority, 36–37, 41
   awareness of audience, 35–36, 40
   enthymematic syllogisms, 40
   ethos appeals, 40
   fluiditiy of thought, 40
   grammatical direct address, 39
   identification with audience, 36
   logos appeals lacking, 40
   arguments of,
      language, reflections on, 41–44
      natural, named and addressed, 47–52
      ordination, reflections on, 44
      scriptural, named and addressed, 44–47
      slavery equated with denying women's ordination, 38–39
      synthesis of, as six numbered propositions, 53
ozer (helper), 152

Palmer, Phoebe, 3, 15, 210
Palmer Street, 78
Pascal, Blaise, 180
Paul, Apostle, 45–47, 135, 148, 168–69, 192, 198
Payton, J. T., 193, 195
Pekin Camp Meeting. *See* camp meetings
Pendleton, NY, vi
Perelandra (Lewis), 160, 166
Perry, NY, 20
Peter, Apostle, 47, 50, 170
Peterson, Brian, 163–65
Peterson, Christopher, 204
Pfouts, Neil E., 67, 75
Phelps, A. A., 123–24
Phoebe, 48, 210
Pike, NY, 111, 198
Plantinga, Alvin, xv, 173, 177–79, 185
Platonism, 148
Pliny the Younger, 51–52
pneuma (spirit), 42
Politics Strangely Warmed: Political Theology in the Wesleyan Spirit (Coates), 101
Pomfret, NY, 77
Populist Saints (Snyder), 55, 61–62, 65–67, 69, 75, 99, 101–5, 107, 109–11, 115–16, 122–24, 129, 132, 138
Porter's Corners, 9
Prayers of the Social Awakening (Rauschenbusch), 128
presbus (elder), 42
Presbyterians, 30, 45, 86, 103
priestly role, 150
   Aaronic, 46
   Christ's, 192
Prince Caspian, 169–70
Progress and Poverty (George), 129
Prohibition. *See* justice (social)
prophetesses, 37, 46, 48
prophets, 37, 46, 48, 124–25, 170

qārā (to call), 156
Quakers, 30, 36
Quintilian, 51

INDEX

Rauschenbusch, Walter, xiv, 119–22, 124–29, 132–36, 138
  abolitionism of, 126
  agrarianism, support for, 125
  economic influences on, 129
  gospel, views on the, 132–38
  pietistic influence on, 122
  prohibition, support for, 126–28
  theological influences on, 136
Redfield, John Wesley, 5, 17, 31, 69, 102, 121, 124
religious diversity, 165, 170, 219, 221, 234
  functional values shared in settings of, 246
  intra-denominational, 27, 103–4, 134–35
  religious beliefs impacted by, 183
religious experience. *See* knowing (general religious)
revival, 3, 30, 103
  abolitionism twin moral crusade of, 123
  camp meetings venue for, 65, 102,
  Christianity and the Social Crisis a sermon of, 132, 134
  Earnest Christian a vehicle for, 66
  formative influence on B. T. Roberts of, 121, 123
  Free Methodist Church spiritual narrative grounded in, 120
  manual labor movement spurred on by, 110
  reformation distinguished from, 131
  social reform connected to, 123, 130–31
Rhetoric of Religion (Burke), 41, 43
Richardson, Jack D., 3, 12–13, 21, 24
Richardson, Robert D., 106
Right of Women to Preach the Gospel, 25–26
river, biblical significance of, 148–151
Roberts, Benjamin T., ix–xviii, 5, 6, 10–27, 31–56, 58, 61–71, 73, 75–92, 94–98, 100–109, 111–17, 119–132, 134, 138, 144, 145, 172–76, 181, 186–90, 192, 198–200, 202, 203, 205, 208, 209, 212, 213, 215, 216, 218–23
  character of, xi, xvii
  acceptance, 106, 187
  action-orientation, ix, x–xi, 21n79, 32, 64–68, 77–99, 102, 104, 116, 121
  ambiguity, comfort with, xii, 32, 41, 102, 112
  assertiveness, x, 16–21, 24, 63–64, 66, 68, 115, 121, 126
  collaboration, 16, 67, 69, 78, 81, 85, 92, 105, 109
  compassion x, 40, 62–63, 65, 66–67, 70, 123, 186–87
  compromise, willingness and ability to forge, 16–17, 19, 33, 112
  creativity, 37, 69, 123
  determination (resilience), ix, x–ix, 21n–22n, 25, 65, 67, 70, 78, 89, 95, 106
  diligence, 66–67, 70, 79, 111–12
  encouragement, 10–11, 20
  generosity, 69–70, 78, 90–91
  gentleness, 14, 17, 19, 36, 106–7
  gratitude, 96, 198
  guilelessness, 20, 40
  humility, 80, 96, 187, 200
  innovation, xii, 64–65, 69–70, 114
  integrity, 20, 25, 64, 82–83, 111, 121
  justice, ix–x, 5, 20, 31, 33, 48–50, 63, 66–68, 69, 115–16, 121, 122–24, 129–30
  loyalty, 15–16, 20, 63–64
  openness, 14, 16, 19–20, 22n80, 37, 41
  patience, 16–17, 20, 33
  persuasiveness, 17, 30–54, 67, 69, 102
  piety (holiness), ix–x, 20, 63–65, 111, 112
  resource-acquisition, 69, 76–99
  child, death of,
    Samuel Roberts, 187
    William Titus Roberts, 77

Roberts, Benjamin T. *(continued)*
  childhood of, 31, 55, 62, 77
  economics of, 129
    debt, reflections on, 91, 98
    Ely, Richard, influence on, 129
    George, Henry, influence on, 129
    manual labor movement, sympathies with, 110–14, 116
    populism, 101, 114
    poverty, concerns about, 130–31
  environmentalism of, 100–117
    Bergen Camp Ground, actions regarding, 105–6
    creation care, views compared to, 100–101, 107
    farming, experience of and affinity with, xiv, 67, 70, 77 (*see also* New York State Farmers' Alliance)
    holiness movement, affinities for, impacts on, 107–8, 114
    nature, attitudes towards, 102, 104, 107, 116–17
    outdoor camp meetings, commitment to, 102–9
  fundraising efforts of, 65, 66–67, 69, 79–80, 87–99, 105, 109
  Methodist Episcopal Church, relationship with,
    attempts to reform, x, 62, 63–64, 69, 104
    expulsion from, x, 64
    membership, 31
    pastoral ministry in, 78, 121
  organizations founded by. *See* camp meetings: Bergen Camp Meeting; Canal Street Mission; Chili Seminary; Earnest Christian; Free Methodist Church; Genesee Campground Association; New York State Farmer's Alliance;
  pastor, service as, 31, 65, 78, 121
  publications of. *See* First Lessons on Money; Ordaining Women; Right of Women to Preach the Gospel; Spiritual Songs and Hymns for Pilgrims; Why Another Sect?
  real estate activity of, 62, 69, 73–99, 104, 105
    mortgages of, 76, 78, 79, 80, 82–83, 88, 90, 115
  social activism of,
    abolitionism, 122–23
    Canal Street Mission established as a ministry to alcoholics, 66
    prohibitionism, 126–28, 130; North Chili Tavern, purchasing and repurposing, 67, 84–85
    railroads, criticism of, 115–16
    renting pews, opposition to, 122, 130–31
    single tax, support of, 129
    slaveholders, banning from church membership, 124
    women's ordination (*see* Free Methodist Church: women, ordained ministry of; Ordaining Women)
  Stowe, Ellen Lois, marriage to 31, 111
    nature, shared love of, 103
    support for calling of, 10–11, 19, 37
  theology of,
    camp meetings, 65, 104, 116
    evangelism and social reform, 130–32
    formalism, religious, 65, 111, 122, 200
    gifts, divine (miraculous),14, 16–17, 19; fanaticism distinguished from, 19
    grace, 192–93
    hell, 172, 175, 186–88
    salvation, connection of social reform to, 130–31
    sanctification, entire, 102
    sin, 129–30, 174, 181
    Wesley, John, comparisons to, 101
Roberts, Benson H., xii, 13, 72, 75, 99, 139

INDEX

Sellew, Emma J, correspondence with, opposing women's ordination, 22–24
Roberts, Ellen Stowe, x, xii, 5, 7–12, 14–16, 19–23, 25–27, 31–32, 37, 61, 69–70, 76–77, 99, 101, 103, 110–12, 118, 121, 139, 225
  Anthony, Susan B., gifting of *Ordaining Women* to, 27
  Earnest Christian, working for, 12
  management of Chili Seminary and B. T. Roberts' ministry, 12
  preaching, call to, of 8–9
  preaching, ministry of, 10–12, 14, 20, 23, 32
  prophecy, gift of, 10
  visions of, 8, 9
  women's ordination, advocacy for, 26–27
Roberts, Florilla, 122
Roberts, Sally, 62, 77
Roberts, Titus, 55, 62, 77
Roberts Wesleyan College, ix–xi, xiii, xvi, 31, 63, 67, 71, 72–73, 75–76, 94, 121, 208, 213, 215, 216, 218–219, 221, 223
Rochester Theological Seminary, 121–122
Roosevelt, Theodore, xiii, 100, 114, 116–117
Rosmarin, David H., 199
Rother, Pauline, 122
Rumsey, Alexander, 82
Rumsey, Cornelius, 81–82
Rumsey farmstead, x, 80–85, 87–88, 90–92, 96, 98
Rushton, Cynda H., 222

šāḥat (destroyed), 168
salvation, 9, 25, 133, 190
  personal nature of, 133–34, 175
  and prevenient grace, 192
  and social reform, 130–34
  this-worldly, 137
šāmar (protect), 150–51, 167
sanctification. *See* grace: varieties of
Sandelowski, Margarete, 213

Scandrett, Joel, 101
Scheier, Michael F., 204
Scherer, Michael, 202
Second German Baptist Church, 122
ṣēlā (rib), 155–56
self-deception, 175
Sellew, Emma J., xii, 13, 27
  calling to preach of, 22
  Chili Seminary, teaching languages at, 22
  Roberts, Benson, correspondence with, opposing women's ordination, 22–24
šēm (name), 156
Seneca Falls Convention, 30
shame, 169
  Fall results in, 162, 167
  and grace-orientation, 194
Sharp, Dores, 134
Shay, Emma F., 4–7, 12
Shelby, NY, 6
Shelly, Judith A., 210, 211, 222
Sheridan, Michael J., 226, 230
Silver Lake, NY, 106
sin, 53, 108, 162, 165, 201
  blinding nature of, 174
  original,
    Augustine's view of, 144, 168
    unscriptural, 144, 167–69
  personal,
    complicity in social sin a form of, 132–33
    selfishness, the core of, 133
    realistic view of, associated with grace-orientation, 194
  social, 125, 132, 169
Sisemore, Timothy A., 194
slavery. *See* justice (social): abolition
Smith, Hart, 78
Smith, Joseph, 120
Smith, Timothy L., 3
Snyder, Howard A., 55, 61–62, 65–67, 69, 75, 101–5, 107–11, 115–16, 122–25, 129, 132, 138, 139, 190, 192, 209, 225
social gospel. *See* justice (social)

social policy practice, religious and spiritual integration in, xvi–xvii, 227–28, 231, 233–238, 240, 246, 248, 249, 251–53
  marginalization of religion and spirituality, 231
    critical theory, a means of exposing, 231
    religion seen as epiphenomenal and anti-modern, 229; religiously motivated activism challenged, 229; Social Movement Theory challenged, 229
    and separation of church and state, 231, 251
    spiritual values not framed as such by practitioners, 249
    spiritual ways of knowing ignored, 231, 247
  Religion and Spirituality in Social Policy Practice model (RSSPP), 236–46, 253
    Formative Phase, 238–39
    Practice Phase, 245–46
    Spiritual Integration Phase, 240–241
    Vocational Phase, 239–40
  research lacuna, 226–27, 230, 247
  skills required for, 240–44
    communicating spiritual values to policymakers, 249–51; separation of church and state paradigm a challenge to, 251
    framing values, 240–41; culture, role in, 241, 250; language, role in, 250
    understanding nuances of religion and spirituality, 241–42
    understanding spiritual ways of knowing, 232, 242–43, 247
    uniting people around shared functional values, 251
  Spiritually Sensitive Community Assessment Instrument (SSCAI) 251–53

values assessed, legitimized, and operationalized by, 251–53
values, both secularly and religiously inspired, able to operate in, 252
values of practitioners, influences on,
  concepts of social justice, 241–42
  defining experiences, 242–44
  framing, 240–41
  religious or spiritual tradition, 241–42
  socialization, 238–239, 246
social work (direct practice), religious and spiritual integration in, 226
  research on, 230
  skills lacking for, 228
  training, effectiveness for, 228
Society for Manual Labor in Literary Institutions, 110
Sousa, Lori, xvi–xvii, 226
Sparkes, Fanny J., 50
Spiritualism, 30, 120
Spiritual Songs and Hymns for Pilgrims (Roberts), 107–8
Spradlin, Jill D., 193–95, 235–36
Stanley, Henry Morton, 48
Stanton, Elizabeth Cady, 102
Staral, Janice M., 208, 212
Stearns, Halsey, 38
Steele, Daniel, 62
Stiles, Loren, xii, 13–21, 69, 102, 105, 111
Stillson farmstead, 84–85
Stowe, Harriet Beecher, 31, 34
Strauss, Anselm, 234, 255
Susquehanna Conference, 21, 88

Tappan, Lewis, 110–11
tardēmâ (deep sleep), 155
temperance, ix, 33, 86, 126
Temperance House, 86–87
Thatcher, George, 106
Theology for the Social Gospel (Rauschenbusch), 122
Thomas, M. Lori, 247
Thomas, Scott M., 226, 230–33
Thompson, Laura Y., 202

Thoreau, Henry D., xii, 100, 106–7
tôlĕdôt (generations), 146
Tonawanda, NY, 9–10
Tongue of Fire (Arthur), 136, 138
Toussaint, Loren L., 202
Trajan, 51–52
tree of the knowledge of good and evil, 145, 157–62, 167
tree of life, 151, 158–60, 166, 167
Tucker, Karen B., 104
Turner, Michael K., 103

Uncle Tom's Cabin (Stowe), 34
Union Street 81, 84–85
Unitarianism, 111

Vande Brake, Timothy, xiii, 100
Van Dussen, D. Gregory, 104–6
Victoria, Queen, 51
virtue, 209
    and grace-orientation, 197
    and nursing, 211–12, 217–19, 223
    in psychology, 193
    social, 135
    and warrant of beliefs, 173, 183
    See also Roberts, B. T.: character
Vokey, Daniel, 227, 231–32, 247

Wade, Jenny, 194, 205
Wald, Kenneth D., 226, 229–30
Walker, Mark S., 211–12
Walton, John H., 155
Watkins, Philip C., 199
Watson, Paul J., 193–94, 214, 225
Weaver, Richard, 44

Weld, Theodore D., 110–11
Wenham, Gordon J., 149
Wesley, Charles, 190, 198
Wesley, John, xv, 48, 101, 114, 120, 130, 145, 190–92, 198, 205
Wesleyan University, x, 31, 121
West Falls Camp Meeting. *See* camp meetings
Wetherald, Clara L., 24
Wheatlake, S. K., 138–39
Wheeler, Libbie, 17
Whitefield, George, 103
Whitesboro, NY, 110
Whitney, Janette, 14, 138
Why Another Sect? (Roberts), 5n7, 62n25, 64n32, 105n25, 106n33
Wilcox, Garrett, W. 82, 85–86
Wilcox, Lydia, 82
Wilcox, William, 84–85
Willard, Frances, 50
Williams, David R., 202
Williams, Leighton, 133
Winslow, Karen S., 144
Wood, Julia, 38

yālad (bringing forth), 163
Yamauchi, Edwin M., 149
yāṣab (pained), 165
Yellow Wallpaper (Gilman), 34
YHWH (Yahweh), 146–50, 152–56, 158–63, 166–67
Yosemite Valley, 100

Zahniser, Clarence H., 8, 13, 16, 21, 75
Zinnbauer, Brian J., 197

www.ingramcontent.com/pod-product-compliance
Lightning Source LLC
Chambersburg PA
CBHW071241230426
43668CB00011B/1536